What to Expect
in
the
PURSUIT *of* God

This book was the result of the combined efforts of Dr. John Olsen and Mrs. Linda Stubblefield, who have worked as my editorial advisors. Both have labored many hours to make my thoughts and heart clear to the reader.

Dr. John Olsen accepted Christ as his Saviour at a church service on March 5, 1939. After high school graduation, Dr. Olsen enrolled in Wilson Jr. College in Chicago in the pre-dental curriculum. His college education was interrupted by his enlistment in the Army Air Force in August 1942.

Dr. Olsen married Ruth Wolff on February 20, 1943, while he was in the Air Force. Their marriage produced three sons and three daughters, all of whom are born-again Christians. Their marriages resulted in 19 grandchildren and 11 great-grandchildren. Ruth Olsen went to Heaven on September 12, 2004.

On February 10, 1972, Dr. Olsen left his career with pharmaceutical distribution when he was hired by Dr. Jack Hyles to become part of the fledgling staff who opened Hyles-Anderson College in August 1972. In May 1984, Dr. Olsen was awarded an honorary Doctor of Laws degree from Baptist Christian College in Shreveport, Louisiana. Dr. Olsen retired on June 1, 2002, after serving as assistant to the president and campus host for most of his 30-plus years of service.

Upon her graduation from Hyles-Anderson College in 1977, Linda Stubblefield began working for Marlene Evans with Christian Womanhood. After working in various capacities, she now serves as the assistant editor of the Christian Womanhood magazine. She is married to David Stubblefield, the academic dean at Hyles-Anderson College. The Stubblefields are the parents of two adult daughters.

What to Expect

IN THE PURSUIT

of God

DR. JACK SCHAAP

CREDITS:
Project Manager: Dr. Bob Marshall
Assistant: Mrs. Rochelle Chalifoux
Transcription: Mrs. Cyndilu Marshall
Page Design and Layout: Mrs. Linda Stubblefield
Proofreading: Mrs. Kelly Cervantes, Mrs. Rena Fish,
and Mrs. Maria Sarver

To order additional books by Dr. Jack Schaap,
please contact:
Hyles Publications
523 Sibley Street
Hammond, Indiana 46320
(219) 932-0711
www.hylespublications.com
e-mail: info@hylespublications.com

Dedication

I learned to pray by praying, but I was inspired to pray by two men. The first is my father, Ken Schaap. Dad was on his knees every morning at 6:00 a.m. during my teen years when I worked with him. I saw the consistency of his prayer time and the character of his private life and the influence of his public life. He inspired me to know the God of my father.

The second man is Bob Becker, my roommate during my studies at Pillsbury Baptist Bible College. Bob was the first to invite me and provoke me to pray from 4:30 a.m. through 7:30 a.m. each morning. These prayer times changed my life. Bob also became one of my prayer partners. We spent many days and hours in prayer when we were in our twenties. These seasons of prayer, along with the example of my father, gave me a foundation of prayer that formed the core of my personal life and my professional work.

Thank you, Dad. Thank you, Bob. The words of this book were inspired by your actions and examples.

"God does nothing but by prayer,
and everything with it."
– John Wesley

Contents

Every true advocate studies, down to the bottom, every case you put into his hands to plead. And much more will he study, till he has mastered, his own case before God. Every true advocate absolutely ransacks the records of the Court also for all former cases in any way similar to this case he has in hand. He puts the judge in remembrance of his own past opinions, and of all his predecessors' past opinions and past judgments. Not only so, but a skilful advocate will study the very temperament and mood of mind at the time; the age; and the very partialities and prejudices of the judge,—so set is every adroit advocate on carrying his case. Altogether, you cannot but see what an advocate has, when he becomes a man of prayer.[1]

Introduction

The renowned evangelist, Dr. Tom Williams, proclaims that prayer is more important than Bible reading. He should know. The content of his messages indicates that he is no stranger to Bible reading and Bible study. Dr. Williams' many wonderful answers to his prayers are proof that he is qualified to make such a statement. Yet, in spite of all of his importunity to God, the lovely Mrs. Williams remained a semi-invalid with the mind of a three-year-old child as a result of a horrible attack of bacterial meningitis many years ago.

The Apostle Paul penned the words, *"Pray without ceasing."* (I Thessalonians 5:17) God simply answered, *"...My grace is sufficient for thee."* (II Corinthians 12:9) and left Paul with the infirmity he so desperately prayed for God to cure.

These two illustrations are proof that God answers all prayers in His own mysterious and awesome way. His purposes are not ours to know until it is God's time to reveal them. Not all of us are Pauls or Tom Williamses, but all of us can attain the prayer level where God says, *"...The effectual fervent prayer of a righteous man availeth much."* (James 5:16)

Realistically, Satan or his emissaries are close by to disrupt and frequently interfere with our prayer concentration. That interference makes effectual prayer very hard work.

Prayer is basically a state of mind or meditation wherein one draws close to God and closes out all mental interference during his talk with his God. Therein God accepts the praying one's praise and gratitude for all that He is and all that He provides. It is the place where one should realize that God is not some abstract legend in some far away "up." God is as real as we are and is as close as the air surrounding us. Prayer is also a tool by which a Christian makes his requests known to God. He can pray for personal needs or wants, and/or he can pray for others' needs or wants. Too often we pray selfish prayers and forget "others." The Bible warns us against that practice.

This book is a guide to creating and using our prayer tools wisely and effectually. "When God has specially promised the thing," said Charles G. Finney, "we are bound to believe we shall receive it when we pray for it. You have no right to put in an 'if,' and say, 'Lord, *if* it be Thy will, give me Thy Holy Spirit.' This is to insult God. To put an 'if' in God's promise when God has put none there, is tantamount to charging God with being insincere. It is like saying, 'O God, if Thou art in earnest in making these promises, grant us the blessing we pray for.' "

Foreword

The primary purpose of this book is to bring the reader into a full understanding of what God wants us to do as prayer warriors. We have assimilated the word *prayer* into our lives almost from the very moment we became Christians. Even the unsaved people talk about saying their prayers. So what do we mean by the word *prayer*?

I believe the vast majority of Christians would say, "Prayer is asking things from God." But surely prayer is much more than merely "getting God to run our errands for us," as someone puts it. It is a higher thing than the beggar knocking at the rich man's door.[2]

In preparing the text for this book, I came across a remarkable story about D. L. Moody written in two books—one by R. A. Torrey and one by S. D. Gordon. Because both accounts of the same story gripped my heart, I want to share the story in its entirety from S. D. Gordon's account.

It was back in the early seventies, when Chicago had been laid in ashes. "The building was not yet up far enough to do much in," he [Moody] said; "so I thought I would slip across the water, and learn what I could from preachers there, so as to do better work here. I had gone over to London, and was running around after men there."

He had not been speaking anywhere, he said, but listening to others. One day, Saturday, at noon, he had gone into the meeting in Exeter Hall on the Strand; felt impelled to speak a little when the meeting was thrown open, and did so. At the close among others who greeted him, one man, a minister, asked him to come and preach for him the next day morning and night, and he said he would. Mr. Moody said, "I went to the morning service and found a large church full of people. And when the time came I began to speak to them. But it seemed the hardest talking ever I did. There was no response in their faces. They seemed as though carved out of stone or ice. And I was having a hard time: and wished I wasn't there; and wished I hadn't promised to speak again at night. But I had promised, and so I went.

At night it was the same thing: house full, people outwardly respectful, but no interest, no response. And I was having a hard time again. When about half-way through my talk there came a change. It seemed as though the windows of heaven had opened and a bit of breath blew down. The atmosphere of the building seemed to change. The people's faces changed. It impressed me so that when I finished speaking I gave the invitation for those who wanted to be Christians to rise. I thought there might be a few. And to my immense surprise the people got up in groups, pew-fulls. I turned to the minister and said, "What does this mean?" He said, "I don't know, I'm sure."

"Well," Mr. Moody said, "They misunderstood me. I'll explain what I meant." So he announced an after-meeting in the room below, explaining who were invited: only those who wanted to be Christians; and putting pretty clearly what he understood that to mean, and dismissed the service.

They went to the lower room. And the people came crowding, jamming in below, filling all available space, seats, aisles and standing room. Mr. Moody talked again a few minutes, and then asked those who would be Christians to rise. This time he knew he had made his meaning clear. They got up in clumps, in groups, by fifties!

Mr. Moody said, "I turned and said to the minister, '*What*

does this mean?' He said, 'I'm sure I don't know'."

Then the minster said to Mr. Moody, "What'll I do with these people? I don't know what to do with them; this is something new."

And he said, "Well, I'd announce a meeting for to-morrow night, and Tuesday night, and see what comes of it. I'm going across the channel to Dublin." And he went, but he had barely stepped off the boat when a cablegram was handed him from the minister saying, "Come back at once. Church packed." So he went back, and stayed ten days. And the result of that ten days, as I recall Mr. Moody's words, was that four hundred were added to that church, and that every church near by felt the impulse of those ten days.

Now what was the explanation of that marvellous Sunday and the days following? It was not Mr. Moody's doing, though he was a leader whom God could and did mightily use. It was not the minister's doing; for he was as greatly surprised as the leader. There was some secret hidden beneath the surface of those ten days. With his usual keenness Mr. Moody set himself to ferret it out.

By and by this incident came to him. A member of the church, a woman, had been taken sick some time before. Then she grew worse. Then the physician told her that she would not recover. That is, she would not die at once, so far as he could judge, but she would be shut in her home for years. And she lay there trying to think what that meant: to be shut in for years. And she thought of her life, and said, "How little I've done for God: practically nothing: and now what can I do shut in here on my back. I can pray."

May I put this word in here as a parenthesis in the story— *with pain to Himself*, against His own first will for us, He allows us to be shut in, because only so can He get our attention from other things to what He wants done; get us to see things, and think things His way. I am compelled to think it is so.

She said, "I *will* pray." And she was led to pray for her church. Her sister, also a member of the church, lived with her, and was her link with the outer world. Sundays, after church service, the sick woman would ask, "Any special interest in church to-day?" "No," was the constant reply. Wednesday nights, after prayer-meetings, "Any special interest in the service to-night? There must have been." "No; nothing new; same old deacons made the same old prayers."

But one Sunday noon the sister came in from service and asked, "Who do you think preached to-day?" "I don't know, who?" "Why, a stranger from America, a man called Moody, I think was the name." And the sick woman's face turned a bit whiter, and her eye looked half scared, and her lip trembled a bit, and she quietly said: "I know what that means. There's something coming to the old church. Don't bring me any dinner. I must spend this afternoon in prayer." And so she did. And that night in the service that startling change came."

Then to Mr. Moody himself, as he sought her out in her sick room, she told how nearly two years before there came into her hands a copy of a paper published in Chicago called the *Watchman* that contained a talk by Mr. Moody in one of the Chicago meetings, Farwell Hall meetings, I think. All she knew was that talk made her heart burn, and there was the name M-o-o-d-y. And she was led to pray that God would send that man into their church in London. As simple a prayer as that.

And the months went by, and a year, and over; still she prayed. Nobody knew of it but herself and God. No change seemed to come. Still she prayed. And of course her prayer wrought its purpose. Every Spirit-suggested prayer does. And that is the touchstone of true prayer. And the Spirit of God moved that man of God over to the seaboard, and across the water and into London, and into their church. Then a bit of special siege-prayer, a sort of last charge up the steep hill, and that night the victory came.

Do you not believe—I believe without a doubt, that some day when the night is gone, and the morning light comes up, and we know as we are known, that we shall find that the largest single factor, in that ten days' work, and in the changing of tens of thousands of lives under Moody's leadership is that woman in her praying. Not the only factor, mind you. Moody was a man of rare leadership, and consecration, and hundreds of faithful ministers and others rallied to his support. But behind and beneath Moody and the others, and to be reckoned with as first was this woman's praying.

Yet I do not know her name. I know Mr. Moody's name, but the name of this one in whom humanly is the secret of it all I do not know. Ah! It is a secret service. We do not know who the great ones are.[3]

R. A. Torrey said, "God is just as ready to hear and answer you as He was to answer that bedridden saint. To whatever church you belong, and whoever your pastor is, you can make him a man of power. If he is a man of power already, you can make him a man of even greater power."[4]

Prayer is one of those topics that seems as though it should be very simple, when in truth, there is so much to understand and learn about God and prayer. We will examine this very familiar word oft used in many different syntaxes, but little understood. As Andrew Murray so succinctly wrote, "The place and power of prayer in the Christian life is too little understood. When we learn to regard it as the highest part of the work entrusted to us—the root and strength of all other work—we will see that there is nothing we need to study and practice more than the art of praying."[5]

Oh, how few find time for prayer! There is time for everything else, time to sleep and time to eat, time to read the newspaper and the novel, time to visit friends, time for everything else under the sun, but —no time for prayer, the most important of all things, the one great essential!

– Oswald J. Smith

The Riddle
of Unanswered Prayer

"Ask, and it shall be given you; seek, and ye shall find; knock, and it shall be opened unto you: For every one that asketh receiveth; and he that seeketh findeth; and to him that knocketh it shall be opened. Or what man is there of you, whom if his son ask bread, will he give him a stone? Or if he ask a fish, will he give him a serpent? If ye then, being evil, know how to give good gifts unto your children, how much more shall your Father which is in heaven give good things to them that ask him? Therefore all things whatsoever ye would that men should do to you, do ye even so to them: for this is the law and the prophets." (Matthew 7:7-12)

Through the years I have been approached by people asking why God does not seem to answer their prayers. Some of these fine people desperately want to serve God. Whether it is the normal, boring, "oatmeal" events or the catastrophic, cataclysmic events of life, everyone needs and wants God to be available in all that life brings—good or bad.

When I was a young teenager, it occurred to me that most people excluded God from most of their life; they were what I now call "periodical Christians." They allow God into a set, acceptable, but limited, zone of their lives. In the matter of prayer, they pray when a need arises that is more than they can handle. Periodical Christians believe in God, but they don't have a prayer life and usually don't read their Bible. The truth is, they don't have much of a Christian life except they tiptoe into church, put on a facade for a few hours on Sunday, and then tiptoe out. These periodical Christians seldom partner with God in the matter of doing great things for Him. "Prayer is a thing so big, so meaning-ful, that it calls for every power of a human soul, and anything which does not do this is unworthy to be called prayer."[1]

I cannot emphasize enough the importance of making God active in all phases of our life. Partnering with God begins with obedience to God in the matters of prayer, consistent Bible read-ing, soul winning, and regular church attendance. We will never include God in the greater capacity of our life until we develop a prayer life with Him. No solid growth can take place in the Christian life unless there is prayer growth. No prayer growth occurs until we realize that effective prayer is hard work, and we are willing to work hard.

God said, "...The effectual fervent prayer of a righteous man availeth much." (James 5:16) The words of this verse signify **ener-getic supplication.** Short prayers were the standard in the Old Testament, according to Bible commentator Adam Clarke. Those who were acquainted with Evangelist John R. Rice would recall his practice of quietly uttering a ten-to-fifteen second prayer every ten to fifteen minutes or so. His prayers were right to the point, and he stayed in constant contact with God.

Many Christians talk about prayer as though they are experts at it. The truth is, we tease about prayer, teach about prayer, and preach about prayer, but until we develop a vital prayer life, we will be spiritually powerless Christians.

Daniel believed in consistent and persistent prayer, for he prayed *three times a day*. He believed in bombarding the throne of God with fervent prayer. Prayer was a habit with him.[2]

Is it any wonder that Daniel's prayers brought about his deliv-erance from the mouths of the lions? He was a spiritually power-ful Christian who obviously had a prayer life! Dr. Tom Williams says, "Many people have a prayer time; few people have a prayer life." A prayer life does not mean going to a monastery, becoming a monk, living in seclusion, and dedicating one's life to the Lord in quiet solitude. No! A prayer life requires energetic supplication—any time, anywhere. The Apostle Peter's prayer, "Lord, save me," when he was sinking into the sea, illustrates perfectly that timely energetic supplication at a most unusual location. Thankfully, God makes available the world of prayer to every believer—not just to Daniel and Peter.

Matthew 7 contains four great, life-changing truths about prayer.

1. **God promises to answer everyone's prayer.** *"Ask, and it shall be given you; seek, and ye shall find; knock, and it shall be opened unto you: For every one that asketh receiveth...."* (Matthew 7:7, 8) Do you believe that everyone who asks receives? Have you ever asked but did not receive? Why? God is no respecter of persons, so why do some people like George Mueller have their prayers answered and others don't? God says everyone who asks receives.

An answer to prayer is a granting of the thing which a child asks of his heavenly Father, according to the directions which his Father has clearly set down. When God answers prayer He says "yes."[3]

2. **God promises better things than for what we asked.** *"...and he that seeketh findeth; and to him that knocketh it shall be opened. Or what man is there of you, whom if his son ask bread, will he give him a stone? Or if he ask a fish, will he give him a serpent? If ye then, being evil, know how to give good gifts unto your children, how much more shall your Father which is in heaven give good things to them that ask him?"* (Matthew 7:8-11)

God is saying, "You might know how to give good gifts, but **I** give better gifts. If someone asked you for a piece of bread, you would at least give him something of that value. I would do better! I would give him something of better quality—a sandwich!"

3. **God promises to give more than for what we ask.** *"If ye*

then, being evil, know how to give good gifts unto your children, how much more shall your Father which is in heaven give good things to them that ask him?" (Matthew 7:11) What a wonderful promise! However, asking Him for $100 and expecting a $1,000,000 will probably not happen! Asking does not work that way.

4. God's promises to hear and answer our prayers are ultimately designed to change us. *"Therefore all things whatsoever ye would that men should do to you, do ye even so to them: for this is the law and the prophets."* (Matthew 7:12) Many people display mottos in their office or in their home that read "Prayer changes things." WRONG! Many Christians anxiously pray "God, I've got to have some things changed by You!" God is not interested in changing the *things* of this world. God is interested in changing the *people* who are in the world. Prayer does **not** change *things*; prayer changes *people*! The reason why God gave us these four promises is not to give us things, but to change us.

In any study of the subject of prayer it is fundamental and basic that we understand that if man will meet the conditions of God and pray, God will respond to his prayer and perhaps even change the course of His direction. This does not mean that an immature Christian can frivolously approach the throne of grace and change God's mind. It does mean that the great omnipotent, omniscient, and omnipresent Jehovah God leans toward His children to hear what they say and longs to have them present their petitions to Him that He may give consideration to their requests.[4]

Technically, the average Christian does not understand why God gives us prayer promises or why God commands us to pray. The problem with the Christian life is that not only do we not know how to pray, we also don't know to pray. Many Christians, by simple, well-disciplined stubbornness and character, determine to pray and have their prayer time even if it "kills" them. They turn the pages of their prayer list, pray methodically for each name and/or circumstance listed, and then go their way.

Our perception of what God is trying do in our prayer life is so limited. We are like the man who said, "I see men as trees walking." We do not see through the eyes of the Lord, so we pray almost meaningless, rote prayers: "God, change my marriage. Change my marriage. Oh God, change my wife. What's the matter with her? God, change that woman." Will God answer that prayer? Does God hear and answer every prayer of everyone who asks? Yes!

God will answer that prayer because God promised to answer every prayer from everyone who asks. However, we fail to remember that the purpose of prayer is to change people not things. Many Christians want to reverse the purpose of prayer and use prayer to change their environment. But God changes the person in the environment.

Prayer was not man's invention; prayer is a tool designed by God. Man wants to steal God's inventions and use them for his own manipulative will and concern. Man tries to steal prayer from God and then has the audacity to try to twist His arm and force Him to answer a selfish prayer like "Make me rich!" In other words, man wants to control the way God chooses to answer prayers.

God says, "I will not let you control anything until I control you." The tool that God uses to get control of you is through your prayers. When you do not pray, God will not control you. God refuses to control the believer who will not use God's tools. God uses the tool of prayer to change you so He can control you and use you to channel His good.

Prayer is so important because it is the believer's way of entering into covenantship with God. Prayer says, "God, control me." As God controls the Christian, God then allows him to be the channel through which God does all of His work. There is no limit to the influence a Christian could have!

Unfortunately, many Christians are caught in the trap of having a very small God. Just how big is your God anyway? I'm tired of "small-God" Christian living because it all bears out in what I call "small-Christian" praying—prayer to change our *things*. We want a better environment, a bigger this, a better that, a more expensive that, etc. "Keep praying," God invites the "small-God" Christian, "but you will not recognize My answer!" Why? Therein lies the answer to the amazing riddle of unanswered prayer!

In my opinion the most important prayer chapter in the entire Bible is Romans chapter 8. The Bible says in verse 26, *"Likewise the Spirit also helpeth our infirmities: for we know not what we should pray for as we ought...."* God commands us to pray, but this verse says we don't even know what to pray for. To help us know how to pray, God has given every Christian a gift—the Holy Spirit residing within him. Verse 26 continues, *"...but the Spirit itself maketh intercession for us with groanings which cannot be uttered. And he that searcheth the hearts knoweth what is the mind of the Spirit, because* **he** *maketh intercession for the saints according to the will of God."* (Romans 8:26, 27) The word "He" in verse 27 is identified in verse 34 which says, *"Who is he that condemneth? It is* **Christ** *that died, yea rather, that is risen again, who is even at the right hand of God, who also maketh intercession for us."* The Bible definitively says that Christ is the One Who is making intercession for us.

What exactly is intercession? "It is a form of prayer in which the petitioner stands between God and some great need."[5] An intercessor is someone who goes to the Father on behalf of someone else. Who goes to the Father on behalf of the saints? Christ! Jesus Christ is the Person Who goes to God and says, "On behalf of _____, Heavenly Father, I come to You." You can fill your name in that blank!

[Romans 8:26 and 27] should give much comfort...even to the weakest saint. The Spirit helps us when we pray. When we are so burdened, so broken with grief and heartache, the Holy Spirit groans within us...and God understands the groanings of the Spirit, even the groanings which cannot be uttered because the Spirit utters (in groanings) requests according to the will of God. The Holy Spirit knows the burden, the desire, the longing of the heart of the believer; therefore, He helps us in such an hour.[6]

A Christian's body is the dwelling place for the Spirit of God. This knowledge is unexplainable; I must simply believe! The Spirit of God inside me understands my infirmities, my problems, and my weaknesses. He knows me better than I know myself!

God placed a resident Presence inside of every believer to know intimately the truth about what the believer in whom He dwells thinks and feels, to reveal his motives and thoughts, to help him with his predicaments, and to probe the deep, dark recesses of his mind. The Holy Spirit, Who lives inside of every believer, knows our infirmities, our weaknesses, our troubles, our anxieties, our fears, our panics, our worries, and our deepest concerns. He knows the things you would never tell your spouse or your best friend. He also knows the things you don't even utter in prayer. He knows you intimately because He created you and because He understands you.

We do not know how to pray, but the Spirit knows how. He is the Master-pray-er. He knows God's will perfectly. He knows what is best to be praying under all circumstances. And He is within you and me. He is thinking thoughts that find no response in us. They cannot be expressed in our lips for they are not in our thinking. He prays with an intensity quite beyond the possibility of language to express. And the heart-searcher—God listening above—knows fully what this praying Spirit is thinking, and wordlessly praying, for they are one.[7]

All three members of our triune God are involved in every believer's prayers. The Holy Spirit intercedes for the Christian. Christ goes to God the Father on behalf of every Christian.

In the middle of this powerful prayer passage, God inserts Romans 8:28 which says, *"And we know that all things work together for good to them that love God, to them who are the called according to his purpose."* Seemingly, this verse doesn't "fit" the context of the chapter. God was saying, "I will not change your things because I am going to use *things* to hurt you."

God will take the events of life such as a job layoff, increased taxes, and marriage difficulties and use them as tools to drive the Christian to his knees—not to pray for God to change things, but to pray for God to use the things to be made manifest in the Christian's life. God intends to change the Christian, not his things. Some of the greatest Christians I know seem to have the most miserable events happen to them, and some of the sorriest Christians I know get along just fine.

The Psalms are filled with references to wicked people prospering wonderfully and believers who suffer terribly. Was Job the best man or worst man living in his age? According to Job 1:1, he was *"...perfect and upright, and one that feared God, and eschewed evil."*

I believe that we can conclude if Job was not the best man, he was one of the best. In spite of these glowing accolades, he lost ten children, the affection of his wife, the loyalty of his friends, those he held dear—nearly everyone in his life! God wanted these horrific losses to change Job! God was putting pressure on Job to drive him to his knees in prayer.

Afflictions are sent to bring us to the throne of grace, to teach us to pray, and to make the word of God's grace precious to us. In the day of our sorrow we must wait upon God, for those comforts which are sufficient to balance our griefs;

Job, when in tears, fell down and worshipped God taking away, as well as giving.[8]

The great truth is that when man prays for God to change things, inevitably the situation becomes worse because God wants to use those negative situations of life to change the person who is praying. For instance, when couples come to me for marriage counseling, I find that usually one is tenderhearted, and one is hardhearted. The one who is tenderhearted, who is begging God for his marriage, usually becomes a more mature, more godly saint, while the other becomes a more hardened, tough, ungodly, backslidden person.

Are the prayers of the tenderhearted one being answered? Yes! Prayer is a tool to make the one who prays more like Christ. Romans 8:29 says, *"For whom he did foreknow, he also did predestinate to be conformed to the image of his Son, that he might be the firstborn among many brethren."* What is the will of God for a Christian? That he would become Christlike; that he would be just like Jesus.

When we are burdened in our minds; when we are oppressed with manifold cares and sorrows; when we are ill-used, humiliated, despised, trampled upon; when we are weary of the world and of ourselves; and then, when, instead of rebelling and raging and repining, we accept our lot as laid on us by God, and according to His invitation take all our burden to Christ in prayer,—that is the way to come to Him. That is to say, we come from pride to humility; and from a heart tossed with tempest to a harbour of rest and peace; and from rebellion to resignation; and from a life of unbelief to a life of faith and love.[9]

When Jesus prayed, did His prayers change all the things on earth like they should be? NO! He was crucified, murdered by His accusers. After He was treated as a treasonous traitor to the country, did things change? NO! Christ was the One Who changed because He was the One Who was praying. He went into the Garden of Gethsemane and prayed, *"...Father, if thou be willing, remove this cup from me: nevertheless not my will, but thine, be done."* (Luke 22:42)

The disciples had quit praying, and they did not change until they held a prayer meeting in the upper room! That is exactly why Jesus said to them, *"...tarry ye in the city of Jerusalem, until ye be endued with power from on high."* (Luke 24:49) Jesus knew that they had forgotten the tool of prayer. Pray! Pray! Keep on praying until you're changed! And when the disciples prayed, the fire of God fell. The people who get changed by prayer are the people who are praying.

As you pray, God is changing you. Truthfully, God is not really interested in that for which you're praying; He is far more interested in the person praying because prayer is the way that God knows an individual's heart. But the reason why we stop praying is that our prayers are so far from what God desires and from what He has promised to answer.

God is not some magic Aladdin's lamp to rub and receive three wishes! "Prayer is not extracting favours from a reluctant God. It is not passing a check in a bank window for money."[10] Many Christians' concept of prayer is so far from the Scriptural truth. Prayer is a tool used to enter into covenant-relationship with God that says, "God, I want to be changed."

> In its simplest analysis, prayer—all prayer—has, must have, two parts. First, a God to give. And, just as certainly, there must be a second factor, *a man to receive.* Man's willingness is God's channel to the earth. There must be an open hand and heart and life *through* which God can give what He longs to [give].[11]

When we pray according to God's will—His will being what

God has already written and wants to accomplish—then will we see our prayers answered. We could see our prayers answered like we have never before seen if we would start praying for God's will to be done as He has already written it. Knowing your prayers are answered because they are in line with the will of the Father is a great way to live! The answer to the riddle of unanswered prayer is that God's answer to prayer is to change people and not things!

Christ teaches us to pray not only by example, by instruction, by command, by promises, but by showing us Himself, the ever-living Intercessor, as our life. It is when we believe this, and go and abide in Him for our prayer-life too, that our fears of not being able to pray aright will vanish, and we shall joyfully and triumphantly trust our Lord to teach us to pray, to be Himself the life and the power of our prayer.

– Andrew Murray

Teach Us to Pray

"And it came to pass, that, as he was praying in a certain place, when he ceased, one of his disciples said unto him, **Lord, teach us to pray**, as John also taught his disciples. And he said unto them, When ye pray, say, Our Father which art in heaven, Hallowed be thy name. Thy kingdom come. Thy will be done, as in heaven, so in earth. Give us day by day our daily bread. And forgive us our sins; for we also forgive every one that is indebted to us. And lead us not into temptation; but deliver us from evil."

(Luke 11:1-4)

Luke tells us that as Jesus was praying in a certain place, when He ceased, one of His disciples said unto Him, "Lord, teach us to *pray*." This disciple had heard Jesus preach, but he did not say, "Lord, teach us to *preach*." He could learn to preach by studying the methods of the Master. But there was something about the praying of Jesus that made the disciple feel that he did not know how to pray, that he had never prayed, and that he could not learn by listening even to the Master as He prayed.

There is a profound something about prayer which never lies upon the surface. To learn it, one must go to the depths of the soul, and climb to the heights of God. –A. C. Dixon[1]

Even the 12 who were closest to Jesus sought His wisdom and teaching about how to pray. When they learned how to pray, one definitive result of their willingness to learn was their being used to turn the world upside down for Him.

I personally believe if I can get every one of my church members to praying and walking with God, each will have his life transformed—just like the disciples. In chapter one, we addressed the fact that prayer does not change things; prayer changes people. The person who changes is the person who is praying. When the disciples learned how to pray, their lives were changed. Prayer is vitally important in the Christian's life.

When a Christian prays more in line with what God wants, his prayers are more apt to be answered. Luke 11 contains a plethora of truths which acquaint a Christian with the matter of getting his prayers answered. "God, Who cannot lie, is bound to answer. He has voluntarily placed Himself under obligation to answer the prayer of him who truly prays."[2]

Schedule a "When" You Pray

The number-one reason why people do not receive answers to their prayers is that they do not pray.

Oh! You can pray anywhere, on the street, in the store, travelling, measuring dry goods, hands in dishwater,—where not? But you are not likely to unless you have been off in some quiet place shut in alone with God.[3]

The Bible does not say "*if* you pray," it says, "*when* you pray."

"Teach us to pray," His disciples requested of Him.

He answered, "*When* ye pray...." Jesus had a "when," and His disciples did not! Dr. Dennis Corle says it so well: "I cannot duplicate the supernatural in the life of Christ, but I can duplicate the natural discipline that He exercised—the discipline of a set time, a solitary place, and a steady, consistent habit."[4]

When do you pray? Is there a "when" in your life? Until you have a "when you pray," your prayers will not be answered. A scheduled prayer time will give you a more effective prayer life than a haphazard, do-it-when-I-find-time prayer life.

Those who pray don't have time; they take time. If we do not take time to pray, then it is because deep in our heart of hearts we regard this as a non-essential.[5]

I decided when I was a young man that I did not want to pray simply when I had to have God's help. I don't believe in praying just when I need it. I did not want to live an emergency, critical, ICU kind of Christian life. Resorting to "I must pray right now" was not how I wanted to live. I decided prayer would not be my last resort. I want prayer to be where I live all the time.

As I study the Bible, I find Jesus Christ always went to the Father for everything. When something good happened, He went to the Father. When something bad happened, He talked to the Father. Jesus constantly brought God into the circle of His world. That is exactly the way I want to live! I want to live like He is with me all the time. One way is by taking advantage of this wonderful privilege called prayer.

The disciples surely lacked in this area of prayer. While Jesus prayed in the Garden of Gethsemane, they slept. When Jesus went to the mountain to pray, they stared in awe and wonderment instead of praying. Time and time again when Jesus was praying, the disciples were otherwise occupied. They seemed consumed with the circle of things that God deemed as unimportant.

After all, He had said, "*Therefore I say unto you, Take no thought for your life, what ye shall eat, or what ye shall drink; nor yet for your body, what ye shall put on. Is not the life more than meat, and the body than raiment?*" (Matthew 6:25) He wanted them to see the eternality of the Christian life—especially the benefits of prayer! "When ye pray," He simply stated. Like Jesus Christ, we must consciously choose a life a prayer.

If someone asked me, "Brother Schaap, when do you pray?" I could confidently answer. "Without ceasing—day and night, all the time, an hour Sunday afternoon, two hours on Monday, an hour on Tuesday, three hours on Wednesday." I must spend hours in prayer. If I do not spend hours in prayer, I know that I cannot possibly pastor this church—or any church for that matter. If I don't pray enough, I cannot get what I need from God. "The preacher who does not season his message with prayer, cannot hope for God's blessings to follow his message."[6]

I can honestly say that my life is spent with prayer. I believe if I were to fall into a great tragedy of sin, it would not be because of what most people would expect. Instead, I would be more likely to become a monk in a monastery. A monk spends his life with his God—studying and praying. I love to pray because I have discovered the joy and the glory of spending time with God. I find no greater joy than in communicating with God. I find no greater thrill than in getting into a harmony of thought and mutual communication with God.

Sad to say, God is such a low priority to most Christians. Everything—television programs, PlayStation games, the job, hobbies, and even the newspaper—takes precedence and priority over God to the average Christian layman. The average Christian woman's priorities include laundry, vacuuming, kitchen work, finding a new outfit, having her nails done, and getting a pedicure—but not prayer. She spends several hours a day on her priorities but not 30 minutes in the prayer closet.

Truthfully, I don't understand that attitude of indifference toward God! In fact, I do not ever want to understand a Christianity where God is low priority. To me, God is everything! God is my life. Colossians 3:4 says, *"When Christ, who is our life, shall appear, then shall ye also appear with him in glory."* God is not an unreachable entity up in the sky faraway somewhere.

He Who counts the hairs of our head, and Who is not too lofty and high to notice the little sparrow which falls to the ground, is not too great and high to note everything which concerns the happiness, the needs and the safety of His children. Prayer brings God into what men are pleased to term the little affairs of life.[7]

God is reachable, touchable, and approachable! Talking to God should be as natural as dialing a telephone number and chatting with a good friend. Unfortunately, I watch too many people devote far too much time to their electronic gadgets like cell phones. Instead of "sweet hour of prayer," it is sweet hours of cell phone. The average Christian should measure the time he spends in daily prayer against the time he spends on his cell phone.

Before the advent of the television, did you pray? I was a junior-aged boy before we purchased our first television. Whatever excuse we want to offer as our reason for not praying, the truth is we can still find time to play with the newest toy on the market, watch a movie, play a DVD, or talk on the telephone. We seem to be able to find time for everything but prayer. God's people must make prayer their priority and do as William Walford penned in his immortal song "Sweet Hour of Prayer" and go to the prayer closet for an hour of prayer.

I say this with a sad heart—I believe one of the outstanding sins in the church today is prayer-lessness among the saints. If God's people spent as much time on their knees as they do before their televisions, I am sure we would have a revival that would shake the world! But a prayer-less church is a power-less church; and by the same token, a prayer-less Christian is a power-less Christian.[8]

I cannot count the times I have been asked, "What in the world would I talk to God about?"

My immediate thought is, "You seem to have no problem talking to your girlfriend or to your spouse or anyone else! Why not God?!" God made everyone with whom you communicate! God is also more interesting than any person He created!

I am always amazed at some married couples who seek coun-sel. When they were dating, no one could keep them off their cell phones. They didn't have a life outside of their cell phones. When they come to the office, they say, "We don't communicate very well." Something was lost between the dating and the wedding altar. They ceased to communicate. Likewise, that lack of com-munication seems to happen to Christians too. For some reason, when we get saved, we stop communicating with God. We find time to eat and sleep! If some Christians would make prayer as big a priority as eating, they would be as rich in their spiritual life as they are in their physical life! If they made a priority of walking with God like they make tiptoeing to the refrigerator, they would definitely have a more spiritual life!

Prayer is no petty duty, put into a corner; no piecemeal performance made out of the fragments of time which have been snatched from business and other engagements of life; but it means that the best of our time, the heart of our time and strength must be given.[9]

My desire is for Christians to walk with God. I want people to have a prayer life. I want every Christian to be able to say, "I have a *when* when I pray." Luke 11 teaches very clearly that every Christian must have a *when* to his prayer life.

Luke 11 also provides some guidelines for the Christian and his prayer life. Verses 2 and 3 say, *"And he said unto them, When ye pray, say, Our Father which art in heaven, Hallowed be thy name. Thy kingdom come. Thy will be done, as in heaven, so in earth. Give us day by day our daily bread."* Notice that the Father is associated with giving bread.

In Luke 11:5 more bread is requested. *"And he said unto them, Which of you shall have a friend, and shall go unto him at midnight, and say unto him, Friend, lend me three loaves."* Verse 11 continues this same theme of asking for bread. *"If a son shall ask bread of any of you that is a father, will he give him a stone?..."* Of course not! That son will receive bread from the hand of his father.

If God had made us plead for our own bread, we would have dwelt on ourselves too much, so God wants us to get our minds off of ourselves. We ask for bread for self one time, and He gives it to us.[10]

Luke 11:13 subtly shifts the focus on physical bread to a much more desirable gift available from God. *"If ye then, being evil, know how to give good gifts unto your children: how much more shall your heavenly Father* **give** *the Holy Spirit to them that ask him?"* In this passage bread refers to the gifts of God, specifically the Holy Spirit. God is offering power—the power of the Holy Spirit to live your life!

Every marriage needs the power of the Holy Spirit! What is needed in child rearing is the power of the Spirit of God! Read every lesson, lecture, and available book; listen to all the accessible cassettes and CDs; and watch all the videos and DVDs about marriage you can find. However, these materials are only helpful if you allow the Spirit of God to help you live what is taught. All of those principles are meaningless if you do not have the power of the Spirit of God helping you. The number-one reason why we must pray is to get God involved in our lives.

Praying, "Father, I want this bread. I want the Holy Spirit of God to help me and to use me in my life," is exactly what God is trying to accomplish! He wants Himself involved in our lives. He's not really interested in providing your daily things; rather, He's trying to change and transform His people by the power of His Spirit. "It does change men to pray and the change which is wrought in them is one of the ways in which God answers their prayers."[11] God is doing a great work on this earth, and that work involves His people's conforming to the image of Jesus Christ.

Say Your Prayers

Luke 11:2 says, *"When ye pray, say...."* The Bible does not say, *"Think* your prayers or *feel* your prayers." God wants Christians to say their prayers. The word *say* means "to verbalize." Speak out—either softly or loudly—depending on the situation. Talk to God like He is a real, living being. Chat with Him.

When I was in high school, I had a difficult time with the reality of God. I would shut my eyes, *think* my prayers, and then say, "I really don't know if I'm praying or not." Finally I pulled two chairs together. I put one chair opposite of me, but facing me. I sat down across from the empty chair and said out loud, "God, if You don't mind, I'm going to pretend that You are sitting in that chair. I'm going to talk to You as though You are actually sitting in that chair." This may sound trite, but I started by saying, "Hello, God! How are You doing? You know who I am; I know Who You are. Let's spend about half an hour talking today." I spent that half hour looking at and talking to that imaginary person sitting in that real chair. This practice helped me get into the habit of talking to God. That practice also transformed my prayer life because I soon realized He truly was real. Soon I did not need the chair or any other prop to feel close to God.

Perhaps like me, you need to arrange two chairs together and say, "This is where I will pray. I will make an appointment with God, and we will start talking in that place." Just start talking to God. Have a plan and a daily prayer list. The plan does not matter—as long as you utilize that plan.

Build the Right Relationships
With God

The Bible indicates several different relationships every Christian can have with God. According to Luke 11, to get your prayers answered, you must have the right relationship with God.

1. **The Creator/Creation Relationship.** This relationship takes place at conception. Every human being has the first of these relationships—the Creator/Creation relationship. God, the Creator, has made everyone. However, that relationship does not mean that everyone is saved or on his way to Heaven. All this relationship means is that every person was conceived and born into this world. When we pray, the Bible does not say to address God as, "Our Creator." We can conclude by reasoning that even though we have been created by God, we have no right to ask or demand God to hear our prayers.

You can be an atheist or an agnostic, but you are still a creation of God. You can be a Baptist preacher, but you're still a creation of God. Keep in mind this relationship as God's creation does not qualify anyone to have his prayers answered.

2. **The Saviour/Redeemed Relationship.** The second relationship we can have with God is that of Saviour/Redeemed. We have the first relationship with God—Creator/Creation—by being born; the second relationship with God can be attained by being born again. We sincerely trust Christ as our Saviour to get this Redeemer relationship. We haven't done anything positive; we just received Christ and got our sins washed away. When we pray, the Bible does not command us or tell us to address God by saying, "Our Redeemer." No! The Bible says when we pray to say, "Our Father." Perhaps you can begin to see why we don't get our prayers answered.

Can a new convert get his prayers answered immediately? Perhaps. However, God is not obligated to answer those prayers though He may choose to do so because He is a kind and gracious God. Our God prefers that we have the correct relationship with Him.

3. **The God/People Relationship.** This relationship takes place at separation. II Corinthians 6:16, 17 reveals the third relationship the Christian can have—a relationship with God as His

people. *"...and I will be their God, and they shall be my people. Wherefore come out from among them, and be ye separate, saith the Lord...."* In verse 17 the word *"them"* is referring to some people God describes in verses 14 and 15. *"Be ye not unequally yoked together with unbelievers: for what fellowship hath righteousness with unrighteousness? and what communion hath light with darkness? And what concord hath Christ with Belial? or what part hath he that believeth with an infidel? And what agreement hath the temple of God with idols? for ye are the temple of the living God; as God hath said...."*

Did you realize that an unbeliever cannot call God "his God?" When an unsaved person prays, "Dear God in Heaven," God turns a deaf ear! God cannot be a person's God until he qualifies for Him to be his God. Being created or redeemed does not make God a person's God. He is not any person's God because that person **calls** Him his God. He becomes your God when you leave the crowd that doesn't call Him their God.

The Bible lists a lineup of people to avoid in II Corinthians 6:14 which says, *"Be ye not unequally yoked together with **unbelievers**...."* The word *unbeliever* does not necessarily mean "someone who is not saved." A born-again unbeliever has been sincerely born again but through pride (or whatever) has not, by faith, allowed God to have control of his life. The word *unbeliever* comes from the Greek word *apistos*, "without faith." An *unbeliever* means "not a faithful man." Simply put, someone who is not believable or someone who is not faithful to God is an *unbeliever*. Sad to say, many church-going teenagers and adults associate with believers who are unbelievers—born-again people who are not the kind of believers with whom God wants them to associate.

Verse 14 continues *"...for what fellowship hath righteousness with unrighteousness?"* A righteous person loves to do right. Conversely, someone who is unrighteous does not like doing right. Someone who does not want to keep the rules is an unrighteous person. The teen who does not want to obey his parents is an unrighteous person. Before a Christian can address God as "his God," he must voluntarily remove himself from the company of unrighteous people. Otherwise, God will only be his Redeemer, and he will have no relationship with God other than the fact that Jesus paid for his sins. Can the disobedient Christian pray? Yes. Is God obligated to answer his prayers? No! The disobedient Christian has not done that which qualifies him to call God his God and his Father.

II Corinthians 6:14 continues to list the kinds of people to avoid: "...what communion hath light with darkness?" The kingdom of darkness is directed by the Devil himself. Gothic music and the dark side of life dominating a person's being is against God's will for that person's life. That is one reason why I do not like books which dramatize the evil, darker side of life. I instruct people **not** to become familiar in any way with the kingdom of darkness. Christians have no business reading and learning about the kingdom of darkness. Christians do not need to turn to fundamental exorcism and the casting out of demons. The best way to cast out demons is to lead someone to a saving knowledge of Christ!

The one concern of the devil is to keep the saints from praying. He fears nothing from prayerless studies, prayerless work, prayerless religion. He laughs at our toil, mocks at our wisdom, but trembles when we pray. –Samuel Chadwick[12]

II Corinthians 6:15, "...what concord hath Christ with Belial?..." The word Belial means "good for nothing, lazy people." God has blessed every kind of human being in the world—from adulterers, fornicators, murderers, to thieves—except for one category: lazy people. God has blessed some liars, but He has never blessed a lazy man. God does not want His people associating with lazy people.

Verse 15 continues, "...what part hath he that believeth with an infidel?" Theologically, the word infidel means "someone who rejects the fact that Jesus Christ is the Son of God," or "someone who rejects the fact that Jesus Christ was virgin born, that Jesus Christ lived a sinless life, that Jesus Christ was crucified on a cross, that Jesus Christ died, was buried, and was resurrected from the dead." An *infidel* is "someone who won't stand with believers and say, 'I'm a Christian.' " An *infidel* is "someone who is afraid to get baptized" because baptism says, "I'm not ashamed to be called a Christian!" An infidel publicly denies Christ.

Are you ashamed of Jesus? It's time for Christian young people to dress appropriately and stop identifying with the worldly crowd which thinks nothing of participating in mixed swimming parties and enjoying unchaperoned dates. What our country needs is for some Christians—young, middle-aged, and older alike—to come out from among them and be separate! Modesty is fast becoming a word of past days. It's time to make God your God. *Who* is *your* God?

I believe Paul was addressing the same type of issues and was upset with Christians when he said in Philippians 3:17-21, *"Brethren, be followers together of me, and mark them which walk so as ye have us for an ensample. (For many walk, of whom I have told you often, and now tell you even weeping, that they are the enemies of the cross of Christ: Whose end is destruction, whose God is their belly, and whose glory is in their shame, who mind earthly things.)"* Our lives should loudly testify that we belong to Jesus! Today's Christians need to adopt a theme song: "Now I belong to Jesus, Jesus belongs to me. / Not for the years of time alone, but for eternity."

II Corinthians 6:16 says, *"And what agreement hath the temple of God with idols?..."* What are *idols*?

An idol is anything that takes the place of God, anything that is the supreme object of our affection. God alone has the right to the supreme place in our hearts.[13]

People are mad about things; they love things. Personally, I would not want to make good friends with people who would rather work on Wednesday night than go to church so they can have *things*. Of course, some people must work on church nights, but for some it is merely a matter of choice. I personally would not allow anyone in my family to work during a church service.

Some students from Hyles-Anderson College, the college which was founded and governed by the First Baptist Church of Hammond, are scheduled to work on church nights. I understand that fact, but none of them should want to work during a church service. Those students should protest about missing church. I would be bothered greatly if my son said, "I have a job, and I *get* to miss Wednesday night church." If I detected one iota of happiness on his part, I would make him quit his job. Don't misunderstand me. I am not opposed to the fact that they have to work; I am opposed to the fact that some want to work during church services. It also bothers me when a young man wants to get a decent-paying job and spend all of that money on a fast, high-priced car instead of designating a good portion to the work of God. Teenage young men should not be driving fast cars that are worth $30,000 to $35,000. Idols!

It's about time that some people lowered their expectations and stopped being intoxicated with things (idols). Get away from the things-oriented crowd because that crowd is not the God-oriented crowd. When you come out from among that crowd, then He will be your God, and you will be His people.

"*Wherefore come out from among them, and be ye separate, saith the Lord, and touch not the unclean thing; and I will receive you* [more closely], *And will be a Father unto you, and ye shall be my sons and daughters, saith the Lord Almighty.*" (II Corinthians 6:17, 18) When you decide to leave the disobedient crowd with their godless ways, God your Redeemer becomes God your Father.

4. The Father/Son or Father/Daughter Relationship. Luke 11:2 introduces this close relationship. "*When ye pray, say, Our Father....*"

It is noteworthy that in the model prayer where we are admonished to pray, *"Our Father which art in heaven,"* this is the first time that the title of Father is attributed to God. It is here that He interjects His desire to have a relationship with us as a father would have with his son. The great heart of God wants us to be intimate with Him![14]

The Bible indicates that God is not obligated to hear our prayers or answer them until we can call Him *"Father."* Getting saved doesn't automatically qualify a Christian to get his prayers answered. He must rid his life of that which denies he is a sold-out, born-again Christian. As his righteousness is enhanced, he separates from wrong habits, and as he takes a stand for Jesus Christ, then he can go the Father and say, "Father, I need some help with some things." God, Who has examined the Christian's life, obligates Himself to hear and answer that Christian's prayer.

John 1:12 says, *"But as many as received him, to them gave he power to become the sons of God, even to them that believe on his name."* The word *power* means "authority." When a person get saved, God gives him power. He gives him the privilege or the right to exercise that authority if he so chooses. That person has the authority to go further in his Christian life, to become a *son*; God is now his Father. When God becomes the Christian's Father, the Christian now has the authority to call on God for help with the other relationships of life.

Prayer means more than a right relationship with God as our Father and our sonship obligations. It implies also right relationship with our fellow man, as brothers.[15]

Every time Jesus prayed, He always talked to "His Father." "Jesus prayed to God as Father. Simply and directly did He approach God in the charmed and revered circle of the Father."[16] Jesus never addressed His Father with statements like, "O Creator God..." or "O Lord of the Universe..." or "O God of all mankind...." Jesus lovingly and simply addressed Him as "Our Father...."

5. The Lord/Servant Relationship. Lordship is when the Christian voluntarily says, "I will obey You because I **fear** You. I will give to you because I am commanded to do so. I owe you a debt of duty, and so I will obey out of fear." *Fear* means "to reverence, to venerate, to treat with deference or reverential obedience." The Christian obeys because of duty.

To wait on God is entirely and unreservedly to refer ourselves to his wise and holy directions and disposals, and cheerfully to acquiesce in them, and comply with them. The servant that waits on his master chooses not his own way, but follows his master, step by step: thus must we wait on God, as those who have no will of our own, but what is wholly resolved into His, and must therefore study to accommodate ourselves to His.[17]

The servant relationship is one of service. At this point, the relationship is no longer one-sided. The Christian who is God's servant says, "God, I want to do something for You. I'll read my Bible, go to church, tell others about Jesus, and tithe." The Christian who reaches this level of relationship with God does what God tells him to do.

6. The Friend/Friend Relationship. The closest relationship available to any Christian and God on this earth is the friendship relationship. In Luke 11:5, the Bible says, *"And he said unto them, Which of you shall have a friend, and shall go unto him at midnight, and say unto him, Friend* [referring to God], *lend me three loaves."* In verse 3, the person praying needs daily bread, singular. In verse 5, he needs "loaves," plural. He did not get the bread from his Father; he got the bread from his friend. What is the difference?

We have already established in this chapter that we have a Creator, a Redeemer, a God, a Father, and a Lord (or Master). At this point, a Christian can go to God and get bread [Holy Spirit] or obtain spiritual investment from God. God wants every Christian not simply to work for Him, but to partner with Him and to invest in His work. When a Christian is more interested in doing so much more than merely having his own personal satisfaction met, he has arrived at the friendship stage. When a Christian reaches the point where he is willing to obey God in all matters, he will have completeness in friendship with his God. Friendship is when a Christian serves God because he loves God. He looks for ways to make God happy.

As we learn to know Jesus better and better, our prayers become quiet, confidential, and blessed conversations with Him, our best Friend, about the things that are on our minds, whether it be our own needs or the needs of others. We experience wonderful peace and security by leaving our difficulties, both great and small, with Him, Who is not only solicitous for our welfare but Who also understands what is best for us.[18]

On this earth, every man has the Creator relationship. Only a Christian can enjoy the benefits of the Redeemer relationship, the God relationship, the Father relationship, the Lord relationship, and the Friend relationship. If, as Christians, we want to influence the world, we cannot attain that goal until we reach the Friend relationship. At that point God knows He can trust us.

———

In prayer, soul meets Soul; man meets God. Between them there is faith and trust. By lifting his prayer heavenward, man expresses his faith in God; by bending earthward to listen, God expresses his trust in the sincerity of man.[19]

The true spirit of prayer is no other than God's own Spirit dwelling in the hearts of the saints. And as this spirit comes from God, so doth it naturally tend to God in holy breathings and pantings. It naturally leads to God, to converse with Him by prayer.

–Jonathan Edwards

Hallowed Be Thy Name

"And it came to pass, that, as he was praying in a certain place, when he ceased, one of his disciples said unto him, Lord, teach us to pray, as John also taught his disciples. And he said unto them, When ye pray, say, Our Father which art in heaven, Hallowed be thy name…." (Luke 11:1, 2)

A young couple in our church who were married on a Saturday, left their honeymoon getaway to be in church on Sunday! They were all snuggled up and sitting close— just like honeymooners do. Frankly, I was amazed at their commitment to be in their home church the day after they were married! I believe that couple showed great wisdom in starting their marriage with a commitment to church.

The lack of commitment to anything marks today's society, and the truth is, people are desperately seeking some form of absolute commitment. To be sure, a good marriage can be built on strong commitment. With commitment comes obligation and expectation. A newly married couple expects fidelity and faithfulness from each other. They expect duties to be performed that benefit one another. They have a legitimate right to expect the completion of some obligations.

Character says, "If we are going to spend our lives together, then we will make a commitment of marriage to each other." A lack of commitment is one reason why couples live together in an unwed situation. A man and a woman, who are desperately seeking commitment, remain uncommitted to each other! Marriage is just one area of life that illustrates the wonderful concept of commitment. The fabric of society must be built on the character of commitment.

Likewise, the Christian's relationship with God must be built on the character of commitment. As a Christian, I want to be totally committed to God. Getting my prayers answered is one direct result of being committed to Him. God gave us a wonderful example of commitment—His Son, Jesus Christ.

Do you think Jesus Christ, the Son of God, was committed to His Father? Absolutely! Do you think Jesus Christ was trying to get His Father to see things His way, or do you think Jesus was trying to see things His Father's way? One Scripture passage that proves Jesus' commitment was His prayer in the Garden of Gethsemane: "...*Father, if thou be willing, remove this cup from me: nevertheless not my will, but thine, be done.*" (Luke 22:42)

> Christ, when He saw that He must die, and that now His time was come, He wore His body out: He cared not, as it were, what became of Him: He wholly spent Himself in preaching all day, and in praying all night, preaching in the temple those terrible parables and praying in the garden such prayers, as the seventeenth of John, and "Thy will be done!" even to a bloody sweat. –Thomas Goodwin[1]

Commitment epitomized Jesus' life. Because Jesus was so committed to the Father's will, the Father was obligated to answer His prayers. No wonder all of Jesus' prayers are answered!

Similarly, that same kind of commitment level must be present in the life of a Christian for his prayers to be answered. When we become totally committed to Christ, we have reached the pinnacle of our relationship with Christ on earth. To get our prayers answered, we must pray with determination. We must get as committed to God as Christ was to His Father.

Commitment is like a two-way street. Let me illustrate. When my wife and I exchanged wedding rings on our wedding day, I obligated myself to care for her. My commitment to her means that I put her first in my life. If I am in the middle of a counseling appointment in my office and the phone rings, I check the code to see if the caller is my wife. If so, I answer the phone because she has my vow of commitment. I am happy to do so because I am committed to her. Our commitment to each other mirrors Jesus' saying, "If you will commit yourself to the Father, He will commit to you."

Luke 11 is not so much a prayer we pray as it is an outline to be followed. Basically, this passage contains instructions on praying. Jesus gives us the pattern prayer in what is commonly known as "The Lord's Prayer."

> In this model, perfect prayer He gives us a form to be followed, and yet one to be filled in and enlarged as we may decide when we pray. The outlines and form are complete, yet it is but an outline, with many a blank, which our needs and convictions are to fill in.[2]

Charles Spurgeon, "The Prince of Preachers," who built London's Metropolitan Tabernacle into the world's largest independent congregation during the nineteenth century, said of the Lord's prayer:

> What clear, sharp outlines it has. There are certain definite mercies, and they do not run into one another. There it stands, and as you look at the whole, it is a magnificent picture—not confusion, but beautiful order. Let it be so with your prayers.[3]

In verse 2, the word *hallowed* means "to show proper respect or reverence," "to hold in high esteem," "to give note," or lastly, "to take notice of that which is special above others of the same category."

God's name is holy. It is the expression in human speech of all that He is, and for that reason it is a thrice holy thing.

That name must never be thought of lightly. It is something to command our loftiest reverence and our purest love. It means that we desire that men shall regard the name of God in its true character, and that such a conception of His name is one of the greatest things for which we can pray. The honor of God's name has been the concern of all men who have been mighty in prayer. God's name is hallowed when He is loved and obeyed, when men live righteously and speak of Him with love and reverence. We are to call Him Father, but to remember that He is a holy Father, and that His name is a holy name.[4]

As a rule, when we talk to God or address Him in prayer, we often use various titles for Him. We might say, "Lord, bless us now," or "Heavenly Father, be with us." We use many different titles; however, we rarely address Him by His name.

Again, let us remind ourselves that when we pray, we are not speaking to some invisible, faraway entity. We are speaking to God our Creator, our Redeemer, our Father—our Heavenly Father. By virtue of His omnipresence, He is *always* right next to us! Christians who no longer have an earthly father can always have access to their Heavenly Father! He is as approachable as an earthly father! Therefore, we should address Him like we might speak to our earthly father. Frequently when we *think* as opposed to *saying* our prayers, our minds tend to drift off to other matters that are often time wasters. However, when we actualize God as our *Heavenly Father*, we can cozy up to Him and share all that is in our heart.

The Names of Jehovah God

Many names have been ascribed to God, but one particular chapter in Psalms tells us His name. Psalm 83:18 says, *"That men may know that thou, whose name alone is JEHOVAH, art the most high over all the earth."* God also has other names. Isaiah 9:6 lists several: *"For unto us a child is born, unto us a son is given: and the government shall be upon his shoulder: and his name shall be called Wonderful, Counsellor, The mighty God, The everlasting Father, The Prince of Peace."* Some people call the Pope "Father"; however, the Pope isn't *"The Everlasting Father."* He isn't even a good substitute because he is a mere mortal man. He may be revered more highly and called by a greater title, but no matter how high the Pope is elevated, he will never be Jehovah. Nobody has that name! God shares some of His names with people, but one name belongs to Him alone—Jehovah God! Jehovah—"the self-existent One"!

Jehovah God, the name of God most frequently used in the Old Testament, was the Old Testament Jesus Christ. When Moses talked to the burning bush in Exodus 3, he was in the very presence of Jesus Christ. Moses was instructed to take off his shoes because he was standing on holy ground. *"Moreover he said, I am the God of thy father, the God of Abraham, the God of Isaac, and the God of Jacob. And Moses hid his face; for he was afraid to look upon God."* (Exodus 3:6)

What does *Jehovah* mean? It means that God likes to show off, and He is the only God who has a right to show off. This passage illustrates the importance of Christians having the right relationship with God when they pray. When praying, Christians had better respect Who Jehovah God is.

The disciples understood the sacredness of reverence due Jehovah God. In fact, the Israelites would not speak the honored and exalted name "Jehovah" or "Yahweh" because the name was so sacred; however, they missed the point! God was performing miracles for them, and His chosen people were not taking note of what He was doing. Christian, when you want your prayers answered, take the time to notice what God has done for you because He enjoys being obligated to give things to people who notice what He does! God is a generous God! God so loved the world that He **GAVE**. The more we recognize that He is a giving God, the more He will give to us.

Six times in the Word of God, the name *Jehovah* is attached to another Hebrew name. God particularly wants us to notice these times. They mark incidents when God did something big for His children—when He met every need of man. For example, if I were to mention the name of Colonel Richard MacCormack,[5] the chairman of the deacon board at First Baptist Church of Hammond, most people automatically think, "He is a retired Air Force colonel." As a commissioned officer, he had power and authority over hundreds of military men and women as well as the power and authority to make major decisions. Likewise, as President of the United States of America, the name of George W. Bush carries weight and authority. If I mention *Jehovah*, the average person would say, "Powerful!" True! However, God has specific names for specific situations.

1. Jehovah-tsidkenu. God has given us His righteousness. *Jehovah-tsidkenu* means "The Lord our righteousness." God said, "When you didn't have any righteousness of your own, I gave Mine to you." God wants us to look at that righteousness of God every day and rejoice, "The Lord saved my soul!"

2. Jehovah-jireh. God has provided your daily bread. The name *Jehovah-jireh* means, "The God Who provides." God sees and provides! Jehovah-jireh means that God sees the needs beforehand and lays up in store so when one of His children asks, He can provide. With God, tomorrow's needs have already been provided. The power and provision of God is all available to us. Unfortunately we tend to forget to appreciate what He has done and will do for us. If we won't notice what God is doing, why should He do more for us? If we won't take time to know what God is doing, why would God want to do more for us?

Suppose a Christian desperately needs an answer to prayer and says, "When are You going to step in and help me?"

God will retort, "When are **you** going to notice what I have already done?"

Saying to God, "I need an answer **now**" won't change His mind about when and how to answer the prayer! God knows you needed His answer when you started nonchalantly praying, and you didn't appreciate Him very much. He wants to be seen as a generous God. Simply put, God wants to be noticed!

How can we expect God to answer our bland, boring, rote repetitions? He wants us to put Him to the test and to give Him requests that only He can answer. What has God done for you? Do you notice the little everyday "boring" things that God does for you?

Recently while I was taking a short trip with some friends, we were walking through a parking lot. "Just a minute! Wait just a minute," I exclaimed. I bent down and picked up a penny. I showed it to those who were with me and said, "God loves me!" When I see a penny, I am always reminded that God loves me!

Jehovah-jireh! When I bow my head in prayer, the need I am presenting to *Jehovah-jireh* has already been seen by Him, has already been provided by Him, has already been protected by Him, and has been ready for distribution—with interest! Down through the ages, God saw us fall to our knees and pray. God placed our future requests in a Heavenly bank account, and He has been adding interest to that investment. What a generous God we have!

3. *Jehovah-shammah.* The Lord is right here! *Jehovah-shammah* means "the Lord is present." This name signifies God's abiding presence with His people. *"Thus saith the LORD, The heaven is my throne, and the earth is my footstool...."* (Isaiah 66:1) God is omnipresent; He is everywhere at the same time.

Imagine for a moment that you are walking outside on a foggy day. How close is the fog to you? The fog, "condensed water vapor in cloudlike masses close to the ground and limiting visibility,"[6] surrounds you. God is a Spirit Who is as close to you as fog. Can you see the end of the fog? Usually not. God is the same—He continues on forever—without any termination. What a God!

Our God is not far off; our God is right here with us. The companionship of God, the partnership of God, and the presence of God describe *Jehovah-shammah.*

4. Jehovah-Shalom. "The Lord is my Peace." God is my "spiritual sigh." When an unusually heavy day or an unusually heavy burden comes, sometimes I will just sigh. If my wife asks, "Is everything okay?" I can answer "Yes" because God brings peace.

Jehovah-Shalom brings peace in troubled marriages. He brings peace to troubled relationships. He brings peace to troubled homes. *"And the peace of God, which passeth all understanding, shall keep your hearts and minds through Christ Jesus."* (Philippians 4:7)

5. Jehovah-nissi. "The Lord is my banner!" God had given Moses and the children of Israel great victory over the Amalekites. With Aaron and Hur assisting Moses, Joshua and the armies of Israel fought the Amalekites and won the victory. *"And Moses built an altar, and called the name of it Jehovah- nissi."* (Exodus 17:15) God gave the victory over Israel's besetting enemies.

Christian, does God give you victory over temptation, trial, and tribulation? Do you go to an old-fashioned altar in search of His divine help? Do you pray, *"Jehovah-nissi,* the Lord is my banner"? The Lord has already given the victory! God is a God Who is victorious!

6. Jehovah-Sabaoth. It is the armies of Heaven! II Kings 6:13-17 tells an account of the Assyrian armies surrounding the city of Dothan. Verse 15 says, *"And when the servant of the man of God was risen early, and gone forth, behold, an host compassed the city both with horses and chariots. And his servant said unto him, Alas, my master! how shall we do?"*

The Assyrians have been called the Romans of Asia. Like the Romans, they were great conquerors. They won their victories in the Roman way, by superb organization, weapons, and equipment. Written records indicate that the Assyrians treated conquered people cruelly. If conquered people rebelled or refused to pay tribute, the Assyrians often destroyed their cities and sent the people to distant parts of the empire. A large region, its land encompassed much of the northern part of modern-day Iraq.[7]

Once the Assyrian troops had battered down a city gate, they showed no mercy. They ruthlessly murdered, tortured, and enslaved their enemies. Their practice of relocating rebellious peoples made them very despised. Any conquered people would forever hate the cruel Assyrians. Their extreme measures of exacting tribute have been some of the most brutal scenes of human cruelty that the world has ever known as seen from archaeological finds. One of the ancient monuments discovered in the ruins of ancient Assyria has this inscription by King Ashurnasirpal which described his methods of warfare:

"In the midst of the mighty mountain I slaughtered them, and, with their blood, dyed the mountain red like wool....I carried off their spoil and their possessions. The heads of the warriors I cut off, and I formed them into a pillar over against the city....I flayed all the chief men who had revolted and I covered the pillar with their skins; some I walled up within the pillar; some I impaled upon the pillar on stakes....Many within the border of my own land I flayed, and I spread their skins upon the walls, and I cut off the limbs of the royal officers who had rebelled."[8]

For obvious reasons, Gehazi, Elisha's servant, was more than a little nervous and apprehensive about the buildup of armies. However, Elisha showed no worry about the unfolding situation at hand. *"And Elisha prayed, and said, Lord, I pray thee, open his eyes, that he may see. And the LORD opened the eyes of the young man; and he saw: and, behold, the mountain was full of horses and chariots of fire round about Elisha.*" (II Kings 6:17) God's armies were available to do Elisha's bidding! *Jehovah-Sabaoth!*

As God reveals Himself to us, He wants us to take notice of how good He has been to us. A God Who has been that good to us is not interested in giving us more of what we already ignore. He wants us to hallow His name and take time to notice Him.

Prayer is a high privilege, a royal prerogative and manifold and eternal are the losses by failure to exercise it. Prayer is the great, universal force to advance God's cause; the reverence which hallows God's name; the ability to do God's will, and the establishment of God's kingdom in the hearts of the children of men.[9]

Prayer is not persuading God. It is not coaxing God. It is not a matter of influencing God to do something for us. It is not overcoming God's reluctance. It is taking hold of God's willingness.[1]

Who Supplies the "Willing"?

"That Christ may dwell in your hearts by faith; that ye, being rooted and grounded in love, May be able to comprehend with all saints what is the breadth, and length, and depth, and height; And to know the love of Christ, which passeth knowledge, that ye might be filled with all the fulness of God. Now unto him that is able to do exceeding abundantly above all that we ask or think, according to the power that worketh in us, Unto him be glory in the church by Christ Jesus throughout all ages, world without end. Amen."
(Ephesians 3:17-21)

In Ephesians 3:20, the word *able* has always bothered me because I have never questioned God's ability. From the time I was a little boy who was reared to be in church, I have always known that God is able. The ability of God has never been the issue; however, I have always *made* it the issue. Why would God say He is able and leave out the obvious word: "willing"? After all, if God is able, is He willing?

I know scores of people who are able to do exceeding above anyone else. Some men of means could invest sizeable amounts of money in the work of the Lord, but they are not willing to do so. Ability must have a partner, and ability's partner is "willingness."

On the other hand, I know scores of people who are willing, but do not seem to have the ability. Many people would love to give God sizeable amounts of money, but they don't have the ability. The bottom line is that they worry about having the ability, but at least they are willing to be used of God. Those two words, *ability* and *willingness*, must partner together.

Every time I have read this passage in Ephesians, I ask myself, "But is God willing?" I say, "God, I have the 'ability' part down. I understand and know that You are able, but God, who is going to supply the 'willing'?"

The Bible tells me that God is willing. In II Peter 3:9, the Bible says, *"The Lord is not slack concerning his promise, as some men count slackness; but is longsuffering to us-ward, **not willing** that any should perish."* However, that example is a "not willing"; God is saying, "I don't want that to happen." I want to see the "is willing" part of God. God says He is able to answer my prayers, but I want to know if He is *willing* to answer my prayers.

We all have a God Who is *able* to answer our prayers. The question is, "Is God willing to answer our prayers?" Is God willing to use us to do great and mighty works?

The entire Bible is a demonstration of God's ability and man's unwillingness. Why else would God include all those accounts of answered prayers in the Bible? Why record the accounts of Daniel and the lion's den, or the Hebrew boys walking in the fiery furnace, or the provision of manna in the morning when the Israelites wandered in the wilderness, or the parting of the Red Sea, or water flowing from the rock? All these stories in the Bible reveal God's ability! **God's ability plus man's willingness gets the job done!**

God never considers the ability of man. God never wondered if man was able to do anything because He knew man was (and is) unable to do anything! Jesus said in John 15:5, *"...for without me ye can do nothing."* But then in Philippians 4:13, He presents another aspect and says, *"I can do all things through Christ which strengtheneth me."* Still, nobody has ever provided ability that God is interested in considering because God is not interested in man's ability; He is interested in man's willingness.

II Corinthians 8:12 says, *"For if there be first a willing mind, it is accepted according to that a man hath, and not according to that he hath not."* God did not look at what man did not have; God said, "I want to know: are you willing?" Unfortunately, too many people offer excuses: "God, if I had more ability, I'd be more willing."

God wants us to stop attaching our willingness to *our* ability because that is exactly why nothing gets done. Rather, He wants us to attach our willingness to *His* ability! After all, He is able to do exceeding abundantly above all that we ask or think. Instead, we are trying to look at our ability and God's willingness, but He doesn't supply the willingness. Mankind supplies the willingness—not the ability!

God wants to know if we are willing to stay on our knees and pray, to get up early and stay up late, and work, and sweat, and toil, and love, and love, and love, and love, and be abused, and be hated, and be scorned, and be ridiculed. He wants to know if we are willing to pay the price. In Luke 22:42, Jesus Christ says, *"...Father, if thou be willing, remove this cup from me: nevertheless not my will, but thine be done."* Christ was *willing* to go to the cross. We are saved today because Christ was willing to go to the cross.

In Gethesemane we see that our Lord, according to His constant habit, consulted and arranged with the Father the work He had to do on earth. First He besought Him in agony and bloody sweat to let the cup pass from Him; when He understood that this could not be, then He prayed for strength to drink it, and surrendered Himself with the words: "Thy will be done." He was able to meet the enemy full of courage and in the power of God gave Himself over to the death of the cross. *He had prayed.*[2]

In Romans 4, the New Testament reiterates the story of Abraham and Sarah from the Old Testament. *"Who against hope believed in hope, that he might become the father of many nations; according to that which was spoken, So shall thy seed be. And being not weak in faith, he considered not his own body now dead, when he was about an hundred years old, neither yet the deadness of Sarah's womb: He staggered not at the promise of God through unbelief; but was strong in faith, giving glory to God; And being fully persuaded that, what he had promised, he was able to perform."* (Romans 4:18-21) Both Abraham and Sarah were far too old to have children when they received the incredible news that the baby they had been promised would finally come into their lives. Both knew God was able. In their case, it wasn't the ability of God to make a 90-year-old woman able to conceive and bear a child. How many 90-year-old women are *willing* to give birth to a baby?!

The promises of God are so great to those who truly pray, when He puts Himself so fully into the hands of the praying ones, that it almost staggers our faith and causes us to hesitate with astonishment. We "stagger at the promises through unbelief."[3]

Unfortunately not too many people were (or are) found willing to do what God wants them to do.

The Scriptures, which I have loved since I was a young boy, contain incredible accounts of great Christians. In all of these stories, God has always intended that *He* supply the ability and that *man* supply the willingness.

- In John 6 a little boy surrenders his sack lunch, and 5,000 men were fed. Quite possibly, the greater miracle was persuading that boy to give up his food! His willingness gave God the ability to feed the people.
- In Exodus 4 Moses was willing to return to Egypt to deliver the Israelites.
- In Daniel 6 Daniel was willing to pray though it meant being punished with the lions' den.
- In Daniel 3 three Hebrew boys were willing to stand for God though it meant the fiery furnace.

These amazing miracles required only two things: God's ability and man's willingness. Every Christian needs to weigh the question: "Am I willing?" The willingness of the Christian exposes God's ability.

Shadrach, Meschach, and Abednego

The Hebrew boys declared, *"...our God whom we serve is able...."* They recognized they had a God Who is able! Of the 50,000 Israelite young men who had been taken captive by Nebuchadnezzar, only three stood! The other 49,997 were bowing down and saying, "God is able," but they were not willing. However, Shadrach, Meshach, and Abednego stood shoulder to shoulder and asked each other, "Are you willing?" Because they believed God was able, they were willing.

The three young men were thrown into the furnace that had been heated seven times hotter than it had ever before been heated! Nebuchadnezzar and all those watching saw that indeed God was able to do exceeding abundantly above all that we ask or think. Those young men believed He was able to deliver them, and they received a bonus! They were delivered without the smell of smoke on their clothes and without a hair being singed!

Of God's *ability* they had no doubt, though of His *plan* they were not quite sure. As a matter of fact, God did not choose to deliver *from* the furnace but *in* it. Their faith believed when it could not see.[4]

Daniel

Daniel 6 records the story of Daniel's illegal praying. Bitter, jealous men who were envious of his leadership position reported him to the king. Because of his decree, the king had to sentence Daniel to death in the lions' den. The king did not sleep all night long for praying, fasting, and worrying about Daniel. When he went to where the lions were kept the next morning, *"...he cried with a lamentable voice unto Daniel:...O Daniel, servant of the living God, is thy God, whom thou servest continually, able to deliver thee from the lions?"* I can just see Daniel as he stretches, yawns, and says, *"O king, live for ever! My God hath sent his angels, and hath shut the lions' mouths, that they have not hurt me: forasmuch as before him innocency was found in me; and also before thee, O king, have I done no hurt."* (Daniel 6:20-22)

Daniel knew His God was able. He was willing to stand and let God's ability be manifested through him.

Elijah

There had been a drought in the land for three years. (Any child could have easily started a fire under those conditions!) Elijah issued a challenge to the false prophets of Baal to ask their gods to send fire to consume their sacrifice, and he would do the same. The false prophets accepted the challenge, and of course, Baal failed miserably. Elijah first *"...repaired the altar of the LORD that was broken down."* (I Kings 18:30) Not only did he rebuild the altar, he also dug a trench around it, *"...as great as would contain two measures of seed."* (I Kings 18:32)

One measure is equal to about four pecks. One peck in liquid measurement is equal to eight quarts or two gallons. In essence Elijah dug a trench that held over 16 gallons of water. God instructed Elijah to pour water on the sacrifice three times. The water ran off the altar and filled the trench. Elijah used every preventive measure available to him to keep the sacrifice from burning! The false prophets of Baal could make no charge that Elijah had deceived them in any way.

Then when Elijah prayed, God heard; and when the fire came down from Heaven, it consumed everything—the animal sacrifice, the wet wood, the altar made of stones, the dust, and the water in the trench. It wasn't just enough for God to consume the sacrifice—that would have been too easy! He showed Himself able by consuming the rocks!

Molten rock reaches temperatures of 800 to 2,160° F. depending on the type of rock. One stroke of lightning measures more than 15,000,000 volts and generates temperatures of 50,000° F. or higher."[5]

God showed His ability when Elijah showed his willingness to stand against Ahab and the prophets of Baal. "God was with Elijah mightily because he was mighty in prayer."[6] When the people saw Elijah's prayer answered, they fell on their faces and they said, *"The LORD, he is the God; the LORD, he is the God."* (I Kings 18:39)

Elijah was in Elijah's praying. The whole man, with all his fiery forces, was in it. Almighty God to him was real. Prayer to him was the means of projecting God in full force on the world, in order to vindicate His name, establish His own being, to avenge His blasphemed name and violated law, and to vindicate His servants.[7]

The reason for Elijah's success is an open secret. Was he thinking of how he would be held up as an example wherever the truth of God was preached? No, he was not thinking of making history; he was thinking only of making Jehovah-followers out of these Baal-worshipers. God's glory was at stake; so he knew God would send the fire.[8]

These are incomparable stories! In all honesty, I must admit that I do not marvel nearly as much at God's ability as I marvel at man's unwillingness. God's willingness was answered on a place called Calvary. His willingness was illustrated on an old rugged cross. God's willingness is not the issue; *man's* willingness is always the issue! Believing God is able is the first phase of partnering with Him. The second phase is man's being willing. Partnering with God means that His ability plus man's willingness makes things—exceeding great and mighty things—happen. Nothing is too tough for God.

When water came from the rock in the wilderness, it didn't gush from limestone or sandstone. That would have been too easy for God! The water surged from a flint rock! Geologists classify flint as a chalcedony. In Revelation 21:19, the Bible mentions that the third foundation of the wall of the new Jerusalem was made of chalcedony—a very hard, even-grained rock. Man valued flint because it produced a spark when struck against some hard metal. Flint rock would be the last place to look for water—all the more reason for God to demonstrate His power and cause water to flow from flint.

When the children of Israel wanted quail, God obliged. The last place to find quail would be in the desert! God sent millions of quail to the desert to feed the Israelites. God was well able to provide! God's ability cannot be explained any more than all the miracles of the Bible can be explained. But one thing is certain, God's ability is always manifested through man's willingness.

If God can do anything but fail, then why do marriages fail? Unwilling partners. Why do finances fail? Unwilling tithers. Why do families fall apart? Unwilling children and parents working as a team. Why do churches fail? Unwilling pastors and staff members! Why does the world go to Hell? Because of unwilling Christians not ready to say, "God, I'll match Your ability by my willingness."

What exactly does a person's willingness have to do with prayer? A Christian goes to his prayer closet and says, "God, You are awesome! I will match Your ability with a willing heart. Here I am, Lord. I will give You my willingness to match Your ability." At that point of surrender, prepare for God to test you.

- Remember the three boys sentenced to die in the fiery furnace for standing? God was checking their willingness!

- Remember Daniel's choosing to pray under the threat of being thrown to the lions? God was checking his willingness!
- Remember Elijah's 63-word prayer that called down fire from Heaven? God was checking his willingness!

We must understand that these men were of like passions—just like you and me.

Throughout the Bible God brings us example after example of men who prayed and got the answer, and then God tells us, "These men were ordinary men, frail men, sinful men, and yet by faith, righteous men. They were men of like passions as we are, but they prayed and their prayers were answered. Therefore, dear frail Christian, take heart and ask great things from God.[9]

Just imagine what God could and would do today if His people were totally, 100 percent willing.

Effective prayer is prayer that attains what it seeks. It is prayer that moves God, effecting its end.

– Charles Finney

God's Recipe
for Answered Prayer

"I exhort therefore, that, first of all, supplications, prayers, intercessions, and giving of thanks, be made for all men; For kings, and for all that are in authority; that we may lead a quiet and peaceable life in all godliness and honesty. For this is good and acceptable in the sight of God our Saviour; Who will have all men to be saved, and to come unto the knowledge of the truth. For there is one God, and one mediator between God and men, the man Christ Jesus; Who gave himself a ransom for all, to be testified in due time. Whereunto I am ordained a preacher, and an apostle, (I speak the truth in Christ, and lie not;) a teacher of the Gentiles in faith and verity." (I Timothy 2:1-7)

When I was a little boy, I gave my heart to God, and God took me up on my offer. I cannot recall any time in my life when God and I were on the "outs" with each other. I have been "put out" with God once or twice, and I am sure He has been "put out" with me many times! Allow me to enlarge upon what can happen when a child or a young person gives his heart to God.

I fret for the young people who, as they go through school, are borne along by the crowd around them. After graduation, these young people usually enroll in college or seek some type of gainful employment. Their bonds of friendships are weakened or even severed as these young people focus on different avenues of life. Many of these young people find themselves more and more alone with fewer and fewer of their comrades-in-arms. Often at that point, their Christianity crumbles. Many of these "lost-to-the-cause-of-Christ" young people got saved, walked an aisle, made a public profession of faith, got baptized, and sat in church with their parents—just like I did. Grade school, junior high, and high school brought years of contentment to them. But the bombshell of high school graduation ushered in a sudden, cataclysmic change.

I attended a public high school, and in all honesty, I basically lived to protect myself. Insults, blasphemous living, premarital intimacy, drunkenness, peer pressure, and drugs enveloped the school property. I watched my friends' childhood faith crumble, and truthfully, I did not wear my faith well outwardly. I cannot say that I was a paragon of moral righteousness as a young Christian. I was a very good boy—partly because I was too scared to do much except walk around in a shell. When I graduated from high school, I really wasn't sure where I was or who I was. I only knew I wanted to go in business with my father; but for reasons I didn't understand then, God put me in a Christian college.

I did not know one other human being on that college campus. I soon discovered their brand of Christianity was different than I had known. I have often wondered why God sent me there. I soon learned that when everything familiar and dear is stripped from you, soon enough you will find out what you have inside of you. I discovered the wonderful truth that I had a strong relationship with my God. I did not wear that relationship on the inside like I did as a high schooler.

While sitting in my dormitory room, I remember picking up my Bible, and with tears running down my face, I said, "God, this is the only thing I have that's from home. I'm lonely, and I'm scared, and I don't want to be here, but God, I have You here. And God, because I have You with me, I can handle anything— the world, the flesh, and all that the Devil throws at me!"

Truthfully, I do not know from where that faith came. It may have come from my parents or my grandparents or from the preachers who came into my life. I don't know exactly where I got the faith that I needed, but I know this: if you don't have an active prayer life, you will not get all that you can out of life.

I Timothy 2:1 says, *"I exhort therefore, that, first of all, supplications, prayers, intercessions, and giving of thanks, be made for all men."* This passage contains four ingredients that God says must be part of every Christian's prayer life. The Bible uses the phrase, *"first of all"* to indicate the proper order of those ingredients. Every lady knows the two main rules of cooking: (1) Have the right ingredients, and (2) Use the ingredients in the proper order. When the wrong ingredients are used or the right ingredients are used in the wrong order, the results often prove disastrous. Likewise, if God's order is not followed, the desired result will not be achieved. The Christian will have an out-of-balance, ineffective prayer life.

Supplication

The number-one ingredient in a Christian's prayer life is supplication. The word *supplication* comes from the word *supple* which means "bendable, flexible, moldable, easily conformable." Modeling clay, which can be rolled, pulled, stretched, and punched, beautifully illustrates the word *supple*. Modeling clay conforms easily to whatever a child wants to form. When a Christian supplicates, he follows God's command to conform, or mold, or bend, or flex.

When I was a little boy, my Grandpa Elgersma owned a trailer park with 100 units. He had a block incinerator building where the families in the trailer park burned their garbage. Once a month Grandpa cleaned out the ashes and the noncombustible items—the glass bottles, the cans, and any other metal debris. Grandpa loaded that rubbish by shovel into a huge trailer which he pulled behind his pickup truck and took to the city dump. The job was messy, stinky, and unenjoyable, as well as hard work.

I often spent Friday night at my grandparents' house, and one Saturday morning Grandpa asked me to help him load the trailer and go to the dump with him.

When I said it didn't sound like much fun, Grandpa nodded, "It's not."

I didn't go. I chose to stay home to play with some of my buddies. About three hours later, I noticed another of my buddies holding what was left of a butter pecan ice cream cone—my favorite! I walked up to him, pointed at the cone, and said, "Where did you get that?"

He said, "Your grandpa asked me if I wanted to go to the dump with him, and I said, 'Sure!' After we finished at the dump, we stopped at Mill's Ice Cream Parlor on the way home."

I ran to my grandpa, and I said, "Grandpa, you didn't tell me you were going to the ice cream store."

"I wasn't planning to go to the ice cream store," he said, "but on the way home I was hot and sweaty, wanted something to cool down myself, so I bought me an ice cream cone and one for your buddy. Too bad you didn't want to go."

I made a promise on the spot that I would never again fail to go to the dump with Grandpa. About a month later in anticipation of going to the dump with Grandpa, I spent Friday night with my grandparents. At 6:00 a.m., I woke up, ran into my grandparents' room, climbed on top of Grandpa's belly, and said, "Grandpa! Grandpa! Get up! It's time to go to the dump!"

To say he was amazed at my eagerness is an understatement. Eventually he got up, had breakfast, did the chores, and finally announced, "Let's go!" We got into his Chevy pickup, hooked up the red trailer, backed up to the incinerator, and opened up the door. He handed me a coal shovel, and we scooped the ashes and all the remnants of the unburned trash into the trailer, pulled a tarp over it, and drove to the dump.

When we arrived at the dump, we found a worse-than-normal

mess because it had rained the night before. The Heinz pickle factory in Holland, Michigan, dumped all of their rotten cucumbers there. Rats ran everywhere, and flies covered the trash. Anywhere we stepped, oozing mud threatened to pull off our shoes. We finally got the trailer unloaded, washed it off with a power hose, and finally got back in the truck. We had worked hard on what had become a hot, humid day.

Grandpa mentioned he was hungry and thirsty and said, "How about you?" I agreed that I was both hungry and thirsty. We decided to go to Mill's Ice Cream Parlor. We went inside and looked at all the barrels full of ice cream flavors, and I found my butter pecan barrel. Grandpa ordered a triple scoop, and I followed suit.

By the time we got home, I had ice cream all over me—telltale proof that I had enjoyed every bit of my triple dip butter pecan ice cream cone! As a matter of fact, I enjoyed many more triple-dip cones—after I learned my lesson!

I learned something about Grandpa that day. I learned if I went with him and helped him, I could get almost anything from him. In fact, I learned I had to be careful what I asked for or what I talked about because Grandpa was very generous. Grandpa liked spoiling his grandkids, and I received wonderful gifts from him and had many delightful times being with him.

Suppose I had gone to my grandfather and said, "Grandfather, I understand you're going to the dump today. I'd like to place my order with you. I'm going to stay home to play with my buddies, but I want you to stop at Mill's Ice Cream Parlor and buy me a triple-dip butter pecan ice cream cone. I would also like a hot dog and an order of French fries." Can you imagine the insult that my grandfather would have felt? Of course, placing an order like that would have been ludicrous.

I often think about that story when I really need something from God. When I go to God and say, "I need something from

You," I am always reminded of Grandpa's asking me to go to the dump and my subsequent refusal. In my mind's eye, I see my boyhood friend walking with the remnants of that butter pecan ice cream cone. I go to my God and say, "Where do You want to go? We'll go any place You want because I need some things from You." When Grandpa found out that I wanted to go with him, he was willing to go with me where I wanted to go. If I convinced Grandpa that I wanted to go where he wanted to go, I could go to him and get most anything I wanted—even a minibike!

That story illustrates exactly what supplication is. Supplication is convincing God you want to go where He is going and that wherever He goes is a delightful place to go.

Years ago when Dr. Hyles traveled every week, he invited me to go with him occasionally. One memorable time we flew to a meeting he had in Texas. We borrowed the pastor's car on Tuesday, and we spent the entire afternoon together driving around, philosophizing, and talking. It was unbearably hot, so we stopped for something to drink. He decided to go to a mall just to walk around and cool down.

As we walked around the mall, he spotted a Dillard's Store for men. I had never been to a Dillard's in my life. He went up to a rack of sport coats, picked one out, and said, "What a handsome sport coat." When I agreed with his good taste, he asked me what size I wore, found one in my size, and told me to try it on. Evidently he liked what he saw because he asked if I had trousers to match. When I said "no," we went together and picked out a pair of trousers. While I was having the sport coat and trousers fitted, he went to pick out a tie. He soon returned with two ties. When I couldn't make up my mind which I liked best, he chuckled and said, "You shop just like your wife!"

"You taught her," I bantered. Before our boys' day out at Dillard's concluded, he had also bought me a pair of shoes.

When I came back home from the trip, I sported a brand new

sport coat, new trousers, new shoes, and two new ties! Let me pose a question: How do you think Dr. Hyles would have felt if I had met him that morning we were to leave and said, "You know, Brother Hyles, I have rethought this trip. My men's softball league is meeting tonight, and I don't want to miss the game. Then I was reading the *TV Guide* and noticed a made-for-television movie is going to be premiered. I just don't want to miss it because it might never be on again. So, if you don't mind, I'm going to stay home and watch television and play baseball. I would love to be with you, but since I won't be going, would you mind picking up a new sport coat, a pair of trousers, and a couple of ties for me. Expensive shoes would be nice, too. I'd be so appreciative." Imagine how my father-in-law would have reacted!

Unfortunately, that is how most Christians pray! We go to God with our lists of what we want and say, "God, I need these." When God asks us to go to the church bus route, or visit the homeless, or stop by the nursing home, or teach a Sunday school class, we sputter, protest, and offer anemic excuses for our unwilling spirit. The day we convince God that we want to bend and flex with His schedule and we want to bend to His wishes, mold to His will, and convince Him that we really mean business, is the day we say, "God, I'm not coming just to see what I can get for me."

I didn't meet my father-in-law with a list of what I wanted. I met him with an eager heart that said, "It doesn't matter where you are going; I just want to go with you." I can guarantee you that he had the wherewithal to give me whatever I wanted—wherever we went. The more I spent time with him, the more I got what I wanted.

If we could ever convince God that we really enjoy being with Him, it would revolutionize our prayer life. "The Lord wants us to pray because He loves to hear us, because it makes us conscious of our dependence on Him, because it therefore makes our union with Him a greater reality."1 If we convinced God that it wasn't an irritation or disruption in our schedule to go to Sunday church or a Wednesday night Bible study, then we would see how much easier it is to get our prayers answered. God wants to partner in prayer with us. For some crazy reason, God likes us a lot and wants to be with us.

Are we not made in the image of God? Hence, whatever is good about us is a reflection of the personality of God. Then if we love to answer the requests of our children, would not God want to answer us? There are so many places in the Bible that show us God wants to be *loved* as we want to be *loved*. He likes *attention* as we like *attention*. He loves *praise* as we love *praise*. He loves *adoration* as we love *adoration*, and yes, He loves to answer His children as we love to answer ours.[2]

As I have already said, when I was a little boy, I gave my heart to God. For some reason, God reached out and said, "I'll take that heart, son," and God and I have never parted ways. I have never become a cynical, skeptical Christian. I am not a pessimistic Christian who wonders why everything stinks in the Christian life. I am an optimistic Christian who wonders why God is so good. I am not the kind of Christian who wonders why bad things happen to good people, though I do wonder why good things happen to anyone.

Before I was ruined and bitter because God didn't come through for me, before I realized that God is a respecter of persons in the matter of prayer—that God only answers some people's prayer, before I realized that the Bible is a dull, boring Book, before I realized that preaching was something to sleep through, before I realized that church was to be avoided, before I realized that soul winning was a task assigned to only gifted people, before I realized the bus route was a pain in the neck and taxing on the wallet, before I realized that the nursing home ministry is a bunch of old, drooling people, before I realized what a schedule interruption it would be to give my heart to God, before I knew what a wearisome ritual Christianity was, I gave my heart to God! I learned the wonderful truth that Christianity is the most enjoyable and delightful exercise and investment of time a person can give. Before I realized that tithing was an interference with my savings plan and offerings were a sacrifice, I realized that God was exceedingly generous and I could never out-give God. I could never out-love, out-spend, or out-care God. In fact, every time I went with God, I found I came back a richer, more blessed man because of our time together! Wanting to spend time with God unlocks His treasures.

Supplication is convincing God that where He is going is where you are already headed. You want to get things from God, and when He doesn't seemingly come through, you say, "God is not in my life because I have financial problems." You have gotten so preoccupied with what you want, that you have forgotten that is not how to get it. You don't get God's attention by trying to get God's attention. You get God's attention by convincing Him you just want His presence. Supplication is convincing God that we want to be with Him and go where He is going.

Prayer

Prayer simply means "getting God involved." When you want God involved, you must first convince Him that you want to be with Him. Then you may go to God and say, "May I bring some things to You?" That is when God will bend His ear to listen to you.

For instance, when you're knocking on doors and going soul winning would be an excellent time to talk to God. I Timothy 2:3, 4 says, *"For this is good and acceptable in the sight of God our Saviour; Who will have all men to be saved, and to come unto the knowledge of the truth. For there is one God, and one mediator between God and men, the man Christ Jesus.*" According to these verses, soul winning is close to the heart of God.

We need to stop relying on the arm of the flesh. Before seeking employment, seek God first! Before running to Dad and saying, "Dad, get me a job!" go to God first and say, "I want to know where You want me to go to work."

If we would start praying about everything, we would soon discover a peace and joy that we had no idea existed. My Bible says, *"In every thing give thanks...,"* and *"Pray without ceasing."* In every area of life, we should be saying, "God, I want to thank You for Your leadership, and I want to know what You want. You have a will in mind for me, and I want to do Your will!" When a Christian convinces God that he wants to do His will, God will show that Christian His will when He is ready to do so.

The word "prayer" really means "a wish directed towards," that is, towards God. All that true prayer seeks is God Himself, for with Him we get all we need. Prayer is simply "the turning of the soul to God."[3]

Intercession

The word *intercession* quite literally means "make a deal." To *intercede* means "to go to God on behalf of someone else and bargain with God for that person." Bargaining with God is saying, "God, someone is in trouble, and You are the only help, God! I am going to put my neck on the line for that individual, God. He needs You badly, God!"

Intercessory prayer—to prevail—is to be unselfish. All prayer says, "Not my will, but Thine, be done."[4]

A former associate of mine who is building a great church in Houston, Texas, tells the story of how he was a rebellious teenager running with a wild crowd. His parents were godly Christians, but by his testimony, he did not care about breaking their hearts. He did not care about anyone except himself. One morning he came home during the early morning hours to change his clothes while his friends waited. He went to his bedroom, changed his clothes, and took out a pair of brand new penny-loafers to wear. When he slipped them on, he discovered they were soaking wet! Angrily he stormed into his parents' room and shouted, "Why are my shoes soaking wet?"

When his mother looked at him with bloodshot, puffy eyes, he said, "It was like daggers going into my heart; I knew immediately why my shoes were wet."

"Son," she said, "Your dad and I love you, but you won't listen to us. Every night while you are out partying, I take your shoes out of the closet, and I pray and I cry over them. Somehow my words haven't gotten through to you; maybe my tears will."

His mind's picture of his mother crying over his shoes broke his sin-hardened heart! That mother interceded for her beloved son.

Mother, when the preaching won't penetrate the ears of your teenager, maybe your tears will penetrate his soul. Fall on your face and say, "God, I don't know how to reach him," and fill his shoes with your tears. It's time some old-fashioned, praying mothers say to God, "I will do whatever it takes—whatever it takes—to get hold of my wandering boy's heart." Until we get back to praying mothers and fathers, this country is without hope. Everything else is futile until you go to your God in your prayer closet, pour out your tears in another's shoes, and bargain with God.

Intercession is always for persons; we supplicate for things, but we intercede for persons. Intercessory prayer rises above a party, an administration, a sect, a college, a corporation; it views all things in the light of eternal and world-embracing principles—principles of righteousness and good and truth—for the good of humanity. Of such prayer there never can be too much.[5]

Another former associate tells an arresting story of serving as a soldier—unsaved and rebellious—in Vietnam. Knowing he was unsaved, his mother was scared to death he would be killed and spend eternity in Hell. She sought counsel from her pastor and said, "Dr. Hyles, you know my son is an unsaved rebel. If he gets killed, I know he will go straight to Hell. What can I do? I don't know how to reach my boy. He won't listen to me."

"Start knocking on doors and winning souls," Dr. Hyles said. "Every time you win a teenage boy or young adult man, say to God, 'I won him to Christ, God. Please watch out for my boy.' "

That good woman won 200 to 500 people a year to Christ. Every time she won a soul, she prayed, "God, I got You another child. Would You get my child saved?"

The time came when her son did get saved. His mother wrote regularly and enclosed tracts in all her letters. He was like Saul who could not stand against the "pricks." (Acts 9:5) That young man who was running from God became a preacher who has been greatly used of God.

Dr. Tom Williams tells an amazing story about a revival where he had been preaching about intercessory prayer—bargaining with God to get people saved. A smartly dressed, obviously well-educated, upper-middle-class woman came to him after the service and said, "Dr. Williams, I need to speak with you a moment about my unsaved husband. You mentioned tonight about praying and interceding for your loved ones to get saved. I want him to be saved."

"Ma'am," Dr. Williams said, "let's pray right now." He knelt at the altar, but she stayed standing. He looked up at her and asked,

"Do you want to kneel beside me?"

"Well, I guess I can," she hesitatingly consented. When she knelt, Dr. Williams began to pray, "Dear God, give this man a heart attack! Give him a stroke. Put him in critical condition. Put him in ICU. Put him flat on his back where he's facing up, and he has no place else to look but to You...."

The woman was so aghast at his prayer, she stopped Dr. Williams and said, "What are you doing?"

"Ma'am, I thought you wanted your husband saved...," he began to explain.

"Oh, yes! I want him saved," she interrupted, "but I don't want him saved like that!"

"Ma'am, I'm sorry," Dr. Williams said sadly, "but until you're willing to put your husband totally in the hands of God and give God permission to do whatever He has to do, then you don't really want your husband saved."

The father of one of our church members would not get saved. He was a stonyhearted man who just would not listen and had no use for the Gospel. Preachers around the country, including Pastor Hyles, tried to win this man to Christ. He was a Mississippi River boat captain—not a mean man, just a tough man—who had no use for the Gospel. Our church member began praying, "God, whatever it takes to get my father saved, do it!" Little did he know that a major catastrophe on the river would confront his father. The river boat almost sank, and that father almost died. Flat on his back with his face pointed toward Heaven, he finally yielded to God. I find it amazing how God can twist the screws tight enough to make a strong man say, "I need You." Intercessory prayer is not for cowards.

When it comes to intercessory prayers, not many examples of them can be found in the Bible. Intercessory prayer is life-and-death prayer. Moses, who bargained with God for the nation of Israel, said, "God, please don't destroy Your people because the

Egyptians and other nations will say, 'Aren't these the people that your God loves?' Think of your friend Abraham. Please don't destroy Your people for Abraham's sake. God, if You must be angry, take Your anger out on me!" *"Yet now, if thou wilt forgive their sin— ; and if not, blot me, I pray thee, out of thy book which thou hast written."* (Exodus 32:32) When I read this powerful Scripture passage, I can almost feel the air pregnant with the intensity of what Moses was about to say. He was saying, "God, if You must send Your people to Hell, send me instead." No wonder God used Moses!

Throughout the book of Hebrews the character of Moses is likened to that of Jesus. That same level of commitment that made Moses say, "I'll go to Hell," is compared to the same Christ Who said, "I'll go to Hell for mankind." He went to the cross and suffered mankind's Hell.

Only one record exists of an individual in the New Testament who prayed this way. The Apostle Paul said, "My heart's prayer is that Israel should be saved. I can wish myself accursed from God for Israel's sake."
The words *accursed from God* mean "unsaved." Paul prayed with the full intent of going to Hell in place of others.

Intercessory prayer bargains with God on behalf of those who don't deserve that kind of prayer. It is very advanced Christianity, and not many people even entertain the thought of praying that way—let alone do it.

The father of John G. Paton knelt every night for years in the little Scotch home and made his intercession. "I have heard," wrote his son in his own autobiography, "that in long after years the worst woman in the village of Torthorwald, then leading an immoral life but since changed by the grace of God, was known to declare that the only thing that kept her from despair and from the hell of the suicide, was when in the dark winter nights she crept close up underneath my father's window, and heard him pleading in family worship that God would convert 'the sinner from the error of wicked ways and polish him as a jewel for the Redeemer's crown.' "

"I felt," she said, "that I was a burden on that good man's heart, and I knew that God would not disappoint him. That thought kept me out of hell and at last led me to the only Saviour."[6]

Is it any wonder that this praying man's son became a famous missionary to the New Hebrides Islands?

Many people sing the words of the song, "For whatever it takes for my will to break, That's what I'd be willing to do," without any thought of what those words really mean. I have never been able to sing that song because I believe I realize the full impact of those words.

The business of Christianity is not about how many possessions we can hang onto. Rather, it's working with God and saying, "God, I don't know the price that has to be paid, but I'm willing to pay it." A God Who put His Son on the line would be happy to have someone join Him. If we cannot find a people who will be willing to pay the price, who will pay it? Very few people understand the price someone has to pay with intercessory prayer.

Thankfulness

Lastly, I Timothy 2:1 concludes with "...*giving of thanks.*" The Bible uses two different expressions about gratitude. One is *thankful*, and one is *giving thanks*. The fact that this verse does not say, "*thankful*" but "*giving thanks*" is of utmost importance. Being *thankful* comes from the swelling of a person's spirit where he is full and bubbling over with gratitude. It is exactly how I felt when my grandfather bought me a Montgomery Ward, 5-horsepower, $175 minibike! The *giving of thanks* is "an act of courtesy bestowed to people."

One day a friend and I went soul winning at Purdue University, and we stopped at a service station to purchase some gasoline. I decided to go inside and buy some snacks. I was standing in line with my choices behind my friend who was waiting to pay for his gasoline. When he stepped up to the counter, the cashier said, "That will be $12.00," so he gave her a large bill; she gave him the change due, and then said, "Next!"

I paid for my food, and we walked out together. We got into the car, but he just sat in the driver's seat. He didn't even start the car. "What's wrong?" I asked.

He said, "I paid for my gas. I gave her a large bill, and she gave me back some change, and then said, 'Next!' "

I was somewhat perplexed by what he said because I had just witnessed the entire exchange.

Then he added, "She didn't even say, 'Thank you,' and she should have."

"She wouldn't have meant it," I scoffed. "You're just a customer."

"You're missing the point," he interrupted. "Because I keep her in business, she *owes* me gratitude! I will never patronize this station again!"

Later, I began thinking about that conversation in reference to giving thanks.

I do not believe there is any sin more offensive to God, or more common among men, than the sin of ingratitude. We do not like it ourselves when we benefit persons, even in a trifling way, if we see clearly that they have no thanksgiving in their hearts. God is like ourselves in this respect; He has perhaps the same feeling in greater measure, for He is the author not of some good, but of all good, not of trifling benefits, but of life and health and home and friends, and a Saviour, and salvation, and keeping,—the author of all good gifts.[7]

God said, "Even if you don't *feel* it, have the courtesy to *say* it!" Are you mature enough that when you get done praying to say, "By the way, thank You for what You are going to do"? God loves gratitude.

If you want to have a happy marriage, a little gratitude goes a long way. If you want to have a happy home, a little gratitude goes a long way. If you want to have happy relationships, a little gratitude goes a long way. Want to have a happy prayer life? A little gratitude goes a long way! Stop whining and start thanking Him for what He has done for you. "Thanksgiving is an encouragement to God to bestow new graces and gifts upon us."[8]

A long time ago I learned that if I convinced God I wanted to be with Him, He liked to answer my prayers. I also discovered that when I put my neck on the line for other people, God liked to answer my prayers. When I told God "Thank You" for what He was going to do before He did it, God liked to answer my prayers. I don't know about you, but I need God to answer some prayers.

Prayer should be the breath of our breathing, the thought of our thinking, the soul of our feeling, and the life of our living, the sound of our hearing, the growth of our growing. Prayer in its magnitude is length without end, width without bounds, height without top, and depth without bottom. Illimitable in its breadth, exhaustless in height, fathomless in depths and infinite in extension.

–Homer W. Hodge[1]

6

Miracle Praying

"*Then was the secret revealed unto Daniel in a night vision. Then Daniel blessed the God of heaven. Daniel answered and said, Blessed be the name of God for ever and ever: for wisdom and might are his: And he changeth the times and the seasons: he removeth kings, and setteth up kings: he giveth wisdom unto the wise, and knowledge to them that know understanding: He revealeth the deep and secret things: he knoweth what is in the darkness, and the light dwelleth with him. I thank thee, and praise thee, O thou God of my fathers, who hast given me wisdom and might, and hast made known unto me now what we desired of thee: for thou hast now made known unto us the king's matter. Therefore Daniel went in unto Arioch, whom the king had ordained to destroy the wise men of Babylon: he went and said thus unto him; Destroy not the wise men of Babylon: bring me in before the king, and I will shew unto the king the interpretation.*"

(Daniel 2:19-24)

The ability of God to perform miracles can be seen throughout the entire Bible. Every grand story in the Book reminds us that God is not the One Who is powerless. Rather, our lack of faith and our lack of prayer makes *us* powerless. The profound account in Daniel 2 helps us to understand God's great ability.

King Nebuchadnezzar dreamed a dream so incredible he awakened very troubled. As is often the case, the more he tried to remember the details, the more he felt the images slip away, and the significance of his dream was lost. He had dreamed a prophetic vision at the hand of God because God wanted to exalt Daniel into a position that would eventually bring salvation to this king. I truly believe this king became a born-again man as a result of Daniel's influence. God's exaltation of Daniel to a position of great influence would help an entire kingdom have righteousness.

King Nebuchadnezzar was so plagued by his inability to remember his dream that he called for his staff and counselors and ordered them to tell him his dream and interpret it or die. Of course, the king's staff of experts could not deliver; they even told him that no man on earth could reveal the dream. When they could not produce the answers, Nebuchadnezzar ordered their deaths as well as the deaths of every other wise man in the land, including Daniel. He ordered Arioch, the captain of the king's guard, to carry out his decree.

When Arioch arrived at Daniel's home, Daniel questioned him about the king's impulsive order. After Arioch explained the situation, Daniel went to see the king to ask for time to ascertain the meaning of the dream. Nebuchadnezzar granted the request, and without delay, Daniel set a procedure in motion to determine the dream and to learn its meaning. Not only was Daniel's life on the line, so were the lives of every wise man in the land.

Daniel needed a great statement from God, and God came through for Daniel in an incredible way! *Miracle praying!* When Daniel desperately needed a miracle from God, he followed a step-by-step procedure that brought results. Likewise, we can avail ourselves of the same results in this business of miracle praying.

1. Daniel made time to pray. *"Then Daniel went in, and desired of the king that he would give him time...."* (Daniel 2:16) He did not waste valuable time ranting, raving, fretting, and worrying. Griping to your family or loved ones, "Why isn't God coming through for me?" does not result in miraculous answers to prayer.

I well remember a time of going into Dr. Hyles' office and

seeing stacks of unopened mail bound by rubber bands. I picked it up and said, "Little behind in your mail, Brother Hyles?" He grabbed it from me and said, "YES! But I'm not behind in my prayer life! How about you?"

I have to admit that I always hated it when he did something like that! I said, "We won't go there!"

Then he added, "I am behind in my mail by design. I plan what not to do because I must have a plan what **to** do! Don't ever get behind on your prayer time!"

Daniel respected the king's authority and his position, and the king respected Daniel enough to grant him time to pray.

2. Daniel enlisted the help of those who had proven themselves. *"Then Daniel went to his house, and made the thing known to Hananiah, Mishael, and Azariah, his companions."* (Daniel 2:17) A total of 50,000 captives were brought from Israel to Babylon in three different deportations: one in 606 B.C., one in 597 B.C., and one in 586 B.C. Nebuchadnezzar's armies invaded Israel three times and took as captives all the college-aged young people and brought them back to Babylon.

Daniel called on only three—Hananiah, Mishael, and Azariah—of those 50,000 captives to pray. He did not call them by their Babylonian names—Shadrach, Meshach, and Abednego. He called them by their Hebrew names because those names reflected the glory and power of God. The three Hebrews were proven men. Daniel knew he needed to fall on his face with his God and beg for His power. Daniel knew he needed an absolute Red-Sea miracle. Daniel knew he could not run from the problem; he had to pursue the will of God in this matter of life and death.

The soothsayers, the magicians, and the astrologers of the Chaldees brought out their curious books and their strange-looking instruments, muttered all sorts of mysterious incantations, but they all failed. What did Daniel do? He set himself to prayer, and knowing that the prayer of a united body of men has more prevalence than the prayer of one, we find that Daniel called together his brethren and bade them unite with him in earnest prayer that God in His infinite mercy would be pleased to open up the vision.[2]

If you needed a miracle, whom would you choose as prayer partners? To whom would you run when you need a miracle? Like Daniel's, your list would probably be very short, wouldn't it? The will of God is found in the house of God, with the man of God, with the Word of God, and with God. The person who runs from his church and refuses to consult his pastor makes a tragic mistake!

If you're a Hananiah, a Mishael, or an Azariah and someone says, "Would you pray for me?" you had better pray for them. When people ask me to pray for them, I either write it down immediately, or I pray for the person right then. What a sacred honor! I would rather have someone pray for me than any other gift or favor he could give to me. I don't know how to give a gift of gratitude big enough for the person who takes my name to God in prayer.

When one man asks another to pray for him, he avows his confidence in the inner life of that man. He says in substance: "I believe you are on good terms with God, that you are God's man and He will hear you."[3]

When Daniel enlisted the help of his proven prayer warriors, they did not concern themselves with whose prayer God would choose to answer. There is no limit to what God can do through those who do not concern themselves with who gets the credit. Far too much competition goes on in churches nowadays concerning who receives the credit. If we would not care who receives the credit, churches would have no limitations!

The way to be successful in the Christian life is to (1) Convince God that where you are is where you want to be, (2) Go to work and build the biggest "whatever" it is you are building, and (3) Give those who helped all the credit for making it the biggest. There is no limit as to how much God can use a man who does not care who gets the credit.

When I was a young preacher boy, I said, "God, if You'll just use me, I don't care to whom You give the credit. I want You to take all the credit Yourself because You are the One Who really deserves it." I am not concerned about receiving any credit or any glory; I am concerned about God's receiving all the glory.

Someone wisely told me years ago, "Treat praise like a quarterback treats a football—receive it and get rid of it as fast as you can because it will kill whoever hangs onto it."

3. Daniel was willing to pay the price at midnight. *"Then was the secret revealed unto Daniel in a night vision...."* (Daniel 2:19) Miracle praying means midnight praying. If you want to have the power of God, you must have God as your friend, and He becomes your friend during the midnight hours.

God and Jacob became well-acquainted during the midnight hours. Twin brothers, Jacob and Esau parted enemies after Jacob defrauded his father for Esau's blessing. Twenty-eight years have passed since Jacob sought refuge with his Uncle Laban. Their reunion was slated to be a life-or-death meeting, and his still-angry brother was coming to meet him with 400 armed men. Rightfully so, Jacob was worried. He was an older, more mature man who could now see the foolishness of his former ways. The night before the brothers would meet, God told Jacob to send his family across the brook Jabbok.

In this dire emergency doubtless God's promise and his vow made long ago came to his mind, and he took himself to an all-night season of prayer. Here comes to our notice that strange, inexplicable incident of the angel struggling with Jacob all night long, till Jacob at last obtained the victory. "I will not let thee go except thou bless me." And then and there, in answer to his earnest, pressing and importunate praying, he was richly blessed personally and his name was changed. But even more than that, God went ahead of Jacob's desire, and strangely moved upon the angry nature of Esau, and lo and behold, when Jacob met him next day, Esau's anger had entirely abated, and he viewed with Jacob in showing kindness to his brother who had wronged him. No explanation of this remarkable change in the heart of Esau is satisfactory which leaves out prayer.[4]

The Bible says in Genesis 32:24, *"And Jacob was left alone; and there wrestled a man with him until the breaking of the day."* I personally believe that man was the Lord Jesus Christ. The next morning Jacob walked with a limp that he would always carry—the result of his wrestling match. That contest changed Jacob—inside and outside. His name was changed from *Jacob*, meaning "trickster" to *Israel*, meaning "prince of God."

Jacob had finally stopped making himself the issue and made God the issue. Jacob learned that as long as he made himself the issue, he deprived himself from having the power of God. Calvary completely covered all of Jacob's past! Jacob learned he could "twist" God's arm. Jacob paid the price to have God's power on his life!

Midnight praying is saying to God, "I'm not leaving until You hear me!" Hebrews says that I am supposed to come boldly to the throne of grace where I can obtain mercy to find help in the time of need. God wants to answer the prayers where we want miracles to make a difference in other people's lives.

4. Daniel prayed believing God would answer. *"Then was the secret revealed unto Daniel in a night vision. Then Daniel blessed* *the God of heaven.... I thank thee, and praise thee, O thou God of my fathers, who hast given me wisdom and might...."* (Daniel 2:19, 23) One half of verse 19 addresses Daniel's prayer. However, four and one-half verses address thanking and praising God! Daniel thanked and praised God *before* the actual miracle had been put into action. Daniel prayed, knowing that God was going to come through for him!

Through the years I have been captivated by a man named Charles G. Finney (1792-1875). He was known as the man who had more power of God on his life than almost any other preacher who had ever lived. He was often known to say that he spent a minimum of three hours after his sermon praising God for what He had done. When I read that statement, I realized immediately that one reason Charles G. Finney was considered a unique and rare man was that he had found a secret that so few people discover. That secret is the power of praise!

I know people who will pay the price to pray at midnight, but not many people will revel in God when the victory has been won. When God answers one of my prayers, I want Him to grow weary of listening to me thanking Him for what He did that *one* time!

I believe the perpetual power of God comes from praying before and praising after. The prayer and praise go together hand in hand. If you pray and do not praise, you will falter and stumble, and the whole cycle has to start over again. If you will pray and then praise, and let the praise be so much more in measure than your prayer was, then you will start seeing wave after crashing wave of blessing rolling on you.

Daniel spent more time praising God for His answer to prayer than Daniel spent praying for an answer. Those who have the mighty power of God have learned the secret that praise is really where the power is! Nothing will unleash God's perennial power like consistent, regular praise.

One reason why so many of our prayers lack power is because we have neglected to return thanks for blessings already received. Our heavenly Father out of a wise regard for our highest welfare oftentimes refuses to answer petitions that we send up to Him in order that we may be brought to a sense of our ingratitude and taught to be thankful. God is deeply grieved by the thanklessness and ingratitude of which so many of us are guilty.[5]

Would you take time to praise God? If you want to see miracles as a result of your praying, (1) Pay the price beforehand, and (2) When God gives you the answer, don't forget Him. Don't turn your back on Him. Don't ever be guilty of the sin of not praising your God!

God can point His finger at me and judge me guilty of many sins, but ingratitude will never be one of them. I know God deserves my praise, and even before He comes through for me, I say, "By the way, God! You are wonderful!" I never want to forget how good God has been to me!

No prayer,—no faith,—no Christ in the heart. Little prayer,—little faith,—little Christ in the heart. Increasing prayer,—increasing faith,—increasing Christ in the heart. Much prayer,—much faith,—much Christ in the heart. Praying always,—faith always,—Christ always.[1]

The Work of Prayer

"And it came to pass, that, as he was praying in a certain place, when he ceased, one of his disciples said unto him, Lord, teach us to pray, as John also taught his disciples. And he said unto them, When ye pray, say, Our Father which art in heaven, Hallowed be thy name. Thy kingdom come. Thy will be done, as in heaven, so in earth. Give us day by day our daily bread. And forgive us our sins; for we also forgive every one that is indebted to us. And lead us not into temptation; but deliver us from evil."

(Luke 11:1-4)

A church is not just a building. A church is people working together as a team. As we learn—as a team—to walk with God, we will open our schedules to build a *life* of prayer—not just a *time* of prayer. Then we will see the miracles happen!

Prayer is one of those intangibles that is almost too "spooky" for most Christians to grasp because they don't understand the concept of talking to a person they cannot see. They don't quite comprehend being able to chat with the Lord. Prayer should be comfortable and understandable enough for every Christian to be easily engaged in it. Prayer is very, very vital to the Christian life.

We get to know people by talking with them. We get to know God in like manner. The highest result of prayer is not deliverance from evil, or the securing of some coveted thing, but knowledge of God.[2]

The whole idea of praying is so misunderstood by God's people that in Jesus' outline for prayer, a very important phrase is almost universally left out of all books written about how to get your prayers answered. I believe this phrase may well be one of the most important lines in this whole formula in Luke 11 on how to pray.

Jesus said, *"Thy kingdom come...."* In other words, He was saying, "God, Your kingdom come" or "Father, Thy kingdom come." Even His disciples did not understand that little phrase. Great confusion about *"the kingdom of God"* marked the disciples' lives. How do I know?

In Acts 1, the same group of men said to Jesus Christ, after He had been crucified and risen and was about to ascend into Heaven, *"...Lord, wilt thou at this time restore again the kingdom to Israel?"* (Acts 1:6) He answered them, *"...It is not for you to know the times or the seasons, which the Father hath put in his own power."* (Acts 1:7) He added that they would receive a different kind of power *"...after that the Holy Ghost is come upon you: and ye shall be witnesses unto me both in Jerusalem, and in all Judaea, and in Samaria, and unto the uttermost part of the earth."* At that time, the disciples still didn't understand this "kingdom-come" principle.

Don't misunderstand me. A kingdom will come. God will establish a kingdom on this earth. Please allow me to establish point-by-point the *work* of prayer and the kingdom setting of prayer. Though God entices us to pray with promises and commands and rewards, prayer is **not** principally for the believer **to receive things from God.** That is not the primary reason God asked us to pray. All our praying for things—for good things, fine things, and comfortable things—is not the major reason God has for us to pray.

In Dr. John R. Rice's classic book, *Prayer: Asking and Receiving,* he writes, "The object of prayer is to ask God and to get things from Him." Dr. Rice had a far higher level of understanding of spiritual matters than I will ever have, and in the area of prayer, I have always loved the practical reality of the statement

"Christians should go to God and get what they ask for." However, Dr. Rice prayed for a son six times, and God gave him six daughters! The man who taught that you should expect God to give you what you ask for could not get a son! Dr. Rice is in Heaven now, and God has probably told him why he only had daughters! My point is that even the people who taught us the wisest concepts about prayer did not always get what they wanted.

The statements, "God wants to give you things," "God wants to bestow blessings on you," and "God wants to make your life full, rich, and abundant" are all true. However, our definitions are so many light-years away from what God thinks and what God is doing that we tend to become confused. So, we go to God, we say our prayers, and we sometimes do not receive the answer that we want.

Christian prayer begins with the assumption that, as an all-wise, all-loving, and all-powerful Father, God knows what is best in every situation that faces us. And the only conclusion for us to draw from this truth is that it will be to the best interest of ourselves and the Kingdom, to trust God's judgment in regard to our persistent petitions. "No" may be the best answer of all, the most wise, the most loving, and the most just.[3]

God is omniscient, and He knows everything. He does not exist in the realm of time as we do. II Peter 3:8 says, *"But, beloved, be not ignorant of this one thing, that one day is with the Lord as a thousand years, and a thousand years as one day."* God knows the past, the present, and the future of every one of His created beings. Thus God knows that sometimes the things for which we pray for will produce disastrous results that we cannot possibly foresee.

Every prayer to God is answered. None is disregarded. Each is considered thoughtfully and in love. Whether the answer be "Yes" or "No," the Christian knows by faith that God has spoken rightly.[4]

Because our request and the answer are at opposite ends of the spectrum, we don't recognize the fact that God has answered our prayers. Since we cannot "see" the answer, we often stop praying.

There is little doubt that failure in the prayer-life is often—always?—due to failure in the spiritual life. So many people harbor much unbelief in the heart regarding the value and effectiveness of prayer; and without faith, prayer is vain.[5]

When we pray, we initiate wars and battles in the heavenlies. The powers of darkness fight the spiritual angels of God. The word *angel* means "messenger," and God uses angels to deliver answers to prayer. These two factions fight and war and clash because the devils do not want the Christian to receive that answer to prayer. Likewise, the demons do not want to see any Christian getting God's active involvement in his life.

Satan's emissaries care nothing about us. Their threat is not the Christian! God is their enemy! What they fear is that when a Christian starts praying, he might accidentally stumble upon the whole purpose of praying, and as a result, he might accidentally team up with God.

Prayer defeats the plans of [Satan]. He cannot successfully stand before it. He trembles when some man of simple faith in God prays.[6]

The Devil and his demons know that if Christians team up with God, nothing can stop the Christian—nothing!

Do we realize that there is nothing the Devil dreads so much as prayer? His great concern is to keep us from praying. He loves to see us "up to our eyes" in work—provided we do not pray. Someone has wisely said, "Satan laughs at our toiling, mocks at our wisdom, but trembles when we pray."[7]

If God's people ever understood why God wants us to pray and the power of prayer, they would realize that it isn't just so a person can go into his prayer closet and flippantly pray for his needs. That's not principally the purpose of prayer; rather, God wants to get involved in his life. God wants to help the Christian. God wants to give him blessings and joys and all of the by-products of the Christian life. But blessings do not come principally by prayer. Blessings come from obedience.

So then, what exactly is prayer? If prayer isn't to make life a little more comfortable and if prayer isn't having God say, "Your wish is My command," then what is it? God teaches us what prayer is in the statement, *"Thy kingdom come."* Like a passport that allows a traveler access to other countries, prayer is the passport that allows the Christian access to God.

We must understand that God has His own agenda. The reason why prayer is so forgotten, so forsaken, and so ignored by God's people is that we are desperately trying to get God on **our** page. We are trying to get God to do things **our** way—like a dog trainer tries to coerce a dog to obey.

We have a God Whose knowledge is infinite. He can put it into the mind of a doctor to prescribe a certain medicine or diet, or method of cure. All the doctor's skill is from God. "He knoweth our frame"—for He made it. He knows it far better than the cleverest doctor or surgeon. He made, and He can restore.

We believe that God desires us to use medical skill, but we also believe that God, by His wonderful knowledge, can heal, and sometimes does heal, without human co-operation. And God must be allowed to work in His own way. We are so apt to tie God down to the way we approve of. God's aim is to glorify His name in answering our prayers. Sometimes He sees that our desire is right, but our petition wrong.[8]

Thankfully, we have a great Saviour who happens to be a great servant to His children, and yes, a personality of God enjoys serving them. However, being a servant is not principally the purpose of God, and certainly not exclusively or principally His personality. Principally, God is the sovereign Lord of Glory and the immortal, omnipotent, King of kings and Lord of lords. Far too often, we do not have God in His rightful position in our minds. We tend to keep pulling God down to a lower pedestal. In other words, we are trying to make God more humanized. We want a blue-jean wearing God Who is a hireling ready to do our bidding. A human God is the wrong God!

Are not our prayers so often ineffective and powerless— and sometimes even prayerless—because we rush unthinkingly and unpreparedly into God's presence, without realizing the majesty and glory of the God Whom we are approaching, and without reflecting upon the exceeding great riches of His glory in Christ Jesus, which we hope to draw upon? We must "think magnificently of God."[9]

As I survey the world around us, I grieve because so many of us need God so desperately and take so little advantage of Him. Some people are some of the most active pray-ers in their church, but they spend a lot of time asking God to change their environment. "Please God," they beg, "give me a new job."

Nothing happens because prayer alone will not bring that coveted job. You get a job by presenting yourself as a very hardworking person to a potential employer. The door is open for anyone who is not afraid to sweat, work hard, be punctual, and show up every day. The person who spends as much time looking for a job as he does praying for a job will have one quickly. Finding a job is not a matter of how much one prays.

God cannot do some things unless we work. He stores the hills with marble, but He has never built a cathedral. He fills the mountains with iron ore, but He never makes a needle or a locomotive. He leaves that to us. We must work.[10]

My point is that many people spend great amounts of time on their knees in their prayer closet and at the church altar. Though they pray for seemingly everything, nothing happens in their life. These good people have not learned that God has His own agenda, and He will not get on their agenda! Though God cares about them very much, He doesn't care about their agenda. God made them to do His work, and the sooner people understand that they were made for God and God was not made for them, the happier they will be, and the more successful they will become in the prayer closet.

What prayer really is crystallized for me when I was working on a special project regarding the academics at Hyles-Anderson College. My heart was so into this project that I worked for many weeks preparing it for Dr. Hyles. The day I was to present this academic program, Dr. Hyles began philosophizing, and I realized his train of thought was completely opposite of the direction my program was taking. "All of my work down the drain," I inwardly groaned. However, I threw my plan into the garbage can and worked on implementing my employer's plan. I realized that my job was not to tell the founder where I thought he should be going; rather, my job was to learn what he wanted, get behind his program, and push as hard as I could.

When I am in my prayer closet, my job is not to go to God and say, "God, I put a lot of time in this prayer. I have given much thought to this project. Let me tell You what You should do for me." When God chats with me, I often find that His talks somehow point me 180° different from where I thought I was coming! Generally, we tend not to like His directional changes.

As we consider the phrase *"Thy kingdom come,"* we need to keep the following thoughts in a proper perspective.

1. God has His own agenda. God has a plan in mind. God is headed in the proper direction to finish that plan, and in effect, He says, "I invite you to come along with Me." Prayer is the method He chooses to allow us to come on board with Him. If we want to get a hold of God in prayer and have our prayers answered, we must understand that prayer is not a tool for us to manipulate God to get what we want! Prayer is our access to God so we can jump on board with His agenda.

God's having an agenda reminds me of the times I went grocery shopping with my mother. Her agenda was to fill her shopping cart with needed items. When I was little, she would put me into the place provided in the cart for youngsters. As we walked through the store aisles, I would see items I liked. I would say, "Mommy, I want Pop-Tarts." She didn't exactly refuse my request; she just chose something else that was better for me—like spinach or green beans. When I got a little older, I was allowed to get more actively involved in my momma's agenda. I was allowed to push her grocery cart. When we got home, I helped unload Momma's agenda, and I discovered some Pop-Tarts and some ice cream! Mom gave me some unexpected blessings. Likewise, we can praise God for His unexpected blessings when we are actively joined with His agenda.

2. Those who desire to assist God with His agenda find prayer the best tool to use. Prayer is the tool to use when focusing on God's agenda because prayer allows the pray-er the passageway to get on board the figurative ship that God sails to His agenda.

3. Very little praying should be for one's self. I was intrigued the first time I heard my father-in-law say that it had been about 20 years since he had prayed for anything for himself. I once asked him to elaborate on that statement. He explained that the purpose of prayer was not for him to twist God's arm to get what he wanted. "That's selfishness," he said, "and that's what's wrong with so much praying—a spiritual tool is actually being used to make Christians more selfish. Some people actually pray their way into backsliding. They become less of a Christian than a non-praying Christian."

The chief object of prayer is to glorify the Lord Jesus. We are to ask in Christ's name "that the Father may be glorified in the Son." (John xiv. 13) We are not to seek wealth or health, prosperity or success, ease or comfort, spirituality or fruitfulness in service simply for our own enjoyment or advancement or popularity, but only for Christ's sake—for His glory.[11]

The more you pray for yourself, the more you focus on your kingdom rather than God's kingdom. Your kingdom is the kingdom of self—self-righteousness, self-rule, self-arrogance, self-conceit, self-pity, self-depression, self-abnegation, self-humiliation, and the problem with all of those "self" words is they all have a common denominator that God hates—"self." God isn't trying to make you a humble Christian; God is trying to make you an obedient Christian.

Thirty-six men had been unexpectedly killed at the battle of Ai, and then Joshua fell on his face. Joshua exhibited great humility, but God ordered Joshua to get up! God knew the unwarranted deaths were the result of disobedience—not prayer. Unfortunately, people generally want to blame everything on prayer as though God doesn't like them, but prayer—the privilege of prayer—is to use a tool to do a job.

Elijah was a man of like passions—like you and me. He prayed, and rain did not fall for three and a half years. God knew that Elijah understood what He was trying to accomplish. The reason why it did not rain is that God told him to pray that it would not rain. *"And Elijah the Tishbite, who was of the inhabitants of Gilead, said unto Ahab, As the LORD God of Israel liveth, before whom I stand, there shall not be dew nor rain these years, but according to my word."* (I Kings 17:1) God needed a human instrument to pray so it would not rain for three and a half years. "Can anyone doubt that this man of God, who shut up and opened the rain clouds by prayer was not praying, when so much was at stake?"[12]

Three and a half years later, God told Elijah to pray for rain. When Elijah prayed, God sent a gully-washer! Once again, God needed a human instrument. Elijah's prayer was comparable to God's placing a hammer in his hands to build God's work. Elijah was not trying to be a great prayer warrior; he was being a great worker for God. The people who perform God's agenda become mighty prayer warriors.

God's heroes are the men and women who pray, who pray when the days are dark and there is not a single rift in the clouds, when the foe seems to triumph and all the host of God seems cowering in defeat; who pray till the tide turns, and then pray on till the call comes from on high.[13]

Why not give God the privilege of being the King not only of His kingdom, but of your life, and let God give you whatever He wants to give you?

4. The kingdom of God is a spiritual kingdom. This kingdom of God is composed of righteousness, peace, and joy in the Holy Ghost. The fact that righteousness does not overwhelm the United States of America is not a problem caused by the Democrats or by the Republicans. Rather, it is a problem of God's people praying for the wrong things. The homosexual movement is a failure of God's people to pray for righteousness from God.

Prayer is to get God's man to do right. God called Nebuchadnezzar, who was an evil king, *"My servant."* Why? Because Nebuchadnezzar got saved and did a great work of righteousness. He made Babylon the greatest kingdom in the world because he served God. God knew Nebuchadnezzar would serve Him one day, and God knew he would do a whole lot of wrong first.

Both peace and joy in the Holy Ghost follow on the heels of righteousness. Why do we have wars and strife in this world? "It is departure from the will of God, the clash of the human will with the divine will and the clash of human wills with each other, that have made the history of this world a story of strife and bloodshed and destruction and misery and sorrow."[14] We have wars and strife for the same reason that we have disagreements and arguments between two people. Domestic disturbances are one of the most dangerous calls to which a police officer can respond. Some of them are small wars. People pray, "Give us peace, peace, peace, peace, peace" when they do not even have complete peace and harmony in their own home life. "No man's prayer is acceptable with God whose life is not well-pleasing before God."[15]

One of the greatest sins in this nation, which is taking it right down to Hell, is peace and prosperity at any price. Some people are willing to have peace at any price. I refuse to have peace in my home at any price. We will not have rock music in my house; we will have war over that issue. Some parents are willing to sell out their values because they want peace in the house. They will allow their 16-year-old son to smoke cigarettes just to keep peace! More than I want peace in my house, I want righteousness to mark my house. The peace of God is what I want, and prayer is a tool to bring peace in times of conflict. I believe with all of my heart that one reason for conflicts in the world is to cause people to desire the Prince of Peace.

Certainly I do not want people to be hurt or killed in battle. Have you ever read the Old Testament? Over a quarter of a million lives were taken in one day; 185,000 on another day; and 23,000 who misbehaved sexually one day. God wanted peace!

Peace with God is ten thousand times more important than peace with or from anyone else. Prayer brings the right kind of peace.

If a person does not have joy in the Holy Ghost, it is because sorrows and sadness exist in this world. Too many people look for joy in artificial substitutes—drugs, liquor, the Internet, pornography, etc. As powerful as God is, He could stop the cocaine traffic or the liquor traffic immediately. Instead, He allows the world to see what the human heart really is. God allows those false substitutes to exist to show the conflict between what our heart says we need and what God says we can have. God creates conflicts to see what we will do with the prayer closet.

I do not pray that God would shut down all the liquor industry; I say, "God, help Christians to do right and find joy in You and Your Word." If we read the Word of God, we would find our joy in the Holy Ghost and in the Words of God.

I thank Him for the conflicts in this world. I thank Him for the temptations, struggles, trials, and testings because they give me an opportunity to stand up and say, "I believe in You."

God's kingdom has to do with Who rules in your heart. If I want to be a greater Christian in prayer, I have to face unrighteousness, strife, and the sorrows of this world so I can push them back by prayer. My grandfather often said, "It's getting gloriously dark." I thank God for the stress, the strife, and the problems of this society because my King can establish great righteousness and great power in a very bleak situation. God delights in making it so bad that only one person can stand and say, "Let God arise and His enemies be scattered!"

Some people are trying to make their lives so comfortable that God says, "If it ever becomes that comfortable, you will be of no value to Me whatsoever."

When we sing "Draw me nearer, nearer, blessed Lord," we are not thinking of the nearness of place, but of the nearness of relationship. It is for increasing degrees of awareness that we pray, for a more perfect consciousness of the divine Presence. We need never shout across the spaces to an absent God. He is nearer than our own soul, closer than our most secret thoughts.

– A. W. Tozer

As in Heaven

"...Thy will be done, as in heaven, so in earth. Give us day by day our daily bread. And forgive us our sins: for we also forgive every one that is indebted to us. And lead us not into temptation; but deliver us from evil." (Luke 11:2-4)

Prayer is such a universal word. I saw a billboard the other day that said, "Pray the rosary." The word *prayer* is associated with all kinds of religions. For instance, the Muslims pray facing Mecca. The traditional Jews go to the Wailing Wall where they pray touching the wall. They also write their prayers on slips of paper and tuck them in the cracks and crevices in that wall. "Praying before God is a more spiritual business than is performed by merely turning to the east or to the west or bowing the knee or entering within walls hallowed for ages."[1] The Mormons, the Jehovah's Witnesses, the Catholics, the Baptists, and every other denomination uses the word *prayer*—even unbelievers.

A traveller in China visited a heathen temple on a great feast-day. Many were the worshippers of the hideous idol enclosed in a sacred shrine. The visitor noticed that most of the devotees brought with them small pieces of paper on which prayers had been written or printed. These they would wrap up in little balls of stiff mud and fling at the idol. He enquired the reason for this strange proceeding, and was told that the if the mud ball stuck fast to the idol, then the prayer would assuredly be answered; but if the mud fell off, the prayer was rejected by the god.

We may smile at this peculiar way of testing the acceptability of a prayer. But is it not a fact that the majority of Christian men and women who pray to a Living God know very little about real prevailing prayer? Yet prayer is the key which unlocks the door of God's treasure house.[2]

Without a doubt the word *prayer* has become over-utilized in conversation. We all talk about saying our prayers, having prayer time, possessing a prayer life, consulting a prayer book, and finding prayer promises. Moms ask, "Did you say your prayers today?" Do you pray before you eat? All this prayer usage makes the word so common that perhaps we become overly familiar with it. As in so much of Christianity, over familiarization with a word or a phrase without depth of understanding engenders not only a misinformation, but also a certain contempt to where it becomes a disserviced word.

The truth is, very few people pray correctly. For instance, we pray before a meal, but in truth, that prayer is not really praying. The person praying is actually saying, "Thanks. Thank You for our food. We appreciate it. Thanks for being good to us. God bless us now. Amen." That is a prayer of gratitude, and certainly expressing gratitude is commendable. Prayer seems to be something that a few special operational people do successfully. They are like the special forces—the Green Berets or the Rangers—of Christianity.

It is very important to understand that prayer is not so much a request for God to change circumstances as it is a request to reveal His intentions. Do you really think God does not have a will about everything? Do you think that a God Who can design chromosomes and DNA does not know what to do about tomorrow? God designed an atom that no man has ever seen. We just manufacture models of what we think it looks like. Scientists have successfully harnessed a little bit of the energy. We can fashion it into a bomb or produce electricity. Do you believe a God Who is that elaborate, that careful, and that incredibly fastidious with His micro-design, would be a God Who does not have a plan for your life?

I read a *National Geographic* magazine that delved into the reasons why the earth is surrounded by a magnetic field. Scientists have only recently discovered that the magnetic field protects the earth when the sun has its "bad days." When the sun expels huge plasma bursts that are 200 billion times more powerful than the Hiroshima atomic bomb, earth can absorb that impact because the magnetic field cushions the shock. The magnetic field keeps us alive! A God Who has thought so carefully how to protect mankind with an ozone layer, a magnetic field, the five zones of the atmosphere (the troposphere, the stratosphere, the mesosphere, the ionosphere, and the exosphere) from the sun's harmful rays and yet also to enjoy the benefits the sun provides, is a God Who has a definite plan for everyone!

God has a definite plan about how we should conduct our life. God's design of every little intricate part of this universe from the far reaches of space and the incredible design of the heavens that can be seen only with a telescope to the most miniscule, infinitesimally small particles of mankind's world that can only be seen with the help of an electron microscope exclaims that He has a plan for every person's life! Not one person has ever been an abstract thought with God. Every person represents an intimate thought.

In Psalm 139, God says in essence that "you are right before My face constantly. I am always beholding you." God is very aware of what He wants to do with every human being. The plan God has for us to do is in this world because we are not in Heaven. We are not in "the sweet by and by"; unfortunately, we're in "the nasty now and now" which has enveloped us. In I Corinthians 13:12 the Bible says, *"For now we see through a glass darkly; but then face to face...."* The dark glass through which we view this world has hidden not only the pure and good things from us, but also the ways God works in our lives. So God devised a plan called prayer which allows us to put light to the dark glass and see as though we are in Heaven beholding Him face to face.

Prayer allows the Christian to see what normal, natural man cannot see. Prayer is not for an individual to see God change His mind to give him what he wants. On the contrary, prayer is for the believer to see what God has intricately laid out so he can behold the marvels of God!

In Heaven, God's will is neither hidden nor corrupted; rather, it is open and obvious. Everyone knows God's will in Heaven, and that knowledge contributes to the glory of Heaven. The will of God is an intricate plan that God has for all the citizens of Heaven.

Even though God never actually said, "I have had billions of years…," God did have billions of years to think, and He developed a plan for every person who has ever lived. His plan is not of a general nature; rather, it is a specific, well-defined, intimate, personal, very detailed will for every human being.

God has a right to lay out our lives. He has made plans for them and unless we resist, He will help us to live out those plans. When we pray we must, either in words or in heart say: "Nevertheless, not as I will but as thou wilt." A stubborn desire to have our own way about *anything* is entirely inconsistent with the act of prayer.[3]

In Luke 11 Jesus was saying to the disciples, "If you disciples want to live on earth as it is in Heaven, stop getting frustrated about God's not coming through! Instead, pray and ask Him to show you what He has already done." As I have already mentioned, prayer is not a tactic to maneuver God into a position where He has to obey man and come through for him with a particular request.

Prayer is not intended as a way to twist God's arm, to get something that is not right. Prayer is intended as a way to find the sweet will of God and ask what God wants to give and ask what will be good for us and pleasing to God. God is far more willing to give than we are to receive. He has abundance of blessings we never seek and have. But we should not insist on anything that we cannot have sweet assurance is the will of God.[4]

Prayer is saying, "God, I believe Your will is not only good for Heaven; I believe it is good for earth." The mature Christian learns to pray in the will of God. Because he does pray in the will of God, he sees how God answers. When our life is not conformed to His will, we cannot recognize God's answers to our prayers.

While He was on earth, Jesus said, *"…My meat is to do the will of him that sent me, and to finish his work."* (John 4:34) *"Then said I, Lo, I come (in the volume of the book it is written of me,) to do thy will, O God."* (Hebrews 10:7) *"Verily, verily, I say unto you, He that believeth on me, the works that I do shall he do also; and greater works than these shall he do; because I go unto my Father."* (John 14:12) Jesus was saying, "I am going to go to My Father and tell Him to do more and more things for you!" Jesus sought to do the will of His Father; likewise, believers should seek to do the will of God.

I don't pray, "God, please do this,…" and "Please do that,…" and "Please…." Most of my praying is, "God, the answer is already there; open my eyes. Show me where we are going and what we are doing, God. Show me what the plan is. I want to jump on board with You. Show me Your plan; I know if I see Your plan, I will revert from begging and weeping to praising and shouting because that's what the life of a Christian is supposed to be." The Bible says in Psalm 22:3, *"…O thou that inhabitest the praises of Israel."* God lives in praise—not in desperation praying.

Certainly, God allows every Christian to pray a desperate

prayer. We experience times of great grief and anguish because we do have a treasured earthen vessel, and this corruptible vessel (our body) is contaminated by sin. It is susceptible to disease, to broken bones, to heartaches, pain, and affliction. God is not caught off guard when one of His children has an accident or receives a diagnosis of cancer. God is not surprised when the doctor says, "You're having a heart attack." God lovingly designed these events because He wants to show the believer He is perfecting something in his life. "Prayer, in every care and anxiety and need of life, with thanksgiving, is the means God has appointed for our obtaining freedom from all anxiety, and the peace of God which passeth all understanding."[5]

God wants to hear our prayers. "We do not cry to a God afar off, a God holding Himself aloof from us."[6] He said in Philippians 4:6, 7, *"Be careful for nothing; but in every thing by prayer and supplication with thanksgiving let your requests be made known unto God. And the peace of God, which passeth all understanding, shall keep your hearts and minds through Christ Jesus."* In this passage the word *requests* is the Greek word *aitema* (ah-ee-tay-mah) meaning "request" or "petition." God says, "Use your petition as a means of conforming to My plan for your life." Too many people use *requests* exclusively for their "gimme" prayers.

Petition is the lowest, the most rudimentary and the most elementary of all kinds of prayers. And it is because we so seldom rise above the rudiments and first principles of divine things that we so seldom think, and so seldom speak, about prayer in any other sense than in that of request and petition and supplications.[7]

God's ways are perfect. God knows exactly what He is doing, and if we would like to be clued in on what He is doing in our life, He graciously gave us a tool called prayer that will reveal what He is doing when He wants to show us. Too many of us have such a humanistic, unjust opinion of our God! We pray accusatory prayers like:

- "Why did You give me poor eyesight?"
- "Why did You give me arthritis?"
- "Why aren't You coming through for me?"
- "Why won't You give me a spouse?"
- "Why did You give me the spouse I have?"
- "Why did You give me so many children?"
- "Why haven't You given us children?"
- "Why won't You give me a better job?"
- "Why won't You change my life?"
- "Why this and why that?"

God is saying, "Would you pray about the matter, please? *In every thing give thanks....*" (I Thessalonians 5:18) Thank God for what He can do. Ask Him to show you His will. He may not change a certain situation, but He can show you what He is doing with you.

God loves us, and thankfully, God puts up with us! He knows we are fragile and weak. He alone knows all the answers to the heartaches of life, and those answers are available to the one who prays! He alone can show us great and mighty things of which we have never even thought. He alone can do exceeding abundantly above all that we ask or think. God wants to show His people what He is capable of doing!

Believe it or not, God does not need our directions as to how or what to do. Did God need Moses' help at the crossing of the Red Sea? Of course not! God did not consult with him one time about His plans. God never needs anyone's help at figuring out what should be done in any situation.

When I pray, it is not a committee meeting where I say, "Now, Lord here is what I think You should do. God, You know I have been on this earth for almost 50 years—almost half a century. You didn't live on earth nearly that long. So God, let me tell You about my scheme...."

That is not praying! If we recorded your prayers, much of the time spent with God is time spent telling Him what He is supposed to do in your life—as though God cannot figure things out. God does not need our directions. He does not need us to tell Him how to lead. He does not need us to tell Him what to do. Praying is not saying, "God, let me tell You what You've got to do!" Rather, prayer is saying, "God, would You please show me what You have already planned for me?"

1. God has a will and a plan for everything on earth—just as He does in Heaven. "...*Thy will be done in earth, as it is in heaven.*" (Matthew 6:10) Every work we perform in Heaven is in accord 100 percent with His will. God has the same kind of will for this earth.

Not only has God a name to be hallowed and a kingdom to be manifested, but a will to be accomplished. We know that the will of God is "good, and acceptable, and perfect," from its broadest purposes to its minutest applications, and that nothing could be more happy, for Heaven or earth, than its fullest realization.[8]

Earth is not God's second job or a secondary thought. Earth and its inhabitants are not God's hobby. God has a plan for us, just like He does in Heaven, and He wants to show us that will.

2. In Heaven the saints do not pray for God to change His will but to reveal more fully His will. I believe those in Heaven pray, but their prayer is, "God, I see so much! Would You please let me see more?"

The Bible says in I Corinthians 2:9, "...*Eye hath not seen, nor ear heard, neither have entered into the heart of man, the things which God hath prepared for them that love him.*" I believe that this verse in part refers to the Word of God that we have in our possession. However, I also believe that the Word of God explains to us that God has a great plan for us in the future; and those in Heaven are praying, "God, show me those things my human eye could not comprehend. Show those things my human ear could not comprehend. Show those things my human senses could not discern. God, show me great and mighty things."

What are the people in Heaven doing? I believe when they smell the flowers, they can actually taste them because all of their sensory organs are magnified far beyond what is normal for earthbound people. Colors are intensified, as is sound. Music of unbelievable beauty fills all of Heaven. Choirs sing with a majesty that surpasses the best choirs on earth. All of Heaven is magnified a hundredfold.

Nobody in Heaven is praying that God would give him a better lifestyle. Heaven's streets are made of pure gold! Nobody says, "I'm poor; I need more money." Far too many prayers prayed on this earth are simply for more money. God says, "You don't need more money. You need My will." "...Man shall not live by bread alone, but by every word that proceedeth out of the mouth of God." (Matthew 4:4)

Heaven's inhabitants don't pray for God to change His will, but to reveal more fully His will. In Heaven they are enjoying the will of God—unlike many Christians here on earth who are trying to change the will of God. The Apostle Paul said in Philippians 4:11 and 12, "Not that I speak in respect of want: for I have learned, in whatsoever state I am, therewith to be content. I know both how to be abased, and I know how to abound: every where and in all things I am instructed both to be full and to be hungry, both to abound and to suffer need."

Contentment is a condition of your heart—not an accumulation of things. The Bible says in I Timothy 6:8 that man should be content with food and raiment. "And having food and raiment let us be therewith content." If you ate a meal today and you are wearing clothes, the Bible says you are supposed to be content. The Bible says that food and clothing are the basis of all contentment.

In I Timothy 6:6, God says, *"But godliness with contentment is great gain."*

God will give you anything you want. But far too often we miss what prayer provides. Prayer is not just a new car, or a new suit of clothes, or some spending money. Certainly we can pray about those types of things. Sometimes we do too much praying instead of working and obeying and applying His principles. Sometimes we use the tool of prayer as a lazy man's way out of work. In case you want to see God working on earth like He does in Heaven, focus on the following:

1. **Give us our bread day by day.** God provides each day's portion from Heaven. We need to start our prayer life each day by saying, "Father, I know this day before me has already been planned and lived by You. God, I know You have already provided for me what I need for this day. Father, show me the daily provision You have made for me."

However, instead of praying that prayer, before you even see what God has given to you, you want to take it back to the store and return it. You egotistically say, "God, I don't want what You gave me. I want You to give me what I know I need." That prayer is an insult to God Almighty! He has already laid up provisions— a beautiful package of the goods—that He knows we need. We need to trust Him to show us what He has already answered.

Every morning, seven days a week, I eat two poached eggs and one other item that varies week by week. Sometimes, I add two English muffins or a bowl of oatmeal or two waffles with fresh maple syrup. As I enjoy this simple breakfast, I want to be aware of the goodness of God. I think about Who made the chicken who laid the egg, and Who provided the sun and the rain so the corn and meal could grow to feed the chicken, and Who gave man the wisdom to know how to bring that chicken to market.

When I think about the elaborate system that God provided to put those two eggs on my table, thankfulness floods my soul. I thank my God for my wife who prepared my breakfast. I thank God for the grocer who sold the eggs. I thank God for the man who had the wisdom to start refrigeration so the eggs could be kept cold. I thank God for the person who invented packaging. I thank God for the sun, and the rain, and the farmer who grew the crop, and the John Deere combine that harvested the crop. I thank God for the farmer. I thank God for the trucker. I thank God for the roof over my head. I never fail to realize that God, in His infinite wisdom, provided a simple breakfast meal for me that required thousands of years of planning!

When I say, "God, give me my daily bread," I am saying, "God, You are amazing!" I can be happy with a simple breakfast or with finding a penny on the ground because when I pray, I recognize what God has already done for me.

Dr. Hyles prayed seven times a day, "God, help me to cross the path of those You would have me help like Jesus would if He were in my shoes."

He was saying, "God, as I begin this day, You have already ordained for me to meet some people. You gave me my personality so I can help them. You gave me the dollar bills in my pocket so I could share with them. You gave me wisdom and training so I can help them. Somehow I am going to enrich their life as though You are enriching their life. Let me be aware of those divine appointments. Father, You have given me doors of opportunities. There are questions to answer, problems to solve, and You have already taught me. You gave me a Book. I was taught to read and write and know the alphabet so I could have right answers."

In all our undertakings we must wait upon Him for direction and success, and by faith and prayer commit our way to him to undertake for us, and Him we must take with us wherever we go.[9]

His prayer was not, "I don't want to meet those people. I want to go golfing and have fun and play." No! His prayer was, "God, You have laid out my life day by day. May I please see the provision You have already given me?" I knew Dr. Hyles was a man who was content. Why? He spent his life doing for others.

What does it take to make you content? Pray that God will open your eyes to see the wonderful privilege that He has made for that day. God loves and is a very affectionate God, and He will tolerate our "demand lists." God will patiently say, "If you don't like what I have for you, I'll try my best to give you what you want." Sometimes we do get what we want. But because we are never satisfied, we continue to make demands of God. After a while, as we run our own lives, make our demands, and tell God what we have to have, we will discover how unhappy we can be as a Christian. We have missed the fullness of His pleasure and the joy of letting Jesus orchestrate what we need every day of our life.

2. Ask for the forgiveness He has already provided. Why do we have to confess our sins? Why must we remind God that we blew it again and why we are such sorry, miserable Christians? "Satan knows that if we honestly confess our sins, they are forgiven, and he knows that if we honestly confess them we cease from them and therefore he fights every inch of the road that a Christian walks toward confession."[10]

God's forgiveness is already there for the mistakes we make! When we make a mistake and say, "God, I'm so sorry," God says, "Already forgiven!"

Why does God ask us to forgive other people? Because God is happy when we forgive someone who has wronged us. Jesus said, "Do you want to know what prayer is like? Let someone wrong you and then say to that person, 'It's all forgiven. Don't worry about it.' " What a wonderful way to live!

Loving forgiveness of my brother is the condition upon which I, a child of God, may ask His forgiveness. When we forgive those who have wronged us, we have gained the mightiest victory possible over the devil. There is nothing God loves and the devil hates more than a man who can forgive.[11]

Those of you who say, "I'll get even with so-and-so!" or "So-and-so did me wrong..." live a very miserable life! "Lack of forgiveness is the equivalent of an impure heart."[12] The person who will not forgive reveals to everyone his image of God. He gives the impression that somehow God says, "You sinned against Me, and I'm angry!" God has never done that! Consider what He did at Calvary! He forgives! He forgives us even before we even sin. No one can understand the depth of God's forgiveness. Two thousand years ago Jesus took care of every sin we would ever commit. "Kindness must be the answer to injury, love the response to malice, and forgiveness the echo to hate, if we would pray in the spirit of Jesus."[13]

3. **Lead us not into temptation but deliver us from evil.** We pray, "Father, You have laid out a path for me today. Show me the path that will keep me away from evil and temptation. When the end of the day comes, I want to be closer to You than I am right now."

Right after we pray that prayer, we flip on the radio and listen to rock music; or turn on the television and listen to ungodly conversation, music, and talk; or we criticize someone, or we associate freely with the wrong crowd or get angry and lose our temper. We then skip church and have the brazenness to wonder why God isn't being very good to us. The answer is simple! God wove a path for us through the obstacles, and we refused to follow His planned path. The Bible says in Psalm 37:23, *"The steps of a good man are ordered by the LORD: and he delighteth in his way."*

The prayer, "Lead us not into temptation," is only pious hypocrisy if we turn from offering it to go deliberately into situations which we know hold for us enticements to sin. This prayer will search our book-shelves, judge the music we listen to, dictate the company we keep. Whatever lowers our resistance to evil, sullies our minds, stirs our passions, cools our ardor for Christ, dims our vision of eternal things, leaves thoughts of evil in our minds, may be no part of our mental diet. We cannot be inviting temptation and praying against it at the same time. We cannot ask God to save us from the precipice so long as we insist on playing at its edge. Prayer has to be honest.[14]

When I was 30 years old, my home church in Holland, Michigan, asked me to become their pastor. I thought the invitation was the answer to a dream of a lifetime. I thought pastoring my home church was the culmination of everything I had always wanted to do. Every preacher boy dreams of going to his home church to pastor. I realized it was my decision to make. My wife and I went to Michigan and went house hunting. We even chose out some houses that we liked. Truthfully, we were dead-set on going there because we thought it was the will of God. I thought we should go, and my parents were in favor of our going.

I began to earnestly pray, "God, I must know the future. God, I really really want to pastor. I'm teaching at a Christian college, and it's a wonderful life, but God, I really want to pastor a church. What do I do?"

I was reading Psalm 106 and came to verse 15, "*And he gave them their request; but sent leanness into their soul.*" That one verse changed my whole focus and prayer. I said, "God, I don't know what I want, and I don't know what You want. I told You what I want, but I'm not sure ten years from now if that will be what I want. God, I do know this: I don't want to reach my golden years and say, 'Why did I insist on having what I wanted?' God, I don't want to have a lean soul. God, what I really want is Your will!"

God will give in and give the Christian what he wants. The entire chapter of Psalm 106 addresses what happened when He gave the children of Israel what they wanted. The culmination of their desires resulted in Psalm 106:15, *"And he gave them their request; but sent leanness into their soul."*

God always purposes our greatest good. Even the prayer offered in ignorance and blindness cannot swerve Him from that, although, when we persistently pray for some harmful thing, our wilfulness may bring it about, and we suffer accordingly. "He gave them their request," says the Psalmist, "but sent leanness into their soul." (Psa. Cvi.[106] 15)[15]

Of course, my dream of a lifetime was fulfilled in His perfect timing. Now I have wonderful opportunities that I would never have had. My soul is fat because I left my decisions to the package God had planned for me. I chose His will. "Prayer is insistence upon God's will being done, and it needs for its practice a man in sympathetic touch with God."[16]

Stop telling God what He must give you. Start asking God to show You what He has already provided for you. "On earth as it is in Heaven" is the richest and happiest way of living. All that the believer needs is the will of God.

If earnest prayer pleases God, then sometimes, surely, He is pleased when the prayer is so earnest that we do not want food nor drink nor sleep nor any other ordinary pleasure. If God is pleased for us to seek Him, then sometimes, surely, it pleases Him for us to lay aside every weight, abstain from everything that might absorb our energy and interest and thought, that we may give ourselves wholly to the matter of prayer.[1]

Four Prayer Partners

The word *pray* or *praying* or *prayer* or some form of it occurs over 500 times in the Bible. Simply study the word *pray* in all its different contexts, and you will discover that what God wants from you is to have a running dialogue with Him about everything in your life. If I were to summarize the whole issue of prayer in some simple statements, to me prayer is God's saying, "Include Me in everything. If you have a good time, include Me. If you have a bad time, call on Me. If life is just a droll, hum-drum, rhythm of an assembly line, let Me participate with you. If life is a festive occasion, a party, or a celebration, please include Me. Just ask Me to be involved in every avenue of your life."

The book of Luke best describes Christ's humanity. Luke makes Him touchable and feelable and reachable. As I read the book of Luke, I find Jesus always bringing His Father into every situation that arises. He prays before He calls the 12 disciples. He prays before He sends the disciples across the water. He pauses to pray before He heals the blind man. Before He goes to the cross, He agonizes in great seasons of prayer. Jesus was bringing His Father into every avenue of His life. Jesus uttered many prayers, but prayer encompassed the whole fabric of His life; a zone did not exist where Jesus was not bringing the Father into it.

As I have studied these many references on prayer in the Bible, I have repeatedly found four partners that are commonly associated with prayer. These four prayer partners were utilized by people who knew how to get things from God. Jesus wants us to pray about everything, but if you want to get His attention, add a prayer partner to your prayer life.

Prayer is hardly ever mentioned in the Bible alone; it is prayer and earnestness; prayer and watchfulness; prayer and thanksgiving. It is an instructive fact that throughout Scripture prayer is always linked with something else.[2]

Fasting

Matthew 17 tells the story of a man with a lunatic son who sought help from Jesus. Matthew 17:15 and 16 reveals the despair of the father: *"Lord, have mercy on my son: for he is lunatick, and sore vexed: for ofttimes he falleth into the fire, and oft into the water. And I brought him to thy disciples, and they could not cure him."*

Jesus alone could cure the boy. *"Then Jesus answered and said, O faithless and perverse generation, how long shall I be with you? how long shall I suffer you? bring him hither to me. And Jesus rebuked the devil; and he departed out of him: and the child was cured from that very hour. Then came the disciples to Jesus apart, and said, Why could not we cast him out? And Jesus said unto them, Because of your unbelief: for verily I say unto you, If ye have faith as a grain of mustard seed, ye shall say unto this mountain, Remove hence to yonder place; and it shall remove; and nothing shall be impossible unto you. Howbeit this kind goeth not out but by prayer and **fasting**."* (Matthew 17:17-21)

Daniel 9:3 states, *"And I set my face unto the Lord God, to seek by prayer and supplications, with **fasting**, and sackcloth, and ashes."* Daniel was a man who knew how to get his prayers answered.

I Corinthians 7 addresses the intimate marital relationship between the husband and wife. *"Defraud ye not one the other, except it be with consent for a time, that ye may give yourselves to **fasting** and prayer; and come together again, that Satan tempt you not for your incontinency."* (I Corinthians 7:5)

Acts 14:23 says, *"And when they had ordained them elders in every church, and had prayed with **fasting**, they commended them to the Lord, on whom they believed."*

The commonality of these four verses is, of course, fasting. What exactly is fasting? Most people believe that fasting is deprivation from eating. Without delving into a deep theological explanation, fasting is depriving yourself of things that are rightfully yours to have. More specifically, fasting is denying yourself those human physical appetites that are right and proper to have in order to set aside a season of extra time to pray.

The purpose of such abstinence for a longer or shorter period of time is to loosen to some degree the ties which bind us to the world of material things and our surroundings as a whole, in order that we may concentrate all our spiritual powers upon the unseen and eternal things. Fasting has not been ordained for God's sake, but for our sakes. Fasting must be voluntary.[3]

Fasting is important because it shows the importance of your prayer. God wants us to show Him that we think praying is important.

If you are not careful, praying can become a monotonous ritual instead of an intimate conversation. When you pray, maybe you use a list that you systematically go through. If you are not careful, that list can become almost like a metronome beat: This missionary here, that pastor there, the sick lady here, and that person there—the one whose name I don't even know, and the person I heard about the other day…done with my prayers! We say our prayers almost like a little mantra—as do the Islamic people when they hear the prayer horn and they all bow toward Mecca. Remind yourself that prayer is important—more important than a rhythmic, ritualistic cadence.

When I was growing up, we had prayer meetings in my home church on Wednesday nights. We did not have a Bible study. We all met together and sang a couple of songs. The teenagers went downstairs for their prayer time. The junior-aged kids went with a lady who entertained them. The men met together, and the ladies met separately. Everyone knelt and prayed. I could barely wait until I was old enough to pray with the men. The sad thing is when I got old enough to pray with the adults, we stopped having our Wednesday night prayer meeting!

Every once in a while I would "sneak" into the men's prayer time with my dad because I loved to hear the men of the church pray. To this day, I love to hear Christians pray. I could always tell who was praying because each individual developed his own particular cadence and nuance of how he prayed. Some used the name "Lord" repetitiously in their prayers. Another used the name "Father." To be sure, there is nothing sinful about praying like that, but occasionally God wants us to drop the cadence and monotony of prayer. He wants to know if the prayer we are praying really matters to us.

He asks us to set aside some things for a season of time that are rightfully ours to have: food, drink, and even romance with our spouse. With that setting aside comes His special attentiveness to our requests. God wants to know if praying is important to us.

How important your prayer request is to you is revealed by what you are willing to give up to pray. What would you give up to pray? If it cost you money to pray, would you pay to talk to God? Some people pay exorbitant amounts for appointments with Christian psychologists and psychiatrists—just to talk to someone. Why not try God?!

If you did have to pay for your salvation, what would you be willing to pay for it? If you had to put a dollar amount on your Christianity, how valuable is your salvation? What is your faith worth? What is your Bible worth to you?

I remember reading a story about two men who lived in Romania when it was a Communist satellite country. These two men wanted a copy of the Bible, and they heard Bibles were available in a certain city in Hungary. They spent almost six months at risk of life, sleeping in haystacks, hiding in people's barns, and swimming the freezing-cold Danube. They had only the clothes on their backs. They finally reached the city, got the Bible, and smuggled it back to Romania. Just imagine the time and effort they went through just to get a copy of the Scripture. The price they paid to get one Bible was enduring six months of deprivation and the constant fear of capture and ultimately death.

In my office I probably have 30 beautiful Bibles—some bound in calfskin or Moroccan leather and some bound in bonded leather. I know how blessed I am to have these copies of the Word of God. What would you do to show God His Bible is important to you?

God is simply saying, "If the matter of praying is important to you, what price would you put on it? Would you give up a meal? Would you give up two meals? Would you give up eating for one day?"

Prayer is the grasping of the invisible. Fasting is the letting go of the visible. One's degree of faith depends on the degree between the visible and the invisible. As we fast, that is, withdraw ourselves from physical appetites and the satisfying of the senses, we are letting go of the visible. There should be seasons when we let go of the visible completely and grasp the invisible with all of our hearts.[4]

God knows prayer is important, but do **you** think prayer is important? How important is it for you to get ahold of God? Have you shown God how important praying is? Have you fasted for that seemingly insurmountable difficulty in your life?

I cannot know if fasting will positively get your prayer answered, but it is always associated with prayer. Fasting is a way for a Christian to show God how important a prayer request is. Pray about everything, but once in a while say, "God, I am going to show You how important praying is; I am going to go without some meals and spend that time with You because I need something from You, God!"

Ask God for wisdom, and ask God to show you His answer by prayer and fasting. *Fasting shows the importance of prayer.*

Alms

Acts chapter 10 introduces an unsaved Gentile military man—a centurion—whose prayer was answered. *"There was a certain man in Caesarea called Cornelius, a centurion of the band called the Italian band, A devout man, and one that feared God with all his house, which gave much alms to the people, and prayed to God alway. He saw in a vision evidently about the ninth hour of the day an angel of God coming in to him, and saying unto him, Cornelius. And when he looked on him, he was afraid, and said, What is it, Lord? And he said unto him, Thy prayers and thine **alms** are come up for a memorial before God. And now send men to Joppa, and call for one Simon, whose surname is Peter."* (Acts 10:1-5)

In verse 30, Cornelius received his answer: *"...Four days ago I was fasting until this hour; and at the ninth hour I prayed in my house, and, behold, a man stood before me in bright clothing, And said, Cornelius, thy prayer is heard, and thine **alms** are had in remembrance in the sight of God."*

If you want to get your prayers answered, try studying the life of an unsaved man whose only relationship with God was that of Creator/ creation, and God chose to answer his prayer! God even sent an angel to Cornelius in answer to his prayer to direct him to the house of Simon Peter. The angel told Cornelius that God had heard his prayer because of his alms.

Alms are the compassionate, quiet, private acts of kindness an individual personally does for someone in need. If you would like to get your prayers answered in a special way, find someone who cannot do anything for you and do something good for that person as you would want God to do for you.

- When was the last time you bought a pair of shoes for a child who didn't have any?
- When was the last time you bought a meal for someone?
- When was the last time you helped someone financially?
- When was the last time you bought groceries for someone who sincerely needed them?
- When was the last time you reached deep in your pocket—even when you didn't have it—and paid someone's power bill?
- When was the last time you sacrificed for someone else without telling anyone what you did? With nobody else knowing, privately and anonymously put money in an envelope with a note that says "put this on somebody's account who needs the money," and place it in the offering plate.

When you give alms, or do any act of charity, wait on God; do it as unto him; give to a disciple in the name of a disciple, to the poor because they belong to Christ. Do it not for the praise of men, but for the glory of God, with a single eye, and an upright heart; direct it to Him, and then your alms as well as your prayers, like those of Cornelius, come up for a memorial before God. Beg of God to accept what you do for the good of others, that your alms may indeed be offerings, may be an "odour of a sweet smell, a sacrifice acceptable, well pleasing to God."[5]

Almsgiving is as important as fasting, prayer, tithes, and offerings. It is your showing God how you want God to treat you. Almsgiving shows the unselfishness of prayer.

Weeping

Hebrews 5:7, which refers to the Lord Jesus Christ, says, *"Who in the days of his flesh, when he had offered up prayers and supplications with **strong crying and tears** unto him that was able to save him from death, and was heard in that he feared."* When Jesus was here on earth, He attracted God's attention by strong crying and tears.

Christian, when was the last time tears accompanied your prayers? When was the last time tears ran down your cheeks while you were trying to pray, but you couldn't get out the words because they were caught in your throat as you were so choked up? The songwriter said, "Tears are a language God understands." God sees the tears of a broken heart. He hears each one drop from your tear-stained face. Tears flowing down the Christian's face is a language that God understands.

Isaiah 38 records one of my favorite Biblical accounts—the story of King Hezekiah and his recovery from a fatal illness. *"In those days was Hezekiah sick unto death. And Isaiah the prophet the son of Amoz came unto him, and said unto him, Thus saith the LORD, Set thine house in order: for thou shalt die, and not live."* (Isaiah 38:1) How much more clear could God make it? "Hezekiah, you are going to die and not live!"

*"Then Hezekiah turned his face toward the wall, and prayed unto the LORD, And said, Remember now, O LORD, I beseech thee, how I have walked before thee in truth and with a perfect heart, and have done that which is good in thy sight. And Hezekiah **wept** sore. Then came the word of the LORD to Isaiah, saying, Go, and say to Hezekiah, Thus saith the LORD, the God of David thy father, I have heard thy prayer, I have seen thy tears: behold, I will add unto thy days fifteen years."* (Isaiah 38:2-5)

Hezekiah knew God answered prayer. When the Assyrian armies attacked his kingdom, his main defense was prayer. God heard his prayer and the prayers of the prophet Isaiah. The angel of the Lord killed 185,000 Assyrians in answer to their prayers.

When the decree came directly from God that he would die, Hezekiah's faith was not staggered for the news. Without delay, he prayed.

The Bible clearly teaches that prayer changes even the plans of God. When Hezekiah turned his face to the wall, wept and prayed, God changed His plan before the prophet had gotten out the front gate, and sent Isaiah back to say, "I have heard thy prayer, I have seen thy tears: behold, I will add unto thy days fifteen years." (Isaiah 38:1-5) God had planned for Hezekiah to die at once but changed His plans in answer to prayer.[6]

Do you cry when you pray? The sincerity of your prayers is measured by the tears that accompany them. I have already mentioned the story about a backslidden teenager who was running from God. Night after night, his mother took his shoes from his closet and prayed over them until she filled them with her tears. What her words could not do to his backslidden heart, her tears accomplished!

Accompanying your prayers with tears provides powerful transportation straight to the heart of God. The words of your prayers reach the ears of God by the liquid of your tears because God fully understands that language.

Hebrews 5 explains how the young Christ child knew that He had to grow up and go to the cross of crucifixion. Understanding the meaning of that personal sacrifice is far greater than any human's diminished mind and mental capacity can comprehend. Christ shuddered at the knowledge that He had to be separated from His Father and face an eternal judgment in a finite moment. Christ prayed until He wept, and that time with His Father gave Him the strength to go to the cross. With whatever we have to face in life, if we will pray until we weep, we will find the strength to face our personal cross. *Tears show the sincerity of prayer.*

Confession of Other People's Sins

Daniel's life warrants a diligent study because he was a man who knew how to get God to listen to him. *"In the first year of Darius the son of Ahasuerus, of the seed of the Medes, which was made king over the realm of the Chaldeans; In the first year of his reign I Daniel understood by books the number of the years, whereof the word of the LORD came to Jeremiah the prophet, that he would accomplish seventy years in the desolations of Jerusalem."* (Daniel 9:1, 2)

Daniel had been studying the book of Jeremiah the prophet, who happened to be a contemporary of Daniel. In Jeremiah 25:11, he read that the children of Israel would be in captivity for 70 years. The thought occurred to Daniel that the 70 years of captivity had nearly passed. Daniel began praying to know the will of God for his people. He wanted to know the future of his nation, and he begged God to reveal His plan.

God answered Daniel's prayer. *"And I set my face unto the Lord God, to seek by prayer and supplications, with fasting, and sackcloth, and ashes: And I prayed unto the LORD my God, and made my confession, and said, O Lord, the great and dreadful God, keeping the covenant and mercy to them that love him, and to them that keep his commandments; We have sinned, and have committed iniquity, and have done wickedly, and have rebelled, even by departing from thy precepts and from thy judgments: Neither have we hearkened unto thy servants the prophets, which spake in thy name to our kings... O Lord, righteousness belongeth unto thee...."* (Daniel 9:3-7)

Why did God answer Daniel's prayer? *"And whiles I was speaking, and praying, and confessing my sin and the sin of my people Israel, and presenting my supplication before the LORD my God for the holy mountain of my God; Yea, whiles I was speaking in prayer, even the man Gabriel, whom I had seen in the vision at the beginning, being caused to fly swiftly, touched me about the time of the evening oblation. And he informed me, and talked with me, and said, O Daniel, I am now come forth to give thee skill and understanding. At the beginning*

*of thy supplications the commandment came forth, and I am come to
shew thee; for thou art greatly beloved...."* (Daniel 9:20-23)

He prayed and confessed not only his sins, but the sins of his
nation. While he was praying and confessing his sins as well as the
sins of his people, Gabriel ["The one who speaks on behalf of
God"] came to Daniel and said, "Daniel, God heard your prayer
the very first day you prayed."

Daniel had prayed 21 days for the answer to that prayer, and
God had heard him on the first day he prayed! "Answers to prayer
are delayed, or denied, out of kindness, *or*, that more may be
given, *or*, that a far larger purpose may be served."[7] Daniel provided another recipe on how to get God's attention in prayer: confessing his sin and the sins of his people.

Teenagers, do you ever confess the sins of your generation? Do
you ever bow your knee to God and say, "God, I'm so sorry! My
generation promotes gangs, fornication, lewdness, rock music,
adultery, and drugs. God, please forgive me and forgive my generation for our foolishness. I'm so sorry You have to be burdened
with the sins of my generation." God would love to hear some
teenager pray that way.

Middle-aged people, do you ever pray and confess the sins of
your generation? Do you bow your knee to God and say, "God, I'm
so sorry that my generation is marked by avarice, wife-swapping,
divorce, adultery, power struggles, jealousy, envy, the desire to get
ahead, covetousness"? Do you ever go to God and say, "I'm sorry
You've put up with these sins." For some reason God hears the
prayers of those who admit the flaws of their generation.

When was the last time you confessed the sins of the
Republican and Democratic parties? Do you ever confess the fact
that we have sinful people in high places? When was the last time
you told God you were sorry that the Supreme Court of the
United States ruled in favor of sodomite sex? When was the last
time you confessed the sin of removing prayer and Bible reading

from the public schools? Saying "That was way before I was born" is not a legitimate excuse!

Six hundred years before Jesus was born, God judged the nation of Israel by sending Babylon to take His people into captivity. One hundred fifty years later, Nehemiah, a man who knew how to get God's attention, came on the scene. Nehemiah heard about his homeland's lying waste and the city of Jerusalem's lying open to marauders and thieves who had taken advantage of the people.

Nehemiah was distressed beyond measure—he goes to God and makes it a subject of prayer. He begins with adoration, makes confession of the sins of his nation, pleads the promises of God, mentions former mercies, and begs for pardoning mercy. Then with an eye to the future—for unquestionably he had planned, the next time he was summoned into the Kings' presence, to ask permission to visit Jerusalem and to do there what was possible to remedy the distressing state of affairs—we hear him pray for something very special: "And prosper I pray thee thy servant this day, and grant him mercy in the sight of this man [the king]. For I was the king's cupbearer." The final result was that the king not only permitted Nehemiah to go back to Jerusalem but furnished him with everything needful for the journey and for the success of the enterprise. The intense, persistent praying of Nehemiah prevailed.[8]

Though he had been born in Babylon and had never been to Jerusalem, Nehemiah fell on his face and begged God's forgiveness, "God, I am so sorry for the sins that caused You to judge our nation—150 years ago."

Allow me the liberty of placing this story in context with America. In Washington, D. C., our sixteenth president's powerful second inaugural address delivered on Saturday, March 4,

1865, is engraved in stone at the Lincoln Memorial. Lincoln eloquently stated,

Yet, if God wills that it [the war] continue until all the wealth piled by the bondsmen's 250 years of unrequited toil shall be sunk, and until every drop of blood drawn with the lash shall be paid by another drawn with the sword, as was said 3,000 years ago, so still it must be said, "The judgments of the Lord are true and righteous all together." With malice toward none, with charity for all, with firmness in the right as God gives us to see the right. Let us strive on to finish the work we are in, to bind up the nation's wounds, to care for him who shall have borne the battle and for his widow and his orphan, to do all which may achieve and cherish a just and lasting peace among ourselves and with all nations."[9]

Mr. Lincoln was saying in essence that the bloodshed of the Civil War was retribution for the sin of slavery. Every stripe that marked a man's back was paid for by the bullets fired during the Civil War. I have no doubt that Lincoln possessed a high understanding of God's sense of justice.

In terms of human casualties, the Civil War cost more than any other American war. About 1 million men were killed or wounded. Deaths, including those from disease, totaled 529,332. By comparison, about 116,500 Americans died in World War I and 405,400 in World War II. The North lost 364,511 men, the South, 164,821. Disease killed more men than bullets did. About 140,000 Union men and 75,000 Confederates died in battle.[10]

Lincoln believed that almost 600,000 Americans died because hundreds of thousands of people were placed under the lash; we felt we had the right to own people. When was the last time you fell on your face and said, "God, over 150 years ago, we had a devastating Civil War. I'm so sorry that my forefathers would take part in activities that would result in a war that viciously divided our nation's families."

Nehemiah did! One-hundred fifty years later, Nehemiah confessed the sins of the civil war that decimated his homeland. He was a man who knew how to get God's attention.

- Have you confessed anyone's sins?
- Have you ever asked God for forgiveness for what Hitler did to His chosen people in the holocaust?
- Have you ever apologized to God for Stalin who murdered 50 million of his own people?
- Have you ever apologized for Fidel Castro who oppresses his people in Cuba?
- Have you ever apologized for the people in Colombia who know of no other way to make a living than by growing the plants that produce cocaine which poisons the minds of Americans?
- Have you ever fallen on your face before God and said, "God, we surely have corrupted this world You gave us. I'm so sorry!"

This kind of prayer may sound unusual, but it is Daniel Christianity and Nehemiah Christianity. The man who prays, "Wrongs have been committed throughout this world even before my lifetime, and God, I am so sorry" is the Christian God hears. This kind of Christianity goes way beyond the thinking of most Christians. God will readily hear the prayers of people who take the time to confess the sins committed by those who came before them.

- Do your prayers include saying, "Oh God, when I think about six million Jews slaughtered, I am so sorry for what we did to Your people"?
- Do your prayers include saying, "When I see the Muslim people blinded by ignorance and blowing up their young

people and killing Israelis for a piece of real estate, God, I am so sorry."

I go through the world and apologize to God because someone needs to go to God and apologize for what we have done with what He has given to us. When I pray and confess the sins of things I did not do, God knows I mean business about praying. Over 2,000 years ago, a Saviour hung on a cross and confessed man's sins all the way back to the Garden of Eden. God saw His Son confess every sin, and God heard His prayers.

Do you want your prayers answered? Team up with these four prayer partners! Nothing will transform your life, your marriage, your family, your home, your job, and your personality more than walking with God and praying without ceasing.

Fasting shows the importance of prayer.
Alms show the unselfishness of prayer.
Tears show the sincerity of prayer.
Confession shows the worthiness of prayer.

He who has the spirit of prayer has the highest interest in the court of heaven. And the only way to retain it is to keep it in constant employment. Apostasy begins in the closet. No man ever backslid from the life and power of Christianity who continued constant and fervent in private prayer. He who prays without ceasing is likely to rejoice evermore.

–Adam Clarke[1]

The Good Neighborhood
of Prayer

*"Rejoice evermore. Pray without ceasing. In every thing give thanks: for this is the will of God in Christ Jesus concerning you. **Quench not the Spirit.** Despise not prophesyings. Prove all things; hold fast that which is good. Abstain from all appearance of evil. And the very God of peace sanctify you wholly; and I pray God your whole spirit and soul and body be preserved blameless unto the coming of our Lord Jesus Christ."* (I Thessalonians 5:16-23)

All of Scripture was forever settled in Heaven and penned by men under the inspiration of God. *"All scripture is given by inspiration of God, and is profitable for doctrine, for reproof, for correction, for instruction in righteousness."* (II Timothy 3:16) God's Word was written in the Koine Greek language of the New Testament era. Koine Greek is to present-day Greek as 1611 A.D. English is to present-day English.

In the Koine Greek language, the eight verses of I Thessalonians 16-23 comprise a paragraph, and that paragraph contains one key statement which is called the purpose sentence or the statement of purpose. The key statement is the reason why the paragraph was written, and verse 19 happens to be the statement of purpose. Verse 19, which says *"Quench not the Spirit,"* also happens to be the central verse of the paragraph, and all the other sentences surrounding verse 19 are built on that sentence.

The Bible says *"Quench not the Spirit,"* and then lists ways not to quench the Spirit.

- If you don't want to quench the Spirit, *"Rejoice evermore."*
- If you don't want to quench the Spirit, *"...give thanks."*

- If you don't want to quench the Spirit, "*Pray without ceasing.*"
- If you don't want to quench the Spirit, "*Despise not prophesyings.*"
- If you don't want to quench the Spirit, "*Prove all things....*"
- If you don't want to quench the Spirit, "*Abstain from all appearance of evil.*"
- If you don't want to quench the Spirit, keep your spirit, soul, and body strong and complete.

Allow me to liken this series of short, pithy verses to living in a neighborhood. If I took you on a tour of my home neighborhood, I would point out some of our key neighbors. Neighborhoods are extremely important. When choosing a neighborhood in which to live, the question to consider is *not* "Is this the best place to build a house?" Rather, "Is this the best place to build our family and rear our children?" is the most important question to weigh. Those with whom you dwell and associate and where you dwell are very important to the Christian life. Good neighbors are more important to me than the house in which I reside.

When my wife and I moved into the neighborhood where we still reside, several funny incidents happened. About a year after we moved there, a widow lady who had been living there moved closer to her family. A new family moved in. A moving van was parked in front of the house, and our new neighbors had been moving furniture all morning. They decided to take a break, and their idea of a break was not getting a glass of cold ice tea. Their idea of a break was to smoke some cigarettes on their back porch, which happens to face our back door. Our daughter, who was about five years old at the time, had been watching the activity all morning.

When they started smoking, she just stared—speechless. I was watching her and thinking, "What is going through that little mind of hers?" Oh, how I wish I would have known! She made up her mind, opened the back door, and tripped right over to these people to whom we had barely spoken, and said in no uncertain terms, "My name is Jaclynn. I'm your neighbor. You're smoking cigarettes. You're going to go to Hell."

I rushed over and said, "Hello! This little girl is the neighbor from next door. She doesn't live here. We're an adoption agency, and we're taking her back! Glad to have you as new neighbors. Welcome to our neighborhood!" They chuckled and were obviously a little embarrassed, and we were more than a little embarrassed. Our first introduction to our neighbors, compliments of our daughter, was a never-to-be-forgotten experience!

People who want to get their prayers answered but live in the wrong neighborhood spiritually will not have their prayers answered consistently. Notice the neighbors who dwell in Prayer's neighborhood and the company Prayer keeps. Take heed of Prayer's neighbors.

1. Find your joy in things eternal. *"Rejoice evermore"* simply means "to build your joy on **eternal** values." Don't get excited because of a trip to Great America; get excited because you own a copy of the Word of God! According to the Bible, Heaven and earth will pass away—Great America rides will shut down—but the Bible will never fail, never end, or never die! Some people live in a neighborhood where their happiness is dependent upon a paycheck, a Christmas bonus, and season tickets to see their favorite team. Build your joy on the fact that your name is written down in Heaven. Build your happiness on that which does not change. Even as permanent as some of our relationships on earth seem to be, we really must maintain our joy on something even more eternal. If you build your life too much on the temporary things of life, you will have an unsteady and an unstable life. Build your joy around Prayer and Prayer's neighbors. Do you want your prayers answered? If so, make good friends with Prayer's neighbors.

2. Be grateful all the time. *"In every thing give thanks: for this is the will of God in Christ Jesus concerning you."* How much simpler can it be stated than "in everything, we are to give thanks"? God doesn't say to give thanks **for** everything; God says to give thanks **in** everything. How grateful are you? *"In every thing give thanks...."* is gratitude in motion. Some people say they have nothing in their lives for which to be grateful. How sad! In order to get prayers answered, one must be grateful!

If you are as ungrateful as I often am, begin by giving thanks to God for temporal gifts you have received from Him, such as physical health, the use of your mental faculties, strength for your daily tasks, and the desire to work, house and home, food and clothing, and the dear ones whom you love and who love you. Begin with these things and you will notice that it becomes easier for you to see and to give thanks for the spiritual gifts which the Lord has showered upon you.[2]

Prayer and his neighbors, Rejoice Evermore and Gratitude get along famously! If you don't get along with Gratitude or Prayer or Rejoice Evermore, more than likely your joy has not been built on eternal things.

3. Don't limit the influence of God in your life. *"Quench not the Spirit."* is pivotal. The word *quench* means "extinguish." In other words, don't extinguish or snuff out or push down or limit the influence of God in your life. Don't quench that light—just like the song we learned in Sunday school.

"This little light of mine; I'm gonna let it shine.
This little of light of mine; I'm gonna let it shine.
Let it shine, let it shine, let it shine.
Hide it under a bushel, NO!
I'm gonna let it shine,
Hide it under a bushel, NO!
I'm gonna let it shine, let it shine...."

We will let that light shine—especially if we want the influence of the Spirit of God in our lives.

4. Magnify preaching. *"Despise not prophesyings."* (Verse 20) *Prophesyings* is simply another word for "preaching." The word *despise* means "don't make little of it." In other words, Paul was saying, "Magnify preaching."

Prayer is our expression of our thoughts to God. Preaching is our expression of our thoughts to men. True preaching is ever the giving away of oneself. True preaching then is dependent on true praying.[3]

Prayer loves preaching! God says, "Don't minimize preaching." Prayer is bothered by church members who leave the church services during invitation.

The truth of the matter is, I'd imagine if you don't like preaching, you probably don't pray. If you don't like Prayer's neighbors, you probably really don't like Prayer or having God's influence on your life.

5. Test, approve, and examine. *"Prove all things. Hold fast that which is good."* (v. 21) The simple teaching of this verse means to test everything, hold fast to the good, and discard everything else. Test which Bible is the right one. I find that the King James Version satisfies all my needs and wants. Hold fast only to that which is good, and discard all the rest!

The Bible teaches us that we are allowed to put God to the test. The example of Gideon in Old Testament days is sufficient to show us that God honors our faith even when that faith is faltering. He allows us to "prove Him" even after a definite promise from Himself.[4]

Having a slightly skeptical nature does not hurt a person. Some people are a little too gullible in life. They believe everything they hear on the news. Check things out, do a little testing, and do a little research and reading. Find the truth! Take your time to make your choices. Seek counsel and advice.

Before you buy a pre-owned car, have it thoroughly inspected by a certified mechanic. Before you buy a house, consult someone like a good construction engineer to be sure there are no faults in the building.

Prayer says, "Check things out before you get into them." Too many times we resort to Prayer because we haven't done our homework. Prayer cannot fix a person's bad or shoddy homework.

6. Recognize evil. Verse 22 says, *"Abstain from all appearance of evil."* Recognize evil in all of its faces and avoid it! God endows man with what I call an unusual "sixth sense" to know when something is bad. However, we can reside in a bad neighborhood so long that our sixth sense has been dulled to the point where it is no longer reliable. At that point only converted, seasoned, veteran, experienced men who have learned to recognize evil can be good neighbors.

Some bad men do reside in your neighborhood! Some people lack the ability to recognize the different faces of evil. "I wouldn't go to a movie theater," you sanctimoniously say, but you have no problem watching daytime soap operas. You would never think of associating with the liberals, but you have no problem listening to their rhetoric on talk-show radio. Women wouldn't think of wearing their britches or their immodest clothing to church, but have no problem stripping half-naked and wearing bikinis while on vacation. Do you honestly believe geography determines morality? Recognize evil!

When a secular university offers a lucrative sports scholarship to a Christian high school athlete, the wise mother and father say, "You don't want to accept that offer, son." There is no such thing as a gift of athleticism in the Bible. When you make decisions based upon your athleticism, you are not making a decision based on Bible teaching. Trust wisdom!

The prophet Balaam is a good example of a man who did not recognize evil when he was confronted by it. Numbers 22:6, 7 says, *"Come now therefore, I pray thee, curse me this people...that I may drive them out of the land...And the elders of Moab and the elders of Midian departed with the rewards of divination* [fortune telling] *in their hand; and they came unto Balaam, and spake unto him the words of Balak."* The people of Moab and their ruler Balak were frightened of the children of Israel. They sought the help of Balaam, who was a prophet, to stop the incursion of the children of Israel. Balaam told them he would pray about the matter.

In no uncertain terms God said, *"...Thou shalt not go with them; thou shalt not curse the people: for they are blessed."* (Numbers 22:12)

Balaam delivered God's message to Balak's emissaries and sent them home. Not to be denied the help of this prophet, Balak sent more emissaries with greater honors and riches. Balaam eventually succumbed to Balak and his gifts and left God's perfect will—despite the fact that God had told him not to go! *"And God's anger was kindled because he went...."* (Numbers 22:22)

God, Who is forever patient, sent an angel to stop him, and Balaam's donkey saw the angel and stopped. Balaam beat the donkey in exasperation, and God gave the donkey the ability to talk. *"...What have I done unto thee, that thou hast smitten me these three times?..."* (Numbers 22:28) Balaam was so thick-headed in his stubbornness, he started conversing with the donkey! He even argued about the matter with the donkey! The Lord opened Balaam's eyes; he saw the angel and realized the error of his way. Balaam used prayer as a cop-out for his lack of discernment. Balaam's folly illustrates how badly Christians need to have a prayer life.

7. **Properly exercise your spirit, soul, and body.** *"And the very God of peace sanctify you wholly; and I pray God your whole spirit and soul and body be preserved blameless unto the coming of our*

Lord Jesus Christ." (I Thessalonians 5:23) "Prayer wonderfully clears the vision; steadies the nerves; defines duty; stiffens the purpose; sweetens and strengthens the spirit."[5] However, prayer does not make up for a Christian's unwillingness to take care of what God has given to him. When a person abuses his body with alcohol, recreational drugs, illicit sexual relationships, etc., for years, prayer cannot suddenly make him a complete transformed man. Though God is gracious, merciful, and kind, prayer cannot take away the mistakes and abuse of a person who has lived his life abusing his body, poisoning his mind, and neglecting his spirit. Prayer does not reside in that neighborhood where a person consistently abuses what God has given him.

The order of "spirit, soul, and body" is very important. God does not frown on someone's working out and being physically fit. However, the question is have you read your Bible as much as you have pumped iron and exercised? How is your spiritual life doing? Is your spiritual exercise as developed as your physical exercise? Do you ever read a good book or listen to decent music? Do you cultivate your soul at all? Do you ever work on your friendships and relationships? As you exercise and work your body, develop your spirit and cultivate a right attitude and a right spirit with people. Have you used your mind? Have you read any sermons or have you pumped poison into your brain? Do you listen to preaching? Do you prove all things?

If we are to obtain from God all that we ask from Him, Christ's words must abide or continue in us. We must study His words, fairly devour His words, let them sink into our thought and into our heart, keep them in our memory, obey them constantly in our life, let them shape and mold our daily life and our every act.[6]

Then we can go to Prayer and say, "Prayer, I've been living in your neighborhood. I have been listening to the preaching and reading some good books, so Prayer, would you help me?" God is more inclined to hear the prayers of those who are walking the stable life, grateful for the good things and for what God is doing for them.

"Rejoice evermore"—find your joy in things eternal. God didn't put you on this earth simply to rejoice. He put you on this earth to be influenced by Him and for Him. You could do that with all these prayer partners—by living in the good neighborhood of Prayer. The key is being influenced by God. "Prayer influences men by influencing God to influence them."[7] *"Pray without ceasing"* means "never give up on prayer." God in His mercy says, "Never give up on prayer."

In what neighborhood do you live? If you really want to know how to pray, you will have to get around Prayer's neighbors. Prayer helps us to influence for God and to be influenced by God. Prayer is the most powerful tool to help with all that God gives me.

Prayer is our highest privilege, our gravest responsibility, and the greatest power God has put into our hands. Prayer, real prayer, is the noblest, the sublimest, the most stupendous act that any creature of God can perform.[8]

In the place of prayer, the soul has aspirations which are sanctified and set aflame, and what is more, kept aflame. Do you wonder that the devil strives with might and main with all that is reasonable—and all that is unreasonable too—to keep us from this soul-hearing, soul-seeing, and soul-activating place of prayer?[1]

The Enemies of Prayer

"*Take, my brethren, the prophets, who have spoken in the name of the Lord, for an example of suffering affliction, and of patience. Behold, we count them happy which endure. Ye have heard of the patience of Job, and have seen the end of the Lord; that the Lord is very pitiful, and of tender mercy. But above all things, my brethren, swear not, neither by heaven, neither by the earth, neither by any other oath: but let your yea be yea; and your nay, nay; lest ye fall into condemnation. Is any among you afflicted? let him pray. Is any merry? let him sing psalms. Is any sick among you? let him call for the elders of the church; and let them pray over him, anointing him with oil in the name of the Lord: And the prayer of faith shall save the sick, and the Lord shall raise him up; and if he have committed sins, they shall be forgiven him. Confess your faults one to another, and pray one for another, that ye may be healed. The effectual fervent prayer of a righteous man availeth much. Elias was a man subject to like passions as we are, and he prayed earnestly that it might not rain: and it rained not on the earth by the space of three years and six months. And he prayed again, and the heaven gave rain, and the earth brought forth her fruit. Brethren, if any of you do err from the truth, and one convert him; Let him know, that he which converteth the sinner from the error of his way shall save a soul from death, and shall hide a multitude of sins.*" (James 5:10-20)

God is eager to entice Christians to get into the business and labor of prayer. I liken it to signing on with a job or being recruited for the armed forces. One of the recruitment devices God uses to get us to pray is to answer our prayers.

God gets us praying, He sees us praying, and He hears our prayers. "Four things let us ever keep in mind: God hears prayers, God heeds prayer, God answers prayer, and God delivers by prayer."[2] He answers that prayer to lead us to further praying, but not because God is selectively or randomly choosing which prayers He wants to answer. God wants to get us into a life of prayer.

I have already made mention of the fact that little children very often get their prayers answered. Little children possess such an unaltered innocence, and of course, the Scripture says, "...Except ye...become as little children...." (Matthew 18:3) In so many arenas, God does not want us to grow up. He actually wants us to be as little children and to come to Him with that same naive, innocent, sweet love and affection that characterizes a little child.

Prayer is the child's request, not to the winds nor to the world, but to the Father. Prayer is the outstretched arms of the child for the Father's help. Prayer is the child's cry calling to the Father's ear, the Father's heart, and to the Father's ability, which the Father is to hear, the Father is to feel, and which the Father is to relieve. Prayer is the seeking of God's great and greatest good, which will not come if we do not pray.[3]

Sad to say, as we age, we tend to lose that childlike characteristic of innocence. With our maturity comes an independence from God Who then sometimes has to step aside or step back and let us learn to be dependent upon Him again. This process even happens in the arena of prayer.

We tend to forget that a life of prayer is spiritual warfare. Prayer is a battle, and God wants to bring us to the front lines of the battlefield. There the Christian inflicts serious damage on the enemy, brings glory to God, and brings righteousness into the kingdom of God and to God's people. To accomplish that goal, God has to toughen the Christian. He starts the process by first giving us answers to our first simple, delightful prayers.

Without a doubt, prayer is a mighty tool—a very mighty weapon in the hands of a righteous Christian. "...*The effectual fervent prayer of a righteous man availeth much.*" (James 5:16) "Nothing is more pleasing to our Father in Heaven than direct, importunate, and persevering prayer."[4] It would be more easy to find a living person who does not breathe than to find a living Christian who does not pray even just a little bit.

There are those who wade in the shallows of prayer, but they soon leave the waters for more exciting activities. "All around us we see a tendency to substitute human gifts and worldly attainments for that supernatural, inward power which comes from on high in answer to earnest prayer."[5] Very few people continue in effectual, fervent prayer. People try fervent prayer like a new computer game or some daring fad or fashion. When the next fad or fashion arrives, prayer is once again set aside as "what I did when I was a younger Christian and needed it more." Usually a Christian comes back to prayer when he has a great need.

Prayer isn't just for little kids; prayer is for everyone. Prayer should be the tool used by all those who are strong in the Lord—the prayer warriors, so to speak. There's a reason why they earn the name "prayer warriors." Nobody ever says, "Let's go be a 'prayer civilian.' " No! The designation for a person who prays fervently is "prayer warrior." Praying is for those who are strong. Prayer is for those who know that it is **the** weapon of strength they have to offer to spiritual endeavors. Prayer should be used not just by those who are so young in age or faith that they are overwhelmed by its effectiveness or so old they have no other activity. Prayer should be every Christian's activity.

Many attempt prayer, but they fall victim to the enemies of prayer. Because prayer is spiritual warfare, it has spiritual enemies. James 5:10-20 reveals two enemies of prayer. Some form of the word *prayer* is found seven times in this passage. Obviously, prayer is one of the principal themes of James chapter 5. Two men of prayer—Job and Elijah—are addressed in this passage for a specific reason. These two men fought the spiritual battle of prayer and conquered the two enemies of prayer. These two enemies keep us from praying and take us wounded from the battlefield. Sometimes that wound is a self-inflicted scratch or a mortal wound from the enemy. That wound we received took us off the front lines away from prayer and caused us to sit idle—a casualty and terrible loss on the battlefield of prayer.

The purpose of prayer is not to persuade or influence God, but to join forces with Him against the enemy. Not towards God, but with God against Satan—that is the main thing to keep in mind in prayer.[6]

Because God is establishing a kingdom, He wants us to work with Him in establishing that kingdom. At this time that kingdom is not a political realm. God will someday establish a real kingdom within this worldly place to replace all the different present-day kingdoms. The kingdom of God is a spiritual kingdom in the hearts of mankind. God is trying to enlarge His spiritual kingdom, and we Christians have great power in that kingdom. We have a King, Jesus Christ, and He can rule in our hearts in His great power. His kingdom is so powerful that the kingdoms of this earth have launched a war against the kingdom of God.

Because he realizes God's omnipotence, Satan uses subtle tactics to try to prevent God's kingdom from being established here on earth. The god of this world knows how powerful God's kingdom is. God's archenemy, Satan, knows that if God's kingdom's residents—the local body of the local church—ever decided to use the weapon of prayer and stepped onto the battlefield, there is no foe that could withstand them. In I Samuel 17 the giant, Goliath, died because the power of prayer was appropriated and the forces of Heaven were marshaled.

There is no doubt whatever that the devil opposes our approach to God in prayer, and does all he can to prevent the prayer of faith. His chief way of hindering us is to try to fill our minds with the thought of our needs, so that they shall not be occupied with thoughts of God, our loving Father, to Whom we pray.[7]

Satan knows that if God's people ever picked up the weapons of prayer and stepped onto the battlefield, he would be done! That is why God said in Romans 8:37, *"...we are more than conquerors..."*! How can a Christian be more than a conqueror? Merely walk on the battlefield, pick up the weapon of prayer, and claim the promise of Isaiah 54:17—*"No weapon that is formed against thee shall prosper...."* We already have the victory! He Who knows the end from the beginning has already declared Himself the victorious Conqueror! "Men of power are without exception men of prayer. God bestows His Holy Spirit in His fullness only on men of prayer."[8]

However, if the Christian willingly sets down the weapon of prayer and leaves the battlefield of prayer, the enemy will encroach around him. The enemy has the power to steal his conversation with the King and to rob the King of His glory. The enemy is allowed to inflict grave and tragic and immortal wounds in the warrior ranks. The kingdom of darkness thereby encroaches into the kingdom of light, and the turncoat warrior brings shame and reproach to his King.

God's child can conquer everything by prayer. Is it any wonder that Satan does his utmost to snatch that weapon from the Christian, or to hinder him the use of it? How now does Satan hinder prayer? By temptation to postpone or curtail it, by bringing in wandering thoughts and all sorts of distractions; through unbelief and hopelessness.[9]

How can the Christian hold fast to the weapon of prayer? What exactly are the enemies of prayer? Both Job and Elijah conquered their enemies, and in conquering their enemies of prayer, they gained the victory for the kingdom of God.

1. Yielding to pressure. Job teaches us that most Christians are unwilling to stay under the pressure. In James 5:11 the Bible says, *"Behold, we count them happy which endure. Ye have heard of the patience of Job, and have seen the end of the Lord; that the Lord is very pitiful, and of tender mercy."* The word *patience* in this verse means "to stay under the weight; stay under the pressure." Those who buckle under the pressure and run are beaten and defeated before they even forsake the battlefield. God does not bless those upon whom He cannot depend. God does not begin to show Himself strong on behalf of those who cut and run. All 42 chapters of Job are a powerful testimony of a man who stood and said, "I refuse to buckle."

Job wished he had never been born and said so in Job 3:3: *"Let the day perish wherein I was born, and the night in which it was said, There is a man child conceived."* But as much as Job felt he should never have been born, he determined he would not turn back. Job had endured an incredible ordeal of losing everything he owned, the untimely deaths of his children, a wife who rebuked him, and criticizing friends. The Bible says when Job prayed for his three friends, God opened the windows of Heaven and poured out a double blessing on him. However, the book of Job is not to teach the Christian how to get a double blessing; rather, the purpose of Job is to teach the Christian how to fight the enemy of prayer. Job's "don't-quit" mentality was the great weapon of victory that he used in prayer.

Prayer really only works when those who want to avail themselves of its power build a platform that says, "I will stand on my commitment level," and refuse to turn back. God never fails, and life is too short to measure the greatness of God. Health problems, financial needs, business failures, marriage difficulties, parenting struggles, employment upsets, and all other negative happenings that a man can endure have no bearing on whether or not a Christian is effective in this kingdom war against darkness. Life is much too short for a man to take measure against God!

I was captivated by a talk I had with a historian who said, "The Chinese look at history so much differently than Americans do. I was talking to a Chinese historian and asked him for his opinion about the American Revolution. He said the Chinese historian merely said, 'It is too early to tell.' "

The American historian was startled by that reply. "That was over 200 years ago," he said. "What do you mean?"

"A mere 200 years old?" the Chinese historian replied. "Our nation has been in existence for 4,000 years. It's far too soon to tell what a short 200-year time frame can determine."

My point is we cannot take our few decades in the ministry and say, "God, I didn't do everything I thought I should do. I did not have all the victories I thought I should have. I didn't have all the conquering power I thought I should have." A man's life is too brief to put God into a package and tell Him whether or not He is a good God! God needs someone on whom He can depend more than He needs someone who bemoans his lack of victory.

The may who says, "All Hell may assail me, but I shall NOT TURN BACK!" is the man to whom God listens because that man understands the purpose of prayer.

Job begged to die and cursed his birthday, but he never buckled! *"In all this Job sinned not, nor charged God foolishly."* (Job 1:22) Job never once shook his fist at God and questioned Him.

- "What right do You have to kill my ten children?"
- "What right do You have to put my wife at odds with me?"
- "What right do You have to kill all of my staff?"
- "What right do You have to take all of my belongings?"
- "What right do You have to make me go bankrupt?"

- "What right do You have to kill all my servants?"
- "What right do You have to take all my health?"

Job never left the battlefield! "By the sufferings of Job millions of others have been comforted and have been assured that God is good and never forsakes His own."[10] Some people set down the weapon, leave the battlefield, go home, and say, "It doesn't work." Prayer is not for cowards nor quitters.

2. Not subduing human passions. The second man mentioned in James 5 is the subject of the second enemy of prayer. James 5:17, 18 says, *"Elias [Elijah] was a man subject to like passions as we are, and he prayed earnestly that it might not rain: and it rained not on the earth by the space of three years and six months. And he prayed again, and the heaven gave rain, and the earth brought forth her fruit."*

Elijah had such power with God because he knew how to control his passions. A lack of self-control has made prayer nothing more than an insignificant "first-aid kit" we run to because we are bleeding badly again. How can we expect to fight the kingdom of darkness with such a weak Christianity? How can we expect to bring in the kingdom of righteousness, joy, peace, and the Holy Ghost? How can we expect to bring in the kingdom of righteousness if we cannot control the television set?!

God says, "Why don't you get control of your passions and realize prayer is a mighty power?"

Prayer gives us the power to say, "God, let's bring kingdom righteousness to America once again. God, let's step into the Supreme Court of the United States and make a statement about re-introducing the Bible and prayer into the public schools again."

Do you think God is so weak that He cannot reverse past decisions? Do you think God's hand is tied by Abbington v. Schemp in 1962? Do you think God is handcuffed because of Roe v. Wade in 1972? We serve the God Who created Roe and Wade!

How did Elijah pray and bring Ahab to his knees? Simple!

Elijah controlled his passions and disciplined his appetites! I have no doubt Elijah wanted to do the same things we want to do, but he did not give in to the temptation. We give in to our desires and passions.

Heroes are people who are victorious over their passions. They succeed at facing the same obstacles used as excuses for other peoples' failures. People who fail are too paralyzed to do anything great for God because their prayer life is consumed with "Mr. Personal Pronoun"—"I," "Me," and "Mine." I need more money!" "I need a happier spouse!" "I want a nicer house!" "I want more…!" "I want a better quality of life." God wants us to use prayer for His kingdom, but we fritter away our prayers on temporal requests like, "Make me happier."

Prayer never loses sight of the infinite relationships and the infinite values. Herein is the test for our praying. The moment prayer becomes request for something purely for self which may be spent upon personal lusts—or if you will have a milder word, upon personal desires—then prayer is outside the will of God.[11]

God says, "Why don't you pick up the weapon of prayer and get some souls saved? Why don't you pick up the weapon of prayer and advance the kingdom of God?"

Prayer is not some tool to make me happy. Happiness is a byproduct of prayer. This business of praying is spiritual warfare—a tool for the kingdom of righteousness. "Prayers are omnipotent forces, world-wide and heaven-reaching."[12] Are you a Job or an Elijah? Can you handle the two enemies of effective prayer—pressure and passion? God's kingdom desperately needs those who can!

It has often been said that prayer is the greatest force in the universe. This is no exaggeration. It will bear constant repetition. In this atomic age when forces are being released that stagger the thought and imagination of man, it is well to remember that prayer transcends all other forces.

– F. J. Huegel[1]

Team Pray-ers

"Likewise, ye husbands, dwell with them according to knowl-edge, giving honour unto the wife, as unto the weaker vessel, and as being heirs together of the grace of life; that your prayers be not hindered. Finally, be ye all of one mind, having compassion one of another, love as brethren, be pitiful, be courteous: Not rendering evil for evil, or railing for railing: but contrariwise blessing; know-ing that ye are thereunto called, that ye should inherit a blessing. For he that will love life, and see good days, let him refrain his tongue from evil, and his lips that they speak no guile: Let him eschew evil, and do good; let him seek peace, and ensue it. For the eyes of the Lord are over the righteous, and his ears are open unto their prayers: but the face of the Lord is against them that do evil. And who is he that will harm you, if ye be followers of that which is good? But and if ye suffer for righteousness' sake, happy are ye: and be not afraid of their terror, neither be troubled; But sanctify the Lord God in your hearts: and be ready always to give an answer to every man that asketh you a reason of the hope that is in you with meekness and fear." (I Peter 3:7-15)

In I Peter 3, which is a lengthy passage of Scripture, we find what I call a team concept of praying. When I use the term "team concept," I do not necessarily mean a group of ten or fif-teen or more people praying together as a group. Certainly the topic of group praying can be found throughout the Scriptures. I personally do not believe group praying should ever take the place of an individual's praying alone with God. Matthew 6 teaches the secret to getting prayers answered is praying in secret, *"...thy*

Father which seeth in secret himself shall reward thee openly." (Matthew 6:4) "The shortest, the surest, the safest way to seek God is to seek Him 'in secret.' "[2] One's secret prayer life is more important than having a group prayer life.

When I pray alone, I may pray in my office or drive around the Chicago area or pass by the houses of church members in the Calumet region to pray for them. I may find a place in the area where I pray for our city. Because I am burdened and in love with this country, once a week I put on a sackcloth outfit and pray for America for several hours in my office. Whether I pray while wearing a suit and tie, or pray alone in my office, or pray while driving in a car, I am praying as a team member. I am not praying alone because I do not live a solitary life.

Romans 14:7 says, *"For none of us liveth to himself, and no man dieth to himself."* Whether we live or die in the Lord, my life is wrapped in yours, and your life is wrapped in mine. We are a team, and our goal is to spread God's Word and to win the lost for Christ.

In this chapter I am addressing group praying as a *team effort.* A team is an organization composed of workers, each of whom has a different talent, assignment, or skill, but collectively they work toward one common goal. If you don't want your prayers to be hindered, you need to understand the concept of team praying. It is not a team of people praying together; rather, it is understanding that we are all part of a team with every member on the same page, and we pull together.

In I Peter 3:7 the Bible says, *"Likewise, ye husbands, dwell with them according to knowledge...that your prayers be not hindered."* The word *hindered* is the same word used in cutting down a tree. *Hindered* means "cut it off" or "cut it short." God does not want any Christian to have shortened prayers; He wants them to have a full measure of prayer. We must each be for the other in spirit and attitude, and our common goal is to spread God's Word and win the lost. The prayers of a man who is not a team pray-er are cut short or cut off.

The roles of every Christian are varied and different. Still, each Christian can be a team pray-er. Being a team pray-er helps one get his prayers answered. Being a team pray-er does not necessarily mean that we pray for things in common. For instance, as the pastor, I must be a team pray-er with all of the members in First Baptist Church. When I go to my prayer closet, I offer my individual, unique, one-of-a- kind prayers to God. Because there is only one senior pastor of First Baptist Church, my prayers will obviously be unique from the prayers of my members. As the pastor of the church, I need certain answers from God that a member would not necessarily need. I may beg and plead with Him to give me wisdom in specific areas my members do not need, but I need to be on the same team with them so that my prayers are not cut short or cut off.

My wife and I are team pray-ers. Though we don't pray a lot together, we are team pray-ers. We beat in sympathetic harmony on the same page. Having a team-praying spirit and mentality is so important in the Christian life.

One Spirit! One Attitude!

I Peter 3:5-7 says, *"For after this manner in the old time the holy women also, who trusted in God, adorned themselves, being in subjection unto their own husbands: Even as Sara obeyed Abraham, calling him lord: whose daughters ye are, as long as ye do well, and are not afraid with any amazement. Likewise, ye husbands, dwell with them according to knowledge, giving honour unto the wife, as unto the weaker vessel, and as being heirs together of the grace of life; that your prayers be not hindered."* Though Peter mentions husbands and wives in this passage, he also addresses all believers. As he writes this passage under the inspiration of the Holy Ghost, he says to all believers, "If you don't want your prayers hindered, then have the same attitude as each other."

God describes that attitude we are supposed to possess as Christians in two words: obedience and honor! Obedience and honor! I am supposed to obey and honor you; you are supposed to obey and honor me. Christians are supposed to obey, honor, and exalt each other. God wants a spirit or an attitude among team pray-ers where everyone has the same attitude of obedience and honor. We each should highly esteem the other.

- How highly esteemed is the teacher in the students' eyes?
- How highly esteemed are the students in the teacher's eyes?
- How highly esteemed is the choir director in the choir's eyes?
- How highly esteemed are the choir members in the choir director's eyes?
- How highly esteemed is the youth director in the eyes of the high schoolers?
- How highly esteemed are the high schoolers in the eyes of the youth director?

The students in the Christian school should be exalted in the eyes of each teacher as that teacher realizes the tremendous honor he has of teaching them and helping them reach the next level of adulthood. Likewise, the students should give honor and respect to their teachers. Such is the basis of team praying. When God hears the prayers of both the teachers and the students, He will not cut them short nor cut them off. Rather, He will give them a full measure of answered prayer.

Each segment of the ministry should highly respect and exalt every other aspect of the ministry. Does the choir esteem the orchestra? Does the orchestra esteem the choir? Does the choir esteem each singing group? Does the singing group esteem the choir?

We may have our particular favorite parts of the ministry. We might like enjoy the church-sponsored youth baseball leagues more than school, or we might like youth activities more than teenage soul winning. However, the teenage soul winners have to highly esteem the activities, and likewise those involved in the activities have to highly esteem the soul winning. The members of the soccer team have to exalt and respect the members of the wrestling team, and the members of the wrestling team should highly exalt and respect the basketball team members. The basketball team members should highly exalt and respect the cheerleading squad. The cheerleading squad should highly respect and exalt the Pep Club. The Pep Club should highly exalt and esteem the youth ministry. The youth ministry should highly exalt and respect the school system.

When we go to God in prayer and say, "God, I really need Your help," He asks, "Are you a team pray-er?"

A father goes to God on behalf of his son, and God asks, "Husband, how highly do you esteem your wife?"

A mother goes to God on behalf of her daughter, and God asks, "Wife, how highly do you esteem your husband?" "God cannot resist a parent's prayer when it is sufficiently backed up with a parent's sanctification."[3]

To be sure, God notices how much of a team pray-er you are. As you pray, you had better understand that God is examining your prayer life—your team effort. God wants to know how you are getting along with people. If you go to your prayer closet, but you do not like someone in the Christian brotherhood of believers and do not highly esteem the other in Christian love, then God will cut short your prayer.

Unkindly feelings toward another hinder God from helping us in the way He desires. A loving life is an essential condition of believing prayer.[4]

Teenagers who want to get their prayers answered, how do you feel about your teachers? How do you feel about your mom and dad? What is your spirit toward your administrator? God says to highly esteem them, to lift them up, and to promote them. Then God will hear your prayers.

I want to highly esteem what God has given us in Hammond, Indiana. I need my prayers answered, so I exalt and promote the people in my eyes. I esteem them in my image. I want them to see and love each other as I see and love them. My prayer for my members is "God, if they would only esteem each other just as much as I think highly of them." I cannot afford to have a problem with anyone because I want my prayers answered! We must want to be of one attitude and one spirit in the attitude of honor and obedience.

I never want to reach a position in life where I believe I have arrived and no longer have to obey anyone. Every Christian should obey the state and local ordinances, and yes, that means obey police officers. I take great pleasure in being obedient. Many people tell me what to do in life. I am not beneath asking someone with more experience for advice! I Peter 5:5 says, "...be subject one to another...." The person who does all the bossing takes all the responsibility! Personally, I like shared responsibility.

When we submit to each other and bend over backward trying to please each other, God says, "Is there anything you would like?" God looks for team pray-ers!

One Mind

"Finally, be ye all of one mind, having compassion one of another, love as brethren, be pitiful ["full of pity"], be courteous: Not rendering evil for evil, or railing for railing: but contrariwise blessing...." (I Peter 3:8, 9) Consider the words compassion, love, and courtesy. When I go to God in prayer and say, "God, I need some help,"

God wonders how courteous I am to the people whose paths I cross day by day.

If your prayers were answered according to how courteous you are, would your prayers be answered? How courteous are you to each other? How courteous are you to your spouse? How much courtesy is evident in your home? How courteous are you to your Sunday school class teacher? How courteous are you to the preacher when you leave the service early?

Courtesy is a Scriptural concept—not a worldly concept. God is watching for compassion, empathy, and reaching out and helping others when you pray.

A person must not offer prayer for another unless he is willing to be used to answer his own prayer. Frequently God places the prayer in our own hands again, so that we rise from our knees with a vocation before us. Florence Nightingale prayed for the suffering soldiers in the Crimean War, only to find a call in her to go to the Crimea as a nurse. Or, if we are not sent to answer our own prayer, God may give us increased insight into the situation so that we now understand, where before we were uncertain.[5]

Many years ago in the summertime, I was preaching at a camp in southern Illinois. When I drove onto the property and parked, I noticed a baseball game going on. As I sat in my car and watched the players, I observed an outfielder who had a very strange gait. As I watched him, I realized that one of his legs was many inches shorter than the other one. Most remarkable, though, were his six-inch-long arms. He had no elbow, just three little protrusions for fingers on the end of his arms. Quite frankly, he was the strangest-looking young man I believe I have ever seen in my life.

I got out of my car and walked over to the camp director, and as we watched the game together, I could not help but look at this young man.

"His name is Chris," the camp director offered.

"Remarkable kid," I commented.

Just then a fly ball was hit straight to Chris who was playing left field. He watched the ball come, stood squarely in front of it, and let the ball hit his chest. The ball fell to the ground, and he kicked it to the short stop, who got the ball and threw it. The coach explained, "He uses his body to play. He's an incredible kid! You will never find him grumpy. In fact, if you want, I'll put you in the same bunkhouse with him so you can be around him."

"I'd like that very much," I agreed. "In fact, can you put my bunk right next to his?"

After I received the directions to the cabin where I would be staying, I went there to begin putting away my belongings. Chris came in and greeted me before I could greet him. A big smile spread across his face. "Hey! Brother Schaap! So glad to have you! I have heard all about you!"

The camp director was right; Chris had a fabulous attitude. Two days later I had gotten up very early to use the shower facilities before all the other campers. I had finished my shower, and I was just putting away my belongings when I heard Chris coming. I opened the door and greeted him, "Good morning!"

"Good morning, Brother Schaap," he said. "I have to get an early start like you because I sorta get pushed out of the way."

As I continued to gather my toiletries, I noticed he was wearing a button-down shirt, trousers, and tennis shoes—like any typical kid. I also noticed that everything he wore was much bigger and baggier than normal. He said, "Can you do me a favor? Would you unbutton my shirt for me?"

"I'd be happy to do that for you," I said. I proceeded to unbutton his shirt for him. "Anything else?"

"No! I can take it all from here by myself." He walked over to a wall and took off his shirt by scraping his body against the wall until his shirt fell to the floor. He went to the edge of the counter, and he patiently worked until he unsnapped the button on the front of his trousers. He reached inside his traveling kit and took out a device about ten inches long with a clamp on one end. He put that device in his mouth, bit down on one end to open the clamp to undo his zipper. He pushed off his trousers using that stick-like device. After he slipped out of his trousers, he put his foot up on the countertop, bent over, and using his mouth, he untied his shoes. Then he took off his socks using his device.

I left to put my kit away. Soon I heard the sound of the shower. I said to myself, "I just have to see how this kid gets dressed." When I heard the shower turn off, I walked back into the shower facilities with plans of using some sort of pretense. Before I could offer an excuse for my being there, Chris said, "You can watch, Brother Schaap. Everyone wants to see how I get dressed at least once."

"Chris, I've already realized that you are a remarkable young man!"

He had on his clean underclothing. His trousers were lying in the floor, so he stepped into them and pulled them up with that stick apparatus. He stepped to the edge of the counter and kept pushing against the edge until the button finally snapped. He used the stick to pull up his zipper. He then threaded a belt through his belt loops using the stick and the wall. It was just incredible to watch. He dropped his socks to the floor, and by stepping on the sock and pushing with the other foot, he finally got them on.

He then stuck his feet in his shoes, placed his foot on the countertop, bent over from the waist, and proceeded to tie his shoes. It took him 15 minutes per shoe, using his tongue, his lips, and his teeth. He laid his shirt on the floor, lay down on it, and stuck his short little arms in the sleeves, stood up, and leaned against the wall to make sure it was on properly. Then he asked me to fasten the buttons for him. I watched this whole elaborate process in amazement.

A college boy was with me on that trip, and he had likewise noticed Chris. He asked if he could borrow my car. When I asked why, he admitted that he wanted to do something for Chris. When I asked him to explain, he said Chris needed a pair of shoes with Velcro fasteners. I handed him my car keys and some cash. He returned after a couple of hours, presented Chris with a beautifully gift-wrapped box, and said, "Brother Schaap and I thought you might need these."

When he opened the box and saw those Velcro-closure tennis shoes, the tears just spurted from his eyes. "I've never had any store-bought clothes," he finally said. "My dad left our family a long time ago, and we have had to live on what the government provides and handouts. All my clothes are hand-me-downs. I've never had a new anything in my life. I've never had a gift-wrapped, store-bought present."

Chris dropped the shoes to the floor. But when he tried to put his foot in the shoes, his foot would not go inside. He wept. We felt sure we had the right size, so I picked up the shoe, looked in them, and discovered the problem. Since he had never owned store-bought shores, he had no idea that new shoes usually have a wad of paper stuck in the front of the shoe. I reached into the shoe and pulled out the wad of paper.

"Why do they put that in shoes?" Chris asked.

"I don't know," I said. "I guess to frustrate people who have never had a new pair of store-bought shoes!"

He stuck his foot inside of one shoe and excitedly said, "Let me practice working with one of them, and then I want you to time me on the second one."

He put his foot on the countertop, bent over at the waist, and with his mouth, he threaded the loop through the opening, pulled back the fastener, then pushed it over to catch, and dropped his foot to the floor. "Time me!" he exclaimed. What had taken him fifteen minutes now took him two minutes! He was sobbing for joy!

When I go to God and say, "I need something very badly, and I really need You to come through for me," I wonder if God ever says, "Have you made anyone incredibly happy because of an act of compassion?"

Just to complete the story, Chris got an opportunity to go to Bob Jones University and graduated with a degree in art. Disney hired him to do cartoon work at Disney World. I have a letter thanking me for a pair of tennis shoes and a photo of him at his desk doing artwork with a pen in his mouth. Chris is now in his thirties, married, and has children.

Your God watches you when you pray, and He says, "Have you ever made anyone feel as good as you want Me to make you feel?"

One Tongue!

"For he that will love life, and see good days, let him refrain his tongue from evil, and his lips that they speak no guile: Let him eschew evil, and do good; let him seek peace, and ensue it." (I Peter 3:10, 11) That one tongue needs to speak with the law of kindness. Love others. Speak well of each other. Teachers, speak well of parents. Parents, speak well of teachers. Be slow to believe any bad reports. Be quick to praise.

One Cause!

"But sanctify the Lord God in your hearts: and be ready always to give an answer to every man that asketh you a reason of the hope that is in you with meekness and fear." (I Peter 3:15) Christians are a people with a cause. Everyone in the church needs to be on the same page, all pushing and pulling the same load in the same direction! Everyone needs to say, "We're each for the other, and all for the Lord!" Christians have one cause!

When you go to your prayer closet and ask God to answer a

very particular and very personal prayer, God asks, "Are you on the same page as the church where you attend?"

- Deacon, are you on the same page with the deacon board?
- Church member, are you on the same page with the preacher?
- Church staff member, are you on the same page with your employer?

We must be joined to one cause of reaching the world with the Gospel!

To men who think praying is their main business and devote time to it according to this high estimate of its importance does God commit the keys of His kingdom, and by them does He work His spiritual wonders in this world.[6]

We want to be able to go into our prayer closet and say, "God, I need You," and God will answer because He knows we are at peace with everyone, we are focused right where He wants us to be, our cause is on target, and we have one spirit, one mind, one tongue, one cause! God can answer our prayer to its full and complete measure.

Albert Einstein, the late, great mathematician and physicist, once said, "The most powerful force in the universe is the power of compound interest." He devised the financial world's "Rule of 72," a mathematical formula used to determine the number of years it takes to double a money investment at various rates of compound interest. Oh, but Einstein was mistaken! No force exists anywhere that can compare with the effectual, fervent prayer of a righteous man! "Prayer is omnipotent; it can do anything that God can! When we pray, God works."[7] Be an effectual, fervent, team pray-er.

A young man had been called to the foreign field. He had not been in the habit of preaching, but he knew one thing, how to prevail with God; and going one day to a friend he said: "I don't see how God can use me on the field. I have no special talent." His friend said: "My brother, God wants men on the field who can pray. There are too many preachers now and too few pray-ers." He went. In his own room in the early dawn a voice was heard weeping and pleading for souls. All through the day, the shut door and the hush that prevailed made you feel like walking softly, for a soul was wrestling with God. Yet to this home, hungry souls would flock, drawn by some irresistible power.

Ah, the mystery was unlocked. In the secret chamber lost souls were pleaded for and claimed. The Holy Ghost knew just where they were and sent them along.

– J. Hudson Taylor[1]

Five Phases of Prayer

"*I cried unto the LORD with my voice; with my voice unto the LORD did I make my supplication. I poured out my complaint before him; I shewed before him my trouble. When my spirit was overwhelmed within me, then thou knewest my path. In the way wherein I walked have they privily laid a snare for me. I looked on my right hand, and beheld, but there was no man that would know me: refuge failed me; no man cared for my soul. I cried unto thee, O LORD: I said, Thou art my refuge and my portion in the land of the living. Attend unto my cry; for I am brought very low: deliver me from my persecutors; for they are stronger than I. Bring my soul out of prison, that I may praise thy name: the righteous shall compass me about; for thou shalt deal bountifully with me.*"

(Psalm 142)

I always enjoyed hearing Dr. Jack Hyles, the pastor of First Baptist Church of Hammond for 41 years and my father-in-law, tell the details of how God led him to candidate at First Baptist Church in 1959. He told how he deliberated about whether or not he should come and candidate when the pulpit committee extended an invitation. He did not like the cold North; it wasn't like his Texas home. "Down in Texas," he would say, "I could see a yellow sun. Up here it just has a little lighter tone of gray because of the soot from the steel mills."

He would make statements like, "The sun didn't rise until people had already gone to work and to school, and it set before they got out!" He would exaggerate and talk about 20 feet of snow and temperatures 40° below zero. He saw the Hammond area as a very glum place. As he was weighing this decision that would change the course of his life, someone told him that he had to go north and give the people a piece of his Texas sunshine, his personality, his zeal, and his vigor for life. He did bring a lot of sunshine to many people, and we who had the privilege of knowing him have all been recipients and beneficiaries of his Texan charm.

Just like Dr. Hyles brought joy to those whose paths he crossed, our job as believers is to bring a lot of sunshine—not just physically, but spiritually—to people living in depressed, tough areas. Northwest Indiana needs the sunshine that Jesus brings spiritually. First Baptist Church sends bus workers to minister to many people with dysfunctional families. Only Jesus can make a difference in these broken hearts, broken homes, and broken lives.

So much of life is filled with negative, negative, negative. Try listening for any positive news item on the radio or television. Try finding a positive newsworthy article in the newspaper. Occasionally, we hear or read one, but usually it is tucked away and barely noticeable. The majority of life seems to be a written script called negativism. And I personally don't want to live my life looking at the negative side of life!

Christianity is not just being optimistic in a pessimistic world, though I am grateful for all of the optimists I know. Believe me, I appreciate those who look at the half-full glass rather than the half-empty glass. However, I do not believe that is what Christianity is. Christianity is a positive life that God starts inside of us when we trust Christ as our Saviour.

Obviously, many believers will experience heavy hearts at one time or another for various reasons. Some who suffer with the loss of a loved one experience a natural sadness. Saying goodbye to a loved one is a part of life; but even in sadness, we can find joy. The Bible teaches that we should not grieve or sorrow as those who have no hope; we sorrow with hope, and that hope puts a positive look on a very negative life. However, Christianity is not putting a positive spin on the negative of life like a political spin master. We can live a positive life in a negative world via the avenue of prayer.

The positive Christian life is not an attitude of the will; it is growth in our relationship with God. Nothing exposes the positive or negative life of a believer as does his prayer life. If I could rip off the facade of the pretend life some Christians present to their family and friends and try to present to God, the reality of how much their prayer life lacked would be exposed. Something else would also be revealed. That exposure would also show a negative life. Every believer who has had his sins forgiven has a home in Heaven where he will walk on golden streets forever! Living a pessimistic, negative life when there is no reason for doing so marks the life of many a Christian.

Prayer calms disturbing forces, allays tormenting fears, brings conflict to an end. Prayer tends to do away with turmoil. Prayer brings the inner calm and furnishes the outward tranquility.[2]

A Christian's prayer life, more than anything else, reveals the quality of his life in a negative world. Prayer is the outstanding determiner for developing a positive Christian life. When I see a Christian who is living a negative life in a negative world, I know for certain that person does not have a strong prayer life. No Christian can have a strong prayer life and live negatively.

When I feel negative pressures on me, I stop what I am doing, change my schedule, go to my prayer closet, and spend time with God. I do not leave that prayer closet until my disposition has changed.

Changing your outlook is not a matter of just psyching yourself up.

- It is not having cheerleaders pump you up for the spiritual game of life like they do at sporting events.

- It is not simply listening to your favorite song and feeling a euphoric adrenalin rush.
- It is not going to your favorite restaurant and eating foods that bring a full, satisfied feeling.
- It is not leaving your present spouse for another.
- It is not winning the lottery or playing at the casino gaming tables trying to find an instant gratification.
- It is not just reading a good novel or watching your favorite television program.

Changing your outlook is not 60 minutes of distraction so you can feel good about life for a while and then slowly slip back into the negativism. A positive life does not come from exercising sheer willpower or enjoying distractions; it comes from prayer power. Until you understand that fact, you will try all the fantasies, fads, and fashions in a futile effort to feel good. You can feel good about a hairstyle, or a new a new outfit, or new shoes, or remodeling your house, or getting a new set of wheels. Certainly any of these can provide a temporary excitement or a fleeting, momentary distraction.

We had the privilege of taking a family vacation at Disney World in 2006. I believe I can say that Disney brings a lot of excitement with watching the parades, visiting the fabulous exhibits like the Hall of Presidents, touring Epcot Center, and watching the fireworks. All the facets of Disney World please the senses and provide a wonderful cornucopia of pleasure. Still, not one of us left Disney World saying, "I am happy as long as I am here."

Places of entertainment like Disney do not bring a positive life. A person can try to find and buy happiness, but at some point, the supply of money is exhausted. Common sense dictates that a person can buy a new car or remodel his house only so often. He cannot spend money he does not have every time he feels a little negative breeze blowing his way. However, there is a power that is with you all the time that you can take advantage of seven days a week, twenty-four hours a day. That power exists for every believer. It is the power of the Spirit of God through the prayer life of the believer! Prayer is not a switch to flip that is either "praying" or "not praying." Many a believer mistakenly thinks his prayer life is characterized by either "I am praying" or "I am not praying."

Just like a child grows into adulthood, a Christian's prayer life has different phases. Understanding these phases will help you understand the power that comes to you through prayer. As prayer grows, so does your positive outlook on life! There are five phases of prayer that develop a positive Christian life.

Desperation Praying

In Psalm 142:1-4, David was seeking the face of God. *"I cried unto the LORD with my voice; with my voice unto the LORD did I make my supplication. I poured out my complaint before him; I shewed before him my trouble. When my spirit was overwhelmed within me, then thou knewest my path. In the way wherein I walked have they privily laid a snare for me. I looked on my right hand, and beheld, but there was no man that would know me: refuge failed me; no man cared for my soul."* This passage illustrates desperation praying.

Desperation praying is tragedy praying—Hurricane Katrina praying. Desperation praying is foxhole praying. To be sure, desperation praying is great praying. Watch a news bulletin on television showing someone who just went through a tragedy. Generally the person being interviewed makes comments like, "I prayed that God...." or "We are praying for...." Almost always prayer or God is mentioned. Isn't it amazing how He is so needed and wanted in the foxhole times but so unwanted in other aspects of life?

God and the Bible were made unwelcome in the public school classroom, but let there be a tragedy like a school shooting where some students and faculty bleed, and the news reporters talk about how the community is praying for the victims. If God or Jesus can't be mentioned in the public school, why are they praying because of the emergency? Because they only need God when human beings cannot come through for them! How incredibly hypocritical! Why is the mention of God so appropriate on the news when the tough times are upon us. Where is He when everything is fine? "The Lord loves the cry of the broken heart because it distinctly recognizes Him as the living God, truly sought after in prayer."[3]

One of the reasons why we live with this tremendous emotional roller coaster of society with its incredible problems is that people look at God as nothing more than a lucky charm! If we learned to bring God into the normal flow of life as we do when we need Him on the "September 11's" of life, we might find our joy would be a little more consistent. Positive Christian living begins with desperation praying. But don't be a desperation praying Christian who only prays for God's help in times of emergency. We need God every day. The song writer said it so beautifully!

"I need Thee, Oh, I need Thee;
Ev'ry hour I need Thee!
O bless me now, my Saviour, I come to Thee!"

God is surely there for us during the desperation times, and God wants to be there for us when we feel incomplete, when we are in the midst of troubling times, and when we are overwhelmed by the circumstances of life. He also wants to be there when we are "underwhelmed." When we say, "God, it is overwhelming today. I need You!" God says, "I can handle the request!" Why not go to God and say, "God, today is underwhelming! It is not even 'whelmed'; it is just an ordinary day, but I know that I still need You."

Desire Praying

Psalm 145:19 says, *"He will fulfil the desire of them that fear him: he also will hear their cry, and will save them."* God asks, "Anything you would like? Ask Me!"

Many Christians grow to this phase of praying, but they are not very good at it. They pray for phenomenal things that they just have to have, and if they don't get their requests fulfilled in just the way they want them on their expected timetable, they feel God doesn't really want to give them their desires. Psalm 37:4 says, *"Delight thyself also in the LORD; and he shall give thee the desires of thine heart."* Do you think God is lying when He says that He will give us the desires of our heart?

When I was a three-year-old boy, Pastor Garland Cofield started a church in Holland, Michigan. My family became part of the starting membership there. When I was three years old, Pastor Cofield took me for an airplane ride. I still remember flying over the city and seeing the lights, and my heart ignited with the love and desire of flying. I received my airplane license when I was 17, and then I stopped flying because I had no real reason to do it. I got busy serving Jesus, but every time a plane flew over, I prayed, "Lord, this is totally selfish and totally undeserved, but there has to be some reason for me to fly. Let me fly again, please."

Our college now owns a plane that we use for the aviation course. I probably get to fly "473 Bravo Charlie BC" for a couple of hours almost every week. My childhood dream since I was three years old became reality. God does let us have the desires of our heart!

I am married to a woman to whom I could have only dreamed of being married. My family is a dream come true. I live in a dream house, drive a dream car, wear a dream wardrobe, and have a dream job. I live a dream life. I can personally testify that God gives us the desires of our heart! Those who think God is an Indian giver do not know God very well!

I live a wonderful life, but not without problems. I am not saying it is healthy all the time. I am not saying it is without loss and death or disappointment. I am simply addressing the fact that the second level of praying is desire praying. What do you want? Tell God! Does that automatically mean He will give you what you want? No, but it's a good place to start. Get God involved as a partner! We need to bring God into every area of our life.

Want to have a happy marriage? Get God involved!

Want to have a happy family? Get God involved!

We take a great growth spurt to a new phase when we bring our desires to God, the One Who truly wants to know our desires. God wants every believer to share his heart's desires with Him.

Dependence Praying

Psalm 146:5 says, *"Happy is he that hath the God of Jacob for his help, whose hope is in the LORD his God."* Dependence praying is where the Christian lives every day saying, "God, I am aware that every breath I draw comes from You. I am aware that the health I do enjoy comes from You. And God, You are not going to hear from me just because I found out I have a medical emergency. You will hear from me because I am glad I am healthy. I know I need You every moment, and God, I want You to know one reason why I am praying is that I need my daily bread."

When Jesus taught His disciples to pray, the mundane thing He instructed them to pray for was bread. *"Our Father which art in heaven, Hallowed be thy name. Thy kingdom come. Thy will be done in earth, as it is in heaven.* **Give us this day our daily bread.***"* (Matthew 6:9-11) How much more basic can we get than asking for daily bread?

To pray for bread, as Jesus used the word, is to pray for every material necessity which affects the living of men, and hence touches both their bodies and souls. It includes proper housing, clothes, good sewerage and a pure water supply, necessary equipment, food, vitamins, transportation, medicine, books, and the like.[4]

As I have already mentioned, He provides the soil, the seed, the rain, and the air. He made the seeds grow, and then provided all the methods and means to put the bread on the table for us to enjoy—from the farmer to the grocer. God provided everything. *"Every good gift and every perfect gift is from above, and cometh down from the Father of lights...."* (James 1:17)

Dependence praying says, "God, I need You for everything." That is why my first prayer in the morning is, "Good morning, God! I love You." Then I thank Him for everything He gives me from hot water to hot water heaters to plumbing—everything I have is a gift from Almighty God! I love this stage of praying. I ask God for everything that I have—even if I already have it in my possession. When I ask God for something, I am reminded that it was given to me by God alone.

Devotion Praying

Psalms 145, 146, 147, 148, 149, and 150 are all examples of devotion praying. They are the prayers of a person who said, "God, I realize now that everything comes from You, and now I will pray because I am devoted to You! My heart loves You."

This is the prayer of a person who loves God as a Person. When we realize He is a person, we develop a relationship with Him and love Him. God is not a mere being, or a spirit, or an influence, or a dynamic force, or a personality. He is a person Who wants to fellowship with us.

Devotion praying says, "God, I am aware today that I need You as much today as I did on '9-11.' God, every moment of my life is occupied with the understanding and awareness that I need You and love You very much."

Distribution Praying

God needs someone to help Him answer prayer. "Prayer is partnership with God in His planet-sized purposes."[5] God answers prayer through the service of people who understand they are partnering with Him. Too many people in the Christian life walk around looking for a handout, saying, "Give me, God. Give me, God. Don't be so tight, God. Give me, God."

This type of person tries to cajole God into loosening His purse strings for him. Sad to say, the only testimony this person has is how he gets things from God for his personal needs. These people need to grow beyond that phase of praying because they greatly limit their usefulness to God.

> God must help man by prayer. He who does not pray, therefore, robs himself of God's help and places God where He cannot help man.[6]

Desperation praying, desire praying, and dependence praying are a great way to live, but we should be getting things from God every day. It shouldn't be a miracle to get something from God.

People wondered why Dr. Jack Hyles lived above the clouds and had such a positive outlook on life. Remember his silent sermon? He would kneel, look to Heaven, and hold out his hands. At that point he would give away what was in his hands and after that hold his open hands toward Heaven for more to give away. Too many people pocket what God gives to them and talk about how good God is to them. That kind of Christianity makes **you** the center of **your** world. It makes **you** the focus of all the attention. It makes **you** more important than the work of God.

Distribution praying says, "God, I am just a pipeline in the 'plumbing' of the Gospel message. I am just one more pipe to distribute the good news and the water of life to those who need it." This world is not for you to see how much you can get out of God.

This world is to see how much you can give of what He has given to you for those who need it. Distribution praying is when your prayer life matures to that stage where you find yourself praying little about personal desires because your desires are wrapped up in God. What you want to do is give to Him.

Praying saints are God's agents for carrying on His saving and providential work on earth. If His agents fail Him, neglecting to pray, then His work fails.[7]

I am more interested in helping others receive the things they want and need from God and being a conduit for His blessings. Certainly I love blessings like everyone else, but that is not the positive life we need. Because most of our praying stops at desperation or rarely goes beyond that phase and almost never goes to distribution, is why we do not live a positive life in a negative world.

Want to live a positive life in a negative world? Join me in growing your prayer life beyond the selfish pettiness of just an emergency kind of prayer life! Join me in distribution praying—co-laboring with God!

Dr. Wilbur Chapman wrote to a friend: "I have learned some great lessons concerning prayer. At one of our missions in England the audiences were exceedingly small. But I received a note saying that an American missionary…was going to pray God's blessing down upon our work. He was known as 'Praying Hyde.' Almost instantly the tide turned. The hall became packed, and at my first invitation fifty men accepted Christ. As we were leaving I said, 'Mr. Hyde, I want you to pray for me.' He came to my room, turned the key in the door, and dropped on his knees, and waited five minutes without a single syllable coming from his lips. I could hear my own heart thumping and his beating. I felt the hot tears running down my face. I knew I was with God. Then, with upturned face, down which the tears were streaming, he said 'O God!' Then for five minutes at least he was still again; and then, when he knew that he was talking with God…there came up from the depth of his heart such petitions for men as I had never heard before. I rose from my knees to know what real prayer was. We believe that prayer is mighty, and we believe it as we never did before."[1]

How to Talk to God

"But whosoever drinketh of the water that I shall give him shall never thirst; but the water that I shall give him shall be in him a well of water springing up into everlasting life. The woman saith unto him, Sir, give me this water, that I thirst not, neither come hither to draw. Jesus saith unto her, Go, call thy husband, and come hither.

The woman answered and said, I have no husband. Jesus said unto her, Thou hast well said, I have no husband: For thou hast had five husbands; and he whom thou now hast is not thy husband: in that saidst thou truly. The woman saith unto him, Sir, I perceive that thou art a prophet. Our fathers worshipped in this mountain; and ye say, that in Jerusalem is the place where men ought to worship.

Jesus saith unto her, Woman, believe me, the hour cometh, when ye shall neither in this mountain, nor yet at Jerusalem, worship the Father. Ye worship ye know not what: we know what we worship: for salvation is of the Jews. But the hour cometh, and now is, when the true worshippers shall worship the Father in spirit and in truth: for the Father seeketh such to worship him. God is a Spirit: and they that worship him must worship him in spirit and in truth. The woman saith unto him, I know that Messias cometh, which is called Christ: when he is come, he will tell us all things. Jesus saith unto her, I that speak unto thee am he."

(John 4:14-26)

Though I have titled this chapter "How to Talk to God," the subtitle and perhaps a more fitting title would be "Where Does Backsliding Begin?" Unfortunately, nearly every

Christian backslides at one point or another in his life.

Young converts are usually so enthusiastic that it doesn't take long before they have made the outward changes they believe necessary in the Christian life. They have changed their music, cleaned up their language, and modified their video and television viewing. They have even made some changes in their friendships. They have tried to change everything about themselves that was displeasing to God. In fact, they have probably heard so many life-changing sermons, they no longer know who they are!

In making all these changes, they have added soul winning, teaching a Sunday school class, or working on a church bus route to their life. Even as they become busy in their service to the Lord., they have so much enthusiasm and excitement about the forgiveness of sin. But after a while it seems like they have done everything there is to do for good and for righteousness. A little discouragement comes when it seems they have no more worlds to conquer, so to speak.

In Plutarch's essay entitled "On Contentment of the Mind," it reads "Alexander cried when he heard Anaxarchus talk about the infinite number of worlds in the universe. One of Alexander's friends asked him what was the matter, and he replied, 'There are so many worlds, and I have not yet conquered even one.' "[2]

Under the leadership of Alexander the Great, the Grecian empire extended into all of the known civilized world from Greece to India. Alexander planned to make Asia and Europe one country and combine the best of the East with the West. He introduced a uniform currency system and encouraged trade. He encouraged the spread of Greek ideas, customs, and laws. To receive recognition as the supreme ruler, he required that the provinces worship him as a god. Shortly thereafter he became ill with malaria in his capital city, Babylon.

Still, Alexander's accomplishments brought him no great joy. He faced revolts from his conquered dominions, he sold entire nations of people into slavery, he uncovered plots against his life, and he signed orders for many executions. Alexander established a pattern of living that ultimately brought about his demise.

Like Alexander, inevitably, at some time in our Christian life, we will probably establish a pattern of living that will take us to a place we do not want to go. For the Christian, that place is usually the place of backsliding. But what exactly does backsliding mean? We typically think of the Christian life as advancing for God, and the term *backsliding* involves a couple of perspectives.

1. The Christian faces the right direction, but he moves away from the direction he faces. This kind of backsliding is difficult for the onlooker to catch because at any given moment, it may look like the person is still moving forward. Everything about the Christian looks right; he is still attending church, and he still carries his Bible. We cannot tell by his posture if the step he is taking is a step moving forward or a step moving backward. If this person does not correct his problem, he will eventually backslide to a point where he crashes—either morally, financially, emotionally, or maritally. Those of us who watch this tragedy say, "So-and-so fell into sin. How did that happen?"

I hate to contradict those who make this type of statement, but that person did not **fall** into sin. He walked right into it. Everyone walks into sin; nobody falls into sin. The person might fall from his last step, but he was walking backward into it. Since he looked the part and kept looking in the right direction, he caught everyone by surprise. As he was deceiving himself, he was trying to deceive others.

2. The Christian looks backward while he pretends to walk forward. Everyone sees this person is backsliding because of the direction he is looking. Everyone can see the tragedy about to happen. He will eventually pivot and turn to go in the direction he is now headed because his heart and his vision are set on going in the wrong direction.

How to Avoid Backsliding

I personally believe that backsliding can be avoided. For that reason I want to address the very onset of backsliding—when it first enters a Christian's mind. At this point, the Christian either halts, turns back, or goes back. The secret of how we have to work with God is contained in John 4:24 which says, *"God is a Spirit: and they that worship him must worship him in spirit and in truth."* Human beings are essentially physical beings. We do have a spirit in us, and if we are saved, we have God's Spirit residing in us.

When we see each other, we don't notice our spirit first. Generally, we first notice another's physical being. We recognize someone's face or peculiar gait or voice. The majority of our recognition is based on the physical attributes of others. I recognize a particular outfit, or I might recognize someone's hairdo or the fact that someone has gained a few pounds. I can usually recognize the fact that someone is on a diet—or not!

With God, the physical is not what God notices first about us. The physical is not the first thing we establish with God because God is not a physical being; God is a Spirit. However, when we communicate with each other, we use a physical device to do so— communication.

Communication is the foundation for all relationships, including one's personal relationship with God. If you are not communicating in a relationship, then your relationship is backsliding— guaranteed. No relationship in life—parent and child, husband and wife, employer and employee—can succeed without good, healthy communication. Every relationship failure is a communication failure.

If you have failed in your marriage, I can safely say you have failed in communicating. Every divorce is the direct result of a couple's failing to communicate; they stop talking. Every couple in an adulterous affair with whom I have counseled says the same thing: "Pastor, we could talk." They talked their way into bed and into marriage troubles.

If you stop talking to your spouse, you probably won't get divorced the next day or the next year. Possibly you might never get divorced, but you will never have the happy relationship that you could have had. Why? You stopped talking.

We have had problems throughout history because of a lack of communication. The Muslim situation in the 2000s is a direct result of a lack of communication. America tries to communicate with F-16s, and the nations on the receiving end don't care for that kind of communication. They try to communicate with us with roadside bombs, and we don't care for that form of communication. Possibly, our two nations could come to an understanding if we would sit down and chat with each other—in other words, communicate! Communicating sounds far better than sending troops to war in an attempt to halt the strife.

When Hitler invaded Poland and Czechoslovakia, he did not want to talk. He wanted to accomplish one goal—annihilate anyone who opposed him. When Hitler tried to invade Britain in September 1940, only the Herculean effort of the Royal Air Force stopped him. Finally America and Britain said, "Enough!" In a joint endeavor, Normandy was invaded on June 6, 1944, all because the Nazis did not want to talk. The same problem is evident in the life of some Christians.

I have yet to meet a couple experiencing marital problems who say, "We talk well with each other." As a rule, people who talk maintain healthy relationships. If a Christian never stops talking to God, more than likely he will not backslide. Generally a Christian falls into deep sin when he stops talking to God.

Whatever affects the intensity of our praying affects the value of our work. "Too busy to pray" is not only the keynote to backsliding, but it mars even the work done. Nothing is well done without prayer for the simple reason that it leaves God out of the account.[3]

One clear truth is very evident in the lives of many Christians, and that is that they do not talk to God. Most Christians would object vehemently to that statement, and say, "I pray before my meals and before I go to bed!"

Yes, I agree. Most Christians do bow their head before meal times and say "Grace." In a little ritual prayer, they thank God for the food. I personally believe these prayers with the same words, spoken in the same rhythm and same cadence, make God want to vomit sometimes! Or because you tag the little ending, "In Jesus' name we pray, amen" on to your prayers, you believe you have prayed. Praying in Jesus' name is a meaningless statement when it comes to praying.

To pray in Jesus' name has nothing to do with a phrase composed of these three words. It means to pray in the light of Jesus' revelation of God, with confidence in the answer—because it will be God's answer.[4]

No formal endings for prayer are required in the Bible! Our spiritual problems arise because we do not know how to talk to God. Too many of us come to God with demands. We have an arrogant attitude toward God. We have a highly defined will, and we go to God with that highly defined will and say, "God, give me what I want." We act like two year olds having a temper tantrum!

A wife is like Rachel who looked at her husband Jacob and said, "Give me children or else…."

Jacob knew he was not in the position to appeal to God and therefore could not give his beloved wife children. We also go to

God with our childish demands and make unreasonable statements like:

- "Give me good grades."
- "Give me a bigger, newer house."
- "Give me a pay raise."
- "Give me position."
- "Give me security."
- "Give me happiness."
- "Give me, give me, give me…"

With our incessant demands, we build a huge barrier between us and God, and those barriers block any communication. Because God is seemingly deaf to our demands, we shake the fist of defiance and refuse to communicate. "Be that way then, God!" we spitefully lash out. God sadly watches us as we backslide—all because we do not know how to talk to Him and do not understand Who He is.

The Bible says in John 4:24, "*God is a Spirit: and they that worship him must worship him in spirit and in truth.*" What is spirit? Spirit is words, and the words you speak represent your spirit. When you speak what is on your mind, you reveal your heart.

Because God is a living Spirit, in order to worship Him you have to learn to use words. The ability to use words with God is where prayer starts. The connection between the prayer life and the Spirit life is close and indissoluble. It is not merely that we receive the Spirit through prayer, but the Spirit life requires, as an indispensable thing, a continuous prayer life.[5]

In case you want to learn how to talk to God, His steps to follow are elementary.

1. God desires worship. What is worship? Many people believe the Sunday morning church service is the time to worship God. That belief couldn't be further from the truth! The purpose of coming to church is to hear preaching; it is a time to listen to the preacher. But worship is not a Christian's sitting in a pew listening to man preaching.

The word *worship* comes from the root word in the Greek that refers to a dog licking the hand of its master. Worship is a sign of affection. If you have ever owned a dog, you will probably agree with me when I say that a dog is somewhat strange. You can beat a dog half to death with a newspaper because he chewed up your best leather shoes. You can shame that dog until he tucks his tail between his legs and hides his head. You can kick him out the side door because he left some "personal presents" on your new carpet. If you open the door, call the dog, and reach out to pet him, he will lick your hand to death. He is affectionately saying, "Is everything okay? I'm sorry. I didn't mean to upset you." A dog forgives so quickly.

God deliberately chose that word to illustrate how He wants us to feel in our conversation and relationship with Him. Yes, God says to the believer, "You are a dog." When the Syrophoenician woman came to him and said she needed His help, He basically ignored her. She was not to be deterred from her purpose; she knew He was the One Who could help her. *"But he answered and said I am not sent but unto the lost sheep of the house of Israel. Then came she and worshipped him, saying, Lord, help me. But he answered and said It is not meet to take the children's bread, and to cast it to dogs. And she said, Truth, Lord: yet the dogs eat of the crumbs which fall from their masters' table. Then Jesus answered and said unto her, O woman, great is thy faith: be it unto thee even as thou wilt...."* (Matthew 15:24-28)

God wants affection and devotion; He wants to know that we love Him.

What is worship? The word *worship* means "I value you," "I think you are worthy." God wants worship, and *worship* is saying, "Thou art worthy, God."

God says, "Worship Me," and the average Christian says, "I want You to do such-and-such for me."

"That is *not* worship," God says.

Because we do not understand the ways God wants us to interact with Him, we backslide. We simply do not understand the mind of God. We believe communicating with God is just prayer, and prayer is the only way to talk to God. Yes, prayer is asking, but merely asking should not be the only level of communication we have with God. Asking is woven in during times of talking to God. Seasons of prayer should be elaborately filled with communication.

How sad that worship is one of the most neglected parts of our life with God! Not worshiping Him is one reason why we backslide. We are also unhappy with the other relationships in our life because we don't worship God. Because we don't want to establish a strong relationship with God, every other relationship in life is shallow and fragile.

Worship is a Christian and his God developing an intimate relationship. Worship is a Christian and God incredibly engrossed in each other and affectionately exchanging words of endearment. Worship is what I call spiritual romance. *"Draw nigh to God, and he will draw nigh to you...."* (James 4:8)

Prayer is the expression of the human heart in conversation with God. The more natural the prayer, the more real He becomes. Prayer is a dialogue between two persons who love each other.[6]

2. God wants to hear words of worship. Quite simply, you worship God with your mouth! You use words to tell God how valuable and worthy He is. Tell Him that you enjoy His presence. He wants to hear it again and again.

When Dr. Hyles preached about the love of God, he often quoted a little ditty: "Tell me if you love me or not; you told me once but I forgot." God has not forgotten, but He wants to hear the Christian profess his love again and again and again because He is worthy.

Seven times in the Bible we are instructed to love God with all of our heart. We are told to love God supremely. We are also told to love our neighbor as ourself. But seven times we are commanded: "...Thou shalt love the Lord thy God with all thy heart, and with all thy soul, and with all thy mind." (Matthew 22:37) The heart is always mentioned first; God wants to know what is on our heart first. He wants to know where He fits in our heart.

A Christian backslides because he does not want to tell God what is on his heart because he knows his heart is filled with everything but God. It is filled with many words, but the words are of the world and every filthy abomination. His heart is not filled with words of affection. Matthew 12:34 definitively declares, "...for out of the abundance of the heart the mouth speaketh." No wonder some Christians do not want to share what is in their heart!

God wants to hear words that show how much He is valued. God wants to know that the heart has a room reserved for Him. Some of the words God would like to hear include:

- "I want to serve You with all my strength."
- "I want to give my energy, sweat, and toil to show You that I love You."
- "I love You with my heart and soul."
- "I love You with feeling and compassion."
- "I am passionate about You, God."
- "I am passionate about Your Book, God."

God wants to know that there is a big place for Him in our heart. Does God fill you to with consuming love and passionate feelings of affection for Him?

In order to fix your relationships, be passionate with God first. God has to be more important to us than anything else on the face of this world. We had better tell God how valuable He is!

As I think about God, I often say to Him, "I love You, God. I am so glad I get to serve You today. I am so glad I get to be Your child. I am so glad I get to live today for You and with You. I hope You are hearing a great volume, a great noise, a great sound of words of praise and worship from Christians all over this world!"

Familiarity and closeness to God gives relish, frequency, point and potency to prayer. Those who know God the best are the richest and most powerful in prayer. Little acquaintance with God, and strangeness and coldness to Him, make prayer a rare and feeble thing.[7]

Tell Him the truth. Tell Him what is in your heart. Tell Him how valuable He is. Tell Him how important He is. Worship Him with words!

God does not always let us get things at our first effort. He would train us and make us strong men by compelling us to work hard for the best things. So also He does not always give us what we ask in answer to the first prayer; He would train us and make us strong men of prayer by compelling us to pray hard for the best things. He makes us *pray through.*[1]

Show Yourself Strong Through Me

"And when thou prayest, thou shalt not be as the hypocrites are: for they love to pray standing in the synagogues and in the corners of the streets, that they may be seen of men. Verily I say unto you, They have their reward. But thou, when thou prayest, enter into thy closet, and when thou hast shut thy door, pray to thy Father which is in secret; and thy Father which seeth in secret shall reward thee openly. But when ye pray, use not vain repetitions, as the heathen do: for they think that they shall be heard for their much speaking. Be not ye therefore like unto them: for your Father knoweth what things ye have need of, before ye ask him. After this manner therefore pray ye: Our Father which art in heaven, Hallowed be thy name. Thy kingdom come. Thy will be done in earth, as it is in heaven. Give us this day our daily bread. And forgive us our debts, as we forgive our debtors. And lead us not into temptation, but deliver us from evil: For thine is the kingdom, and the power, and the glory, for ever. Amen." (Matthew 6:5-13)

Communicating with God is not simply saying, "Give me…" or consulting a prayer list of 450 names, or reminding God about all the people on earth who need Him, or reminding Him that we have personal needs. The Bible says, *"…for your Father knoweth what things ye have need of, before ye ask him."* From Matthew 6:8, we can surmise that the big issue of prayer should not be reminding Him about what we need. Unfortunately, most of our praying is exactly that—reminding God of what we need!

If God knows our condition already and does not need our prayers to keep Him informed, why do we come to Him in prayer at all? The reason is that prayer is not to be thought of as primarily a process of asking and getting. It is first of all a fellowship between God and ourselves, a fellowship in which we lay bare our hearts. We shall do our share of asking and experience more than our share of receiving, but it is communion with God that comes first in Christian prayer. *And out of this communion we emerge as changed persons!* Something happens to us when we pray.[2]

Still, we pray as though God has no idea what to do in our life! Seemingly our prayers miss the whole point! In the Bible when Jesus prayed to God, His Father, His praying had real purpose, and real conversation took place. Jesus was talking to Someone Whom He knew very well and very intimately.

On the other hand, we talk to God so callously and as though He has no plans whatsoever. "God couldn't possibly have planned this! God, let me tell You what You should do," we dictate.

- "God, please heal so and so."
- "God, what are You doing?"
- "God, where were You when we had that accident?"
- "God, where are You when I need You so much?"
- "God, You don't have any compassion or You would care about me and my needs!"

We treat God as though He has no compassion. "God couldn't possibly care about situations like we do," we humbly declare. We insult God with these kinds of prayers and statements! *"God is our refuge and strength, a very present help in trouble."* (Psalm 46:1)

Our prayer lives are filled with conversations that are arrogant, conceited, and proud, and they are an affront to God! I believe I would disconnect if I were God! He is more merciful and kind than any human being ever thought of being. He is just to the unjust as well as to the just. That is why God puts up with the foolishness of man.

One of the things Jesus criticized the most while He walked on the earth was the foolish way in which man prays! He did not want Christians to pray like the Pharisees who wanted to be noticed in their spirituality. He also instructed Christians not to pray like the hypocrites who prayed for the glory of men. (Matthew 6:2) Jesus instructed Christians to pray alone!

The prayer life is a lonely life. Samuel Chadwick [the principal of Cliff College, England] used to say, "True prayer is a lonely business." The hypocrite requires an audience when he prays. He wants to be heard when he wants to pray. He must impress. True prayer requires sincerity. True prayer requires purity.[3]

We then pout because God doesn't answer our prayers the way we think He should. God loves us, but that doesn't obligate Him to give us anything. He is a good God whether or not we ever acknowledge that fact. So exactly how should we talk to God?

1. We should pray to know God's will. Prayers like, "God, what would You like me to do about this matter?" should punctuate our prayer life.

People come to me and ask, "Pastor, what would you like done in this situation?" I like to hear that question, but sometimes I have to say, "I don't know." Thankfully, our God never says, "I don't know" because God is knowledge, wisdom, and understanding, and He knows exactly what He wants to do in every situation. God has an opinion about every matter and a will in every circumstance of life.

When we lift up our souls to God in prayer it gives God an opportunity to do what He will in us and with us. It is putting ourselves at God's disposal.[4]

At this writing, one of our very good deacons is critically ill and in ICU in a local hospital. "Father, what do You want?" should be our prayer regarding this good man. However, generally our prayer in such a case would be, "Please God, heal him!" Frankly, if I were to call for a vote about this man by the members of First Baptist Church, I dare say 100 percent of them would want him to be healed. God knows our wishes, but just maybe God's opinion on the matter is far different than ours!

Please don't misunderstand me! Family and friends need to pour out their heart to Him! When Dr. Hyles faced his open-heart surgery, I prayed that he would recover from that surgery. I doubt if anyone prayed that he would die. If prayer could heal a man, Dr. Hyles would still be walking on this earth. However, God has the final vote, and God's vote is always the majority.

When we say that God hears prayer, we do not mean that He always gives us literally what we ask for. We do mean, however, that He gives us what is best for us and if He does not give us the mercy we ask for in silver, He bestows it upon us in gold.[5]

Stop asking, "What do You want, God?" He wants us to pray that His will be done on earth as it is in Heaven! Pray, "God, I want to know Your will," because far too often we ignore God's will.

2. Don't pray so hard to get your will. I don't believe God minds our saying what we would like. We should go to God and say, "God, may I ask You a question? Can we talk about what You would like to talk about? What is important to You, God?" He desperately wants us to care about what He cares about! God wants us to know His will! "Prayer is the means by which the will of God comes to rule in our own hearts and makes us vessels meet for the Master's use."[6]

I often make statements like, "Tell me what Your opinion is,

God. What I want more than anything in the world is to know Your will in the matter."

Unfortunately, most of our prayers revolve around wants like, "Oh, God, please give me a date with so-and-so," or "Please come through for me, God."

When God doesn't give us what we want, we get so bent out of shape. Merely ask God to show you His will and then don't push your will so hard.

3. Pray that God will be glorified. The word *glory* best describes God's desire in hearing our prayers. God wants to show off how wonderful He is by answering our prayers. God wants people to know what He has done and Who He is. His greatness is why we sing songs like, "How Great Thou Art."

"O Lord my God, when I in awesome wonder
Consider all the worlds Thy hands have made,
I see the stars, I hear the rolling thunder,
Thy pow'r throughout the universe displayed.

Then sings my soul, my Savior God to Thee;
How great Thou art, how great Thou art!"

Praying is to glorify God! "Prayer concerns God, Whose purposes and plans are conditioned on prayer. His will and His glory are bound up in praying."[7] *"And lead us not into temptation, but deliver us from evil: For thine is the kingdom, and the power, and the **glory**, for ever. Amen."* (Matthew 6:13)

The purpose of praying is to magnify God. That is why Paul says in Philippians 1:20, *"...so now also Christ shall be **magnified** in my body, whether it be by life, or by death,"* and *"Whether therefore ye eat, or drink, or whatsoever ye do, do all to the **glory** of God."* (I Corinthians 10:31)

Allow me to list several more of the many references that refer to the glory of the Lord.

- *"That, according as it is written, He that glorieth, let him **glory** in the Lord."* (I Corinthians 1:31)
- *"But we all, with open face beholding as in a glass the **glory** of the Lord, are changed into the same image from glory to glory."* (II Corinthians 3:18)
- *"But he that glorieth, let him **glory** in the Lord."* (II Corinthians 10:17)
- *"It is not expedient for me doubtless to **glory**. I will come to visions and revelations of the Lord."* (II Corinthians 12:1)
- *"But God forbid that I should **glory**, save in the cross of our Lord Jesus Christ, by whom the world is crucified unto me, and I unto the world."* (Galatians 6:14)
- *"That the God of our Lord Jesus Christ, the Father of **glory**, may give unto you the spirit of wisdom and revelation in the knowledge of him."* (Ephesians 1:17)
- *"And that every tongue should confess that Jesus Christ is Lord, to the **glory** of God the Father."* (Philippians 2:11)
- *"Who shall be punished with everlasting destruction from the presence of the Lord, and from the **glory** of his power."* (II Thessalonians 1:9)
- *"Whereunto he called you by our gospel, to the obtaining of the **glory** of our Lord Jesus Christ."* (II Thessalonians 2:14)
- *"And the Lord shall deliver me from every evil work, and will preserve me unto his heavenly kingdom: to whom be **glory** for ever and ever. Amen."* (II Timothy 4:18)
- *"Thou art worthy, O Lord, to receive **glory**...."* (Revelation 4:11)

When you pray, what God is wanting is not a list of demands of how He must make you happy, but a heartfelt petition, "God, somehow through this circumstance, would You magnify Your name?"

I am afraid that most Christians in general are not very interested in glorifying Jesus Christ. They are simply seeking an acceptable level of comfort relative to the world in which they live. Instead of worrying about their comfort level, they should pray that God would be glorified. They should pray that God would use them as a platform on which He can perform. II Chronicles 16:9 says, *"For the eyes of the LORD run to and fro throughout the whole earth, to shew himself strong in the behalf of them whose heart is perfect toward him."* God is looking for people who are mature enough to let their life on earth be a platform on which He can stand and show the whole world how wonderful He is. Too many Christians buckle under pressure.

My prayer is, "God, be glorified! God, would You please use me to show others how incredible You are!" "Perhaps the richest thing about prayer is not the receiving of our request but the means of receiving it; that is, fellowship with the very God of Gods and the Creator of the universe."[8]

Unfortunately, too many of our prayers are an admission that we are buckling. Too many people pray, "Oh, God, I don't think I can take anymore. I have reached the end of my rope." Don't look at emergency circumstances with despair; look at them as opportunities for God to show off!

A loved one receives a negative medical diagnosis—because God wants to do something greater than just simply heal! When Lazarus died, Jesus cried. Human emotion is part of the process of bringing glory to God. After Jesus wept, He made a shocking statement: "Lazarus is asleep!" He glorified Himself through Lazarus' death and resurrection. God does not make light of the intense pain of sorrow. He never minimizes any pain we feel; however, He does minimize the **length** of the pain. A powerful promise is given in II Corinthians 4:17 which says, *"For our light affliction, **which is but for a moment**, worketh for us a far more exceeding and eternal weight of glory."* We have a Saviour Who knows the meaning of pain and heartache. God wants to use our heartache to show how wonderful He is!

If the circumstances that come into a person's life result in God's glory, then he has accomplished the purpose for being on this earth. God did not put one person on this earth to be happy; He only put us here to glorify Him. It is our welcome duty to go to Him through every circumstance and say, "God, if You would be so kind to show me what You want to do and do it through me, I promise You can count on me to show everyone how great You are. What would You like to do?" "Prayer at its highest is a two-way conversation."[9] Talk to God!

A private soldier, bearing an important message across that shell-swept hell of "no man's land," sought refuge and a brief respite in a war-dismantled church, where, to his astonishment, he found kneeling at the altar an officer of first rank, whom, when arising, after long communion with the God of armies, he recognized as Marshal Foch, Commander-in-Chief of all the allied forces.[1]

Why God Wants Me to Pray

"In those days was Hezekiah sick unto death. And the prophet Isaiah the son of Amoz came to him, and said unto him, Thus saith the LORD, *Set thine house in order; for thou shalt die, and not live. Then he turned his face to the wall, and prayed unto the* LORD, *saying, I beseech thee, O* LORD, *remember now how I have walked before thee in truth and with a perfect heart, and have done that which is good in thy sight. And Hezekiah wept sore. And it came to pass, afore Isaiah was gone out into the middle court, that the word of the* LORD *came to him, saying, Turn again, and tell Hezekiah the captain of my people, Thus saith the* LORD, *the God of David thy father, I have heard thy prayer, I have seen thy tears: behold, I will heal thee: on the third day thou shalt go up unto the house of the* LORD. *And I will add unto thy days fifteen years; and I will deliver thee and this city out of the hand of the king of Assyria; and I will defend this city for mine own sake, and for my servant David's sake."* (II Kings 20:1-6)

Job asked, "What profit is there in prayer?" We can list all the obvious reasons why we should pray; unfortunately, many of us have stopped praying because those reasons have no real merit concerning prayer. So why should I pray?

- Because I am supposed to pray.
- Because my parents instructed me to say my prayers when I was a little boy.
- Because it a Baptist thing, and I am a Baptist. I have to do what Baptists do.

From these lame answers, we can readily ascertain that many of us simply do not have any real Biblical understanding of what prayer is. Prayer has obviously become very ritualistic to some people. Catholics genuflect during the service or bow at kneeling benches, or do the sign of the cross, or go through the rosary. Why? Because these rituals are the mark of good Catholics. Good Baptists walk an aisle during the invitation, kneel at the altar, and do something they call prayer.

I have always liked to hear people pray. Many seasoned veteran Christians have learned how to really pray, and being in the presence of someone who knows how to pray is a tremendous joy and delight. I enjoyed hearing my father pray—especially when I was a little boy. I have already mentioned our Wednesday night prayer meetings at my home church. When we all divided to pray, I always wanted to go with my dad and the men because I wanted to hear them pray. It was obvious to me, even as a young boy, that they had many years of talking to God because they were so comfortable and natural with God.

When revival services were announced, our church members used to meet for what we called cottage prayer meetings. We would go to a member's house and take two or three hours just to pray for the upcoming meeting. The host and hostess always prepared something to eat, and we would fellowship for a few minutes, but we would always get down to business and pray. I loved it when they started praying, and the men's prayers were punctuated by long periods of silence. The men began to push away the cares of the world and began to talk to Someone Who was very real but not visible. I listened to them in awe. They knew the art of truly communicating with God.

True prayer is neither a mere mental exercise nor a vocal performance. It is far deeper than that—it is spiritual transaction with the Creator of heaven and earth.[2]

However, most people do not understand this business of talk-ing with God. Far too often prayer is mechanical communication. In praying—public or private—having a familiarity and comfort-ableness in talking to God is so important.

Are you comfortable talking to God? Or has your prayer life developed a rhythmic cadence of the mechanical yackety-yack that you must finish with the words "in Jesus' name"?

If I pray in the name of Jesus,—that is, if I request things from God, relying upon His power, His merits, I am asking in His name. If I make these same requests, relying upon my own merits, upon my own worth or works, then I am not asking in His name; I am asking in my own name. In the latter case I have no promise. In the former case I have. "If ye shall ask any thing *in my name*, I will do it." (John 14:14)[3]

Christians need to walk out of the lethargy and apathy of the so-called mechanicalness of Christianity. In II Kings 20, God gra-ciously provides an example of a king who knew the power of prayer. King Hezekiah also realized the importance of consulting with God's man. In the opening of this chapter, the man of God, Isaiah, had walked into the king's bedroom, and in brief, no uncertain terms, had told Hezekiah to put his affairs in order because he was going to die. The king said nothing to Isaiah, but as soon as the prophet left his quarters, Hezekiah turned his head to the wall and began to pray.

The very next verse forever records Hezekiah's prayer because I believe God was impressed. Before Isaiah could leave through the palace gates, God told him to return and tell the king, "*I have heard thy prayer.*" Isaiah turned around, re-entered the king's pri-vate quarters to tell him that God had seen his tears and had heard his prayer. God added 15 years to Hezekiah's life.

Obviously Hezekiah's fatal illness must have been the will of God, but his prayer changed God's mind. This amazing account reveals the power of prayer and God's willingness to listen to what a human being thinks about a particular matter. This account also contains some practical ideas about why every Christian should pray.

1. We should pray, first of all, to acknowledge God. We should pray because we need to acknowledge that God is real and present. The Bible says, *"...for he that cometh to God must believe that he is...."* When you do not pray, you are what I call a practicing atheist. When we do not talk to God, we are not acknowledging Him. E. M. Bounds [1835-1913] said, "Not to pray is a denial of God, a denial of His existence, a denial of His nature, and a denial of His purposes toward mankind."[4]

Proverbs 3:6 says *"In all thy ways acknowledge him, and he shall direct thy paths."* The word *acknowledge* comes from the word "to know" or "knowledge." It simply means to admit or to recognize or to know that He is there. God says, "Talk to Me!"

When you pray, you are not talking to an empty chair. You are talking to a real person. When you pray to God, you are saying, "I just want You to know that by the very fact I am talking to You, I am admitting I believe You exist. You are real." I am reminded of a chorus I have always loved:

> "It's real, it's real, oh, I know it's real.
> Praise God the doubts are settled
> For I know, I know it's real."

Acknowledging God is like waving to your neighbor. Sometimes when I back out of our driveway, I see my neighbor. If he glances at me, I always wave at him. Maybe I do not want to become best friends with him, but it is just common courtesy to acknowledge my neighbor exists. Occasionally, I get out of my car to shake his hand, and we chat about the weather or our lawns. There are many reasons why I talk to my neighbor. Good talking is important.

Our duty in the Christian life is to acknowledge God. "Prayer's real purpose is to put God at the center of our attention, and forget ourselves."[5] If I were to summarize the Christian's life in one sentence, it is to demonstrate that I believe in God. I am supposed to tell the whole world in testimony by word and by deed that I believe there is a real God, and all of us will answer to Him someday. Because I know I will have to answer to God someday, I conduct myself the way I do in my marriage. That is the reason why I conduct myself the way I do as a pastor. That is why I conduct myself as I do as a father. That is why I conduct myself the way I do as an employer. By the way I live my life, I want to acknowledge the fact that there is a God, and I have to answer to Him someday.

2. **We should pray in order to consider His will.** Prayer is the Christian's way of saying, "I would like to hear Your opinion on the matter." We need to let God know that His opinion is more important than ours. "When men reflect upon what God is and upon what they are, and honestly confess their own failures in view of God's character, they naturally find it easy to submit to the will of God."[6] People should talk through a subject—even in a disagreement—to acknowledge that each person present has a valid opinion. When one party says, "I don't agree with that assessment," or "How can you think that way?" even the negative acknowledgment is still an acknowledgment that another's opinion exists. To say, "I don't agree" is to say, "I understand what you said."

The Bible says every Christian may pour out his complaint to God; he can cast his burden on Him; he can open his mouth wide to God, and God will fill it. The bottom line is that a Christian can tell God what he is thinking, but every Christian should want to know what God has to say as well. God should be more important than anyone.

When you do not pray, you are saying to God, "I don't want to hear what You have to say!" Not praying is such a casual, calloused insult to God. When you don't pray, you are missing out on the opportunity that the King of the universe, not just a mere mortal, wants to hear your opinion and thoughts. Very few people of prominence care about what others have to say on any matter.

It is common courtesy to ask another for his opinion if he requests yours. For instance, occasionally some of my assistant pastors and I meet with the mayor of Hammond and some of his advisors. The mayor often opens the conversation with a statement like, "I would like to hear your opinion on such-and-such a subject."

"I appreciate your interest in that matter, Mayor," I answer. "This is my opinion." When I finish giving my thoughts, I always add, "And Mayor, I would really like to hear your opinion as well."

That is exactly what praying is. It is a Christian's saying, "God, I can't believe You want to hear what I have to say, but here goes. And would You please tell me what You think about the matter?"

Why should you pray? Because Someone Who is truly important wants to hear your opinion about life's matters! In Psalm 142:2, David said, *"I poured out my complaint before him; I shewed before him my trouble."*

Just like David, you can pour out your soul to God, give Him your heart, and show Him everything. Once you have poured out everything in your heart, then it is time to ask Him, "God, now that I have that off my chest, what do You think about that matter, God?" When you don't pray, you are saying you do not want or need to hear God's opinion. Personally, I would love to know God's opinion about everything!

I wonder how many times I have said or thought how much I would love to sit down with Dr. Jack Hyles, ouir former pastor, now and discuss this ministry. I would love to have the opportunity to say, "Can I talk to you about such and such?" I would love to hear what he has to say! I would like to give him a tour of our new auditorium, and to be honest, I would like to know his feelings about what we have done with the ministry that he left us when he went to Heaven.

But One Who is far greater than Dr. Hyles wants to know *my* opinion. And that far greater Someone Who is infinitely greater, really wants to hear what *you* have to say. Why should you pray? Because He wants to hear from you, and you should want to know what He has to say.

3. We should pray to partner with God. Prayer is my earthly partnership with God. I am employed by God, as is every Christian! The Bible says in I Corinthians 3:9, *"For we are labourers together with God...."* That verse indicates that we have a partnership with God. To *co-labor* means "we are on the same team partnering to do God's work." That verse is not addressed specifically to a pastor; it addresses the believers. We can partner with God through faith promise giving, through paying our tithes and giving our offerings, through serving on bus routes, through teaching in Sunday school classes, but a major way we can partner is through the avenue of prayer.

When I pray, I feel like I am entering into labor with God. I feel like I am saying, "God, You and I have something big to do, and my part includes talking to You about this great work."

God says, "Talk to Me; we are doing a great work."

When you talk to God, you don't get Gabriel or Michael; you get God!

I was counseling with a church member who was going through some very trying circumstances. When he finished explaining, he asked, "Have I properly conveyed to you the gravity of the situation?"

"I believe so," I said. "My cell number is.... Write it down."

The man was incredulous. "You are taking my situation serious," he said.

Yes, I did take his problem seriously, and he has called me. But far more exciting to me is the knowledge that I can get God's attention at any time, and I don't even need a cell number! God gives me direct access to Him! When I am talking to God, He says, "I am listening to you! What do you want to talk about?" "Prayer is not given us as a burden to be borne, or an irksome duty to fulfil, but to be a joy and power to which there is no limit."[7] We have personal, unlimited access to Him at all times!

4. We should pray because all good relationships are built on good communication. If you want to get along well with God, you must start talking to Him. Too many Christians believe that praying is asking for things, and indeed, that is part of prayer. But when you talk to those nearest and dearest to you, do you always ask for things? Of course not!

I am interested in building a relationship based on the fact that the Bible tells me God wants to talk to me! "In the interaction of life and prayer will be found the secret of power, and the realization of fellowship with God will never be more than a theory save as prayer becomes a practice."[8]

Consequently, I say to Him, "Lord, if You want a relationship with me, You have one! Let's talk!" I can chat with Him. I can laugh with Him. Every Christian can humor with God.

We can go to God and talk about subjects as mundane as the weather. When we say, "Thanks for the nice weather," He can reply, "You are welcome; I did it. I know."

"You are awesome, God! I noticed!"

God would love to have a personal relationship with you! Having a personal relationship is just being aware that God is there, and you bring Him into the conversation. God wants to build a relationship with you. Start talking to Him!

5. We should pray because God wants to measure our passion and sincerity. God wants to find out if there is anything about which we care. Weeping over sad movies, getting upset if your child doesn't get to play on his little league team, or getting angry with a referee's call in a sport's event in the whole scope of eternality are really rather insignificant! All the things that are truly important that you will someday see as important, such as the lost souls in foreign countries or your neighbors or your loved ones or your marriage or your family, are somehow lost to view in the day-to-day living of life. A lot of griping goes on, but not a lot of praying goes on. God can find out where your passion level is merely by checking your prayer life.

I sometimes wonder, "When does God decide to start using a young man?" We lived on a farm that we were turning into another business, and I would go sit on a hill—even during inclement weather—so I could just be alone to talk to God. As I was bundling up to go out, my mother would say, "Where in the world are you going?"

She never stopped me when I would answer, "I am going out to run my dog for a while." She knew.

I did not go out every day or even every week, but I wanted to be alone with God frequently. I wonder if perhaps God saw a young man who was not interested in watching television or videos when most everyone else was. I wonder if God wondered, "Why would a young boy go out in a snowstorm to pray?"

I sometimes wonder if God saw me as a freshman at college who took the challenge of another young man who said, "I dare you to pray with me for three hours." I went with him and prayed in a classroom for three hours, and that is when I began to really talk with God. I wonder if God said then, "I have found a young man whose passion is in Me." Let me hear you pray, and I will tell you if you have a passion for anything!

When struggling married couples seek counsel, I want to say, "Let me listen to you pray for your marriage, and I will decide whether or not I want to help you." I don't say that, but I do wonder if some of these couples seeking help ever spent 60 minutes at one time praying for their marriage. It is too easy to run to the pastor's office and ask him for six points that will guarantee a happy marriage. When I fall on my face and pray for some of these struggling couples, I tell the Lord, "Forgive them! I doubt if they are spending any time praying for their marriage, but God I want You to see that I mean business." I don't know if I can pray another's marriage to become strong, but this I know—God knows I am concerned about the matter! "One of the mightiest instrumentalities for the world's advance is intercessory prayer—prayer for others."[9]

- When parents seek counsel about a wayward child, I want to say, "Let me hear you pray for your son, and I will tell you what is wrong with your son."
- Before you tell me why your bus route isn't productive, I want to hear you pray for your bus route.
- Before you tell me that teaching is not your field and it has been a tough year in the classroom, I want to hear you pray for your students.
- Before you tell me that the mission field where you went is a hard area and you didn't realize how hard before you chose to go there, I want to hear you pray for that mission field. Before a missionary receives my money, I really would like to hear him pray for the mission field to see if he is really passionate about his field.

God has His intercessors everywhere. They are to be found often in unexpected places, in men and women who have learned the secret, and who by familiar intercourse with God are channels of blessing to men: but the majority of us are not praying.[10]

Most people are experienced at emergency praying, but I will be honest with you, we are reaching the day and age where even desperation praying is seldom accessed. It is much easier to rely upon the pastor. Is God in the pastor's pocket or something? Does the pastor carry God along in a briefcase?

Something about God says, "I want to know if you have a passion for anything." God also knows how to find out if you do; He listens to you pray.

Why should I talk to God? I talk to God because I feel strongly about some things in life! I feel strongly about my marriage, so God hears me pray about my marriage. I feel strongly about this ministry, so God hears me pray about this ministry.

If God chooses to bless a ministry based upon the passion of your prayer life, will that ministry grow to overflowing? Based on the prayers of His people, God determines the passion and the intensity of their hearts. God blesses His people about as intensely as they pray. In other words, your marriage is about as passionate as your prayer life. If your prayer life is mechanical, formal, boring, monotonous, ritualistic, like a little litany, probably your marriage is too. Everything about your life is boring because the lack of passion that you show in the prayer closet is translated into the reality of where you work and where you live. "Prayer is not a little habit pinned on to us while we were tied to our mother's apron strings; neither is it a little decent quarter of a minute's grace said over an hour's dinner, but it is a most serious work of our most serious years."[11]

Do you want to turn the world upside down? Turn it upside down in your prayer closet! When your prayer closet is aflame with the passion of your life and wet with the tears of sincerity, then God will say, "I heard your prayer, and I saw your tears."

To be much *for* God, we must be much *with* God. Jesus, that lone figure fasting in the wilderness, knew strong crying, along with tears. Can one be moved with compassion and not know tears?[12]

God says He collects our tears and puts them in a bottle. Is your bottle as dry as dust? When you go to Heaven someday and God says, "Bring Me the bottle where we collected his tears. I want to measure his reward by the passion of his tears." Will the angel bring Him an empty flask? Did you know that God will give you rewards in Heaven by the passion of your prayer life on earth? Truthfully, nearly everything you have is based on your prayer life. "Prayer is the special means by which God intends us to receive His blessings."[13]

Dr. John R. Rice, the founder and editor of *The Sword of the Lord* said, "Every problem in the Christian life is a prayer problem." I didn't understand that statement for a long time, but I have learned that as I passionately pray in my prayer closet, God pours out blessings on my public ministry. *"But thou, when thou prayest, enter into thy closet, and when thou hast shut thy door, pray to thy Father which is in secret; and thy Father which seeth in secret shall reward thee openly."* (Matthew 6:6) God will translate blessings and convert passionate private praying into public blessing.

To be little with God in prayer is to be little for God in service. Much secret prayer means much public power.[14]

When a problem such as a serious illness comes and the doctor's words are ominous and threatening, the non-praying Christian drops to his knees and begs, "Oh God, please help me. Please heal me!" God notes those prayers and says, "We finally found some passion; let's keep that loved one ill." I personally believe many people stay ill because it is the only way God can find out if a person is passionate about anything. When God hangs death in front of someone, all of a sudden, that person gets scared and starts praying.

We have all seen church members who paid little attention to God when all was going well, when health was good, the purse full and business flourishing. But when adversity crowded in upon them, when sickness hovered over the home, when the crape was on the door, or when all their plans and air-castles were in the dust, they called upon God and wondered why He did not hear them. It seems hard to say, but it is a blessing that God does not answer under such conditions. Nothing could be more hurtful than for God's favors to be at the beck and call of such praying. The way into the inner sanctuary is the way of holy living and constant communion. To answer under any other conditions would be to put a premium upon sinful neglect, and give the keys of the treasury to those who would "consume it upon their lusts."[15]

I know I have told God a hundred times, "You may make me sick. You may give me an incurable illness, but You will never have to give me a disease that gets me more passionate about praying than does good health!" God doesn't have to do anything to awaken me! When I go to my prayer closet and lie down before God, I pray passionately and cry because I know God is looking for someone who is passionate about the Christian life. If you really want to see your ministry grow, pray! Pray passionately! Pray with tears!

    6. We should pray as we use our life as leverage. The Bible is filled with men who said, "God, may I tell You how I live?" In II Kings 20:3, Hezekiah said, *"I beseech thee, O LORD, remember now how I have walked before thee in truth and with a perfect heart, and have done that which is good in thy sight."* God heard his prayers, saw his tears, and sent Isaiah to tell him He would give him 15 more years. Isaiah learned that Hezekiah had leverage to his prayer because he prayed and God listened!

    Hezekiah had deliberately and willfully chosen a different direction than the one his father had chosen. Whereas his father was an abomination, Hezekiah walked before God in truth. He had lived a righteous life, and he used the life he lived to give leverage to his prayers.

    Living a righteous and holy life is not just a "cute" way of living.

A Christian doesn't say "no" to sin because he is not "into" sin. We are all sinners conceived in iniquity and born in sin! *"O wretched man that I am! who shall deliver me from the body of this death?"* (Romans 7:24) We all have the same flesh, the same temptations, the same afflictions, and the same passions. *"Elias was a man subject to like passions as we are, and he prayed...."* (James 5:17) Elijah was a righteous man, and righteous men pray because they don't want to waste righteous living.

I go to God and say, "God, I need some things, and You know what nobody else does." Of course God knows my flaws, my weaknesses, and yes, He knows I fail Him again and again. But the life I live is a life lived to leverage and torque my prayer life all that much more. That is one reason why I talk to God.

If you ever have the feeling that your prayers bounce off from Heaven and God doesn't hear your prayers, how do you live? Dr. Dennis Corle says, "God will not leave the path of holiness to walk with me, but if I will enter the path of holiness, He is waiting for me to walk with Him."[16]

A man who does not attend First Baptist Church of Hammond called me on the phone and said, "I have an emergency, and I don't live in your area, but I know you. God hears your prayers. Would you promise to pray ten minutes for me right now?"

I asked, "What kind of life do you live? I have lived righteously to get my prayers answered. I don't want to waste my prayer time on someone who doesn't live for Him."

Righteous living leverages prayer, and unrighteous living receives the deaf ear of God. I liken it to going to the bank. I pray because I have a life that God examines, and if I do something right, that is like depositing money in a bank. Righteousness is like accruing or accumulating credit. Suppose your car has been repossessed, you haven't made your mortgage payment in nine months, and you are about to default on your house. So you go to the bank and say, "I want to get a loan." The loan officer asks pertinent questions like: "Do you have a job? Do you work anywhere? Do you have any savings? Do you have any gold or silver? Do you have certificates, stocks, bond, or collateral like an automobile?" When the answer to each of these questions is a resounding "no," that loan officer will no doubt say, "I have no money available for you."

That person's life does not back up his request. Likewise, when a Christian's life doesn't back up his prayer requests, God doesn't care to listen. He turns a deaf ear. It is not just the praying; it is the living that goes with the praying! We believe in righteous living because we believe God hears prayer.

Praying awakens conscience, stirs the heart, and tends to correct evil ways and to promote good living. No man will pray long and continue in sin. Praying breaks up bad living, while bad living breaks down prayer. Praying goes into bankruptcy when a man goes to sinning.[17]

A teenage boy said to me, "Brother Schaap, I just don't agree with your convictions and standards. I like you, but I just don't like what our church believes."

As we talked, I casually interjected, "You don't pray, do you?" He looked startled.

I continued, "People who live the way you live don't pray. I live my life because I pray and because I believe God hears prayers. Do you honestly think that I live the way I do because I don't think living the way you do is fun? You think somehow that my flesh would not enjoy indulging in all that you do? You really think that sometime during my 70 years on earth that I would not enjoy going to Vegas and gambling?"

We may denounce that kind of living in our preaching, but the flesh enjoys sin. Hebrews 11:25 calls it enjoying "...*the pleasure of sin for a season.*" Yes, sin may be pleasurable, but I believe that God hears prayers, and that is why I diligently labor to steer clear of sin. I need too much from God to indulge in a worldly lifestyle, and I pray because I have leveraged my prayers with my living. You can too!

7. We should pray because prayer teaches us that God wants us to obey Him. Hebrews 5 tells us that Jesus learned obedience. "The man of obedience is the man whom God will hear."[18] God wants us to pray so we will learn to listen to Him. Prayer is hard, but Christians need to do the hard things! "True prayer is laborious, careless of personal interests, loyal to the truth and willing to risk all and dare all for God."[19]

If your obedience were measured by your prayer life, how obedient are you? Praying people who have a problem obeying authority are people who do not pray. Prayer requires a discipline of obedience that is the highest form of obedience because nobody sees you when you pray except God. If you can pray, you can do anything for God! If you have the power to get yourself out of bed to talk to Almighty God, it will not be a great difficulty for you to knock on the door of a lost sinner.

If we have an obedience problem, prayer will take care of it. If you have a child who has a hard time obeying, pray with him! If you can get your child to talk to God, he won't have any problem talking to his teachers. I believe that lack of prayer is the root of every problem we face.

8. We should pray because prayer helps us to see and appreciate God's promises. See Hagar as she takes her son Ishmael away from Abraham's household. The water bottle ran dry, the food ran out, and nothing was left in the knapsack. She left her son sitting under a bush because she knew he was going to die. She sat down to weep in private. As she wept, God heard the prayer of her son and pointed out a well to her. The well had always been there, but she didn't see the well until God heard the voice of her son and saw her tears.

Prayer and helplessness are inseparable. Only he who is helpless can truly pray.[20]

We will not see the opportunities God has for us or the solutions to our problems until He sees us pray like Hagar prayed. Because tears are a language God understands, He will hear the prayer. God has an answer. God doesn't have to invent answers; He already knows what we need. He has already stored all the solutions we will ever need to any problem we will ever confront. The reason why we do not see the answer is that we do not pray.

9. **We should pray because God, for some strange reason, loves our company.** The Bible says we were made for His pleasure. If I could humor God or please Him or if I thought that I could bring pleasure to Him, I would do it, and I know God finds pleasure in the prayers of His saints. He finds great pleasure in one's pouring out his heart to Him.

We have made prayer so complicated, and the simple truth is that there is a God Who loves us and wants to supply our needs and our wants in exchange for our total dedication and surrender to Him and our abiding in Him.[21]

Have you ever watched a kid play a video game? How intense is he? Have you ever prayed like that? If you prayed as intensely as you play, you would bring great pleasure to your God!

God would say, "I like that! What did you need?"

Unfortunately, we pray pathetically; we pray like losers play. We don't get much from God because our prayers lack intensity and passion. Have you ever heard someone pray with such intensity that you were embarrassed to be in the vicinity? That person's prayer was much too personal and far too passionate for you to be in his presence. Passion in prayer is what God desires from us.

We don't believe that a feeble mortal cry could enter into the ears of the Lord God of the heavens and earth. We find it impossible to believe that mortal man could stand on the gleaming pavement of Heaven, that the infinite God could be moved by the pleas of sinful man. We find it hard to believe that before Him the angels veil their faces, but that by prayer the armies of Heaven could be called to arms and that divine majesty could obey the orders of a worm-like man. We find it difficult to believe that our prayers could restrain the powers of evil and that the wheels of Providence could alter their course at the request of man, and all of this happens because some feeble sinner saved by grace kneels before the throne of grace and brings his petition to God![1]

17

Ask for It

"Ask, and it shall be given you; seek, and ye shall find; knock, and it shall be opened unto you: For every one that asketh receiveth; and he that seeketh findeth; and to him that knocketh it shall be opened. Or what man is there of you, whom if his son ask bread, will he give him a stone? Or if he ask a fish, will he give him a serpent? If ye then, being evil, know how to give good gifts unto your children, how much more shall your Father which is in heaven give good things to them that ask him? Therefore all things whatsoever ye would that men should do to you, do ye even so to them: for this is the law and the prophets." (Matthew 7:7-12)

Matthew 7 should be on the lips of every believer because that Scripture should be in the heart of every believer. *"Ask, and it...."* Ask for **it**. *"Ask, and it shall be given you."* What in the world is *"it"*? **It** is whatever you are not praying for because **it** isn't very important to you, or **it** isn't very needed in your life because **it** isn't very big to you. You don't ask for **it**, and as a result, you don't get **it**.

I want **it**. To the degree I want **it**, I ask for **it**. If you don't want **it**, then you probably won't ask for **it**. To the degree you do not ask for **it**, you will not receive **it** from God. It is just that simple!

What is **it** that you want from God? What is **it** that you must have from God? What is **it** that drives you to your prayer closet or drives you to talk and talk to God? What is **it** that drives you to seek God and beg, "God, I need **it** bad!"

There are some things I need from God—badly. Because I think I need **it** and because I believe God wants me to have **it**, I talk to Him. We are about as good at talking to God as we want **it** from God.

Dr. John R. Rice, the editor of the *Sword of the Lord*, told the story of how he was in a committee meeting to discuss holding a citywide campaign. He asked pertinent questions like, "Who will lead the singing, who will play the organ, who will conduct the music, etc." When it came down to "Who will lead in prayer?" one of the committee members said, "Get Dr. So-and-so; he is able in prayer."

Dr. Rice said, "Deliver me from people who are able in prayer. They drone on and on like reading a poem at a baccalaureate service. It bores the graduates, and it bores God."

God simply says, *"Ask, and it shall be given you."*

The reason we do not pray much and talk much to God is that there is no **it** that we really feel we need. Prayer is asking for **it**. The reason why that prayer promise is next to meaningless to us is that we have asked for things that really aren't necessary in our life.

You pray, "Bless my mama, my daddy, and my grandpa, too." Would you know if God was blessing them? Would you recognize a real answer to the prayers if God took your prayers literally?

"God, be with Grandpa," you pray. What exactly do you mean when you say, "Be with Grandpa"? Are you asking God to wake him up or knock him off so you get an inheritance? What do you mean when you pray, "Be with Grandpa"?

We pray, "God, be in our meeting tonight." Where exactly would you want Him to be? Do you want Him to sit in the choir or in an auditorium pew? What a nebulous way to pray!

What is **it** that you cannot live without? What is **it** that you must have God do for you? The **it** is what you must have from God that is right and proper to have. "Dear God, I must have **it**. I must have Your power. I must have Your wisdom. I must have **it**." If there is not an **it** in your life, there is probably no prayer in your life. Your prayer without an **it** is probably a monotonous, nebulous litany of reading names and situations. When **it** is not important, neither is prayer. If I ain't got to have **it**, I ain't going to pray! It's that simple!

What is **it** that God alone can do that you must have from Him?

- Broken marriage? How many times have you prayed for **it**?
- Wayward son? How many times have you prayed for **it** to be changed?

Unfortunately, **it** must not be very important to us because we don't actively pray about the things where God says, "I would give **it** to you if you asked." My Bible says in Matthew 7, *"Ask, and it shall be given you."*

When we don't ask, God must believe that the things He can do for us must not be very important. **It** must not be very big because the bigness of **it** measures how big our God is! If I have a big request, then I must have a big God for **it**. For some Christians, God must be very tiny because He is seemingly not really needed. I feel sure I can say without reservation that 99.9 percent of the things a Christian believes he needs in life are not necessary!

Our life is consumed with a pettiness and a smallness that relegates God to a small corner of our life and says, "God, You know I think You are a wonderful God, but the truth of the matter is, I really cannot think of anything for You to do. Well, I would like a million dollars, but most preachers say that is a foolish prayer so I am not going to pray for that."

I do! I will match the millions He gives me against yours! I intend to keep picking up those pennies because my dad always said, "A man finds a penny and won't stoop to pick it up. Why should God give him a million dollars?" Whenever I see a penny, I pick it up and say, "God, don't forget that million dollars please?"

You may think, "That is silly," but I like my way far better than yours! I like my way of doing **it**, rather than your way of doing **it**. I like my way of praying better than your way of not praying. I like my way of living close to God better than your way of living far away from God.

When I get to my office, the counseling starts, and people ask me to help them. When I ask some people, "How is God getting along with you, and how are you getting along with God?" the tears begin to roll down their faces, and the answer is the same. "Not very well."

I cannot help but think that it is amazing how people will wait as long as it takes to see me or any counselor, for that matter, and they won't talk with God! These good people seeking help don't need me at all compared to how much they need God! I am dirt. I am a sinner! There is nothing that I could possibly do for them that God couldn't do a billion times better!

A very good family in our church went through a tragedy, and the wife said to my wife and me, "I want to thank you for being our pastor and pastor's wife. You are God's skin to us."

Certainly, I am honored to be "God's skin" in her eyes, and I appreciate that wonderful compliment. Coming from her, it was a high honor. But we have a God Who has more than just skin! We have a God Who has omnipotent power and unlimited wisdom. This God can transform a life, transform a marriage, transform a job, and transform living. We have access to a great, big, wonderful God!

God's only condition and limitation of prayer is found in the character of the one who prays. The measure of our faith and praying is the measure of His giving.[2]

What do you want God to do? Tell Him, and your request should be something you must have God do. If God isn't needed, He will find someone who does want and need Him! God is the ultimate mover and shaker!

You say, "Well, I pray. I prayed for good health, and I have cancer." How many times did you pray for **it**?

- Preacher, how much did you pray for your sermon that you preached? How many hours were you on your face begging almighty God to do the spiritually impossible because you cannot do **it**?
- Mothers, how much do you pray for your children on any given day? When was the last time you spent an hour a week in prayer for each child?
- Soul winner, who in your life needs to get saved?

In his book *Prevailing Prayer*, Dwight L. Moody tells the story of a wife living in England who had an unconverted husband. She resolved that she would pray every day for 12 months for his conversion.

Every day at twelve o'clock she went to her room alone and cried to God. Her husband would not allow her to speak to him on the subject; but she could speak to God on his behalf. It may be that you have a friend who does not wish to be spoken with about his salvation; you can do as this woman did—go and pray to God about it.

The twelve months passed away, and there was no sign of his yielding. She resolved to pray for six months longer; so every day she went alone and prayed for the conversion of her husband. The six months passed, and still there was no sign, no answer. The question arose in her mind, could she give him up? "No," she said; "I will pray for him as long as God gives me breath."

That very day, when he came home to dinner, instead of going into the dining room, he went upstairs. She waited, and waited, and waited; but he did not come down to dinner. Finally she went to his room, and found him on his knees crying to God to have mercy upon him. God convicted him of sin; he not only became a Christian, but the Word of God had free course, and was glorified in him. God used him mightily. That was God answering the prayers of this Christian wife; she knocked, and knocked, and knocked, till the answer came.[3]

Matthew 7:7-12 tells us one of many ways of how to get **it** from God. In the context of praying, however, verse 12 does not seem to fit. The verse starts with the word *therefore*, so that word automatically connects verse 12 with the prayer passage. *"Therefore all things whatsoever ye would that men should do to you, do ye even so to them: for this is the law and the prophets."* (Matthew 7:12) A great prayer lesson can be found in this passage concluding with verse 12.

Since I want **it** from God, He says, "Show Me how badly you want **it**. I want you to seek and find."

What exactly do "seek and find" in verse 7 mean relative to asking? I had never found a proper connection until I carefully studied the *therefore* of verse 12. I believe God is saying, if you want **it** from Him, find what **it** is for someone else, and get **it** for that person. Seek a way to get for another what he thinks he must have and find a way to do the same for others. When God sees the energy and the effort expended to help others get what they believe will help them, then afterward go to God, and He will measure out the same amount of energy and bestow the same amount of effort in getting **it** for you!

That kind of praying will change one's prayer life! Is there anything that you have helped someone else get to the same fervent degree that you are asking God to give **it** to you? We live in a very selfish society today. A gentleman might pick up a heavy item for someone in an effort to be courteous or leave a good tip for the waitress in a restaurant or even say "thank you," but that is not what God is promoting. God is saying when someone cross-es your path and you discover he needs something which you can give, how diligently do you seek a way to satisfy that person's need? To that degree, God will work at satisfying it for you.

Is it any wonder Dr. Hyles' prayers were answered? If he even remotely suspicioned that someone wanted an item, that need was usually met within a short amount of time. Pastor Hyles was masterful at meeting needs. If he saw someone wearing a pair of worn shoes or a threadbare suit, he often met that need. If he heard someone was on his way to a funeral out of town, money in an envelope "mysteriously" arrived to help with travel expenses. Someone, namely Dr. Hyles, was being diligent to seek a way to find it for the person he was helping. No wonder when he went to God and said, "God, I need it from You," God answered his request.

God looks to see how we provide for other people, not how we provide for ourselves and ours. Verse 12 is addressing people we don't necessarily feel obligated to help. God watches how we ful-fill the requests of other people, and then He satisfies our prayers with the same energy that we expend satisfying other people's requests.

A troubled marriage is the direct result of two people who stop providing for each other. She wants him to provide for her, to talk to her, and to give her what she believes she deserves. Then why doesn't she give to him in the same manner in which she hopes he will give to her? When she likewise gives what he wants, God will hear their prayers.

This society of Christian people is so filled with an abundance of Christians who know nothing about getting it from God. Torrey said, "Prayer is God's appointed way for obtaining things, and the great secret of all lack in our experience, in our life and in our work is neglect of prayer."[4]

If we Christians don't pray, who do you think prays? If we

don't need the power of God, who does?! If we don't need **it**, who does?! I want the blessings of God! I would rather die than not have **it**, and God knows my heart. Does God know about any **it** that you must have from Him?

Here is the great secret of success. Work with all your might; but trust not in the least in your work. Pray with all your might for the blessing of God; but work, at the same time, with all diligence, with all patience, with all perseverance. Pray then, and work. Work and pray. And still again pray, and then work. And so on all the days of your life. The result will surely be, abundant blessing. Whether you see much fruit or little fruit, such kind of service will be blessed.

– George Mueller

How to Multiply the Blessing

"Thus the LORD saved Hezekiah and the inhabitants of Jerusalem from the hand of Sennacherib the king of Assyria, and from the hand of all other, and guided them on every side. And many brought gifts unto the LORD to Jerusalem, and presents to Hezekiah king of Judah: so that he was magnified in the sight of all nations from thenceforth. In those days Hezekiah was sick to the death, and prayed unto the LORD: and he spake unto him, and he gave him a sign. But Hezekiah rendered not again according to the benefit done unto him; for his heart was lifted up: therefore there was wrath upon him, and upon Judah and Jerusalem. Notwithstanding Hezekiah humbled himself for the pride of his heart, both he and the inhabitants of Jerusalem, so that the wrath of the LORD came not upon them in the days of Hezekiah…Howbeit in the business of the ambassadors of the princes of Babylon, who sent unto him to enquire of the wonder that was done in the land, God left him, to try him, that he might know all that was in his heart." (II Chronicles 32:22-26, 31)

Thirty years ago when I was a youth director, I planned an activity called "Bigger and Better." Everyone who attended the activity was formed into a two-member team. Each team received one penny. For 90 minutes, each team exchanged the penny for something bigger and better and more valuable than the penny. Whoever came back at the end of the activity with the most valuable and largest item was declared the winner of the contest.

One team returned with a refrigerator in the back of a pickup! The team had first traded their penny for an old toaster, and they traded that for a surfboard. That was traded for a fancy watch, and for their last trade, the person with whom they were dickering said, "I will take what you have for a refrigerator."

The last team to come in arrived in a Kenworth truck! The truck driver blew his air horn as he pulled up and he said, "I have a couple of people who say they are on something called a 'Bigger and Better' activity." He held up a penny and said, "They gave me this penny in exchange for leasing my truck!" Since I hadn't given any stipulations on leasing or owning, they won the contest! After all, the truck was worth about $100,000! That trucker was a good sport as we all piled into the cab and took turns riding around the neighborhood for an hour and a half.

With God, a prayer request is much like that "Bigger-and-Better" game. Every answer to prayer opens up another opportunity that requires a greater need and greater resources.

I remember when I was dating the young lady who is now my wife. Our first date was at a youth revival. After the conclusion of the revival, I bought her a strawberry milkshake. We went on three dates that first week. Then I sat with her in church the following Sunday. To say that I was enjoying our dating is an understatement!

In the course of these four dates, I learned that she had a junior-senior banquet to attend. Of course I wanted to take her, and I wanted to do it right with proper transportation, a tuxedo, and flowers. So I called my dad and asked for a sizeable loan. "Son," he said, "that is a lot of money. How long have you been dating this girl?"

I hedged and said we had had four or five dates, and I failed to mention they were all in one week!

"Son, before I give you that much money, I have a question. Is she 'the one'?"

I assured him that I had indeed found "the one"! Our dating

became a "Bigger-and-Better" activity each time!

Every date I had with my future wife opened another door that eventually opened the door to matrimony, and that opened a door to child rearing, and that opened the door of ministry. The doors of my life have kept on opening until the prayers and requests I make to God are so much larger than the prayers I made in 1979 when I got married.

If you are growing in the Lord, you will need more from God. If you need more from God but you are not receiving from God, then you are a famished Christian. You are hungry for His blessing or depriving yourself of His blessing, and your trying to grow in the Lord will fail. Have you watched some Christians who enter a ministry of service such as the bus ministry, give it all they have, God blesses them in a wonderful way, and the bus route skyrockets? But then, almost as quickly, it plateaus and then gradually starts dying.

Some people excuse the failure by saying, "People have a season of blessing." Personally, I am not interested in big peaks; I am interested in sustained building. I want the blessings of God to be like a little snowball that, as it rolls down a mountain of snow, becomes bigger and bigger—so big the person rolling it can no longer handle it. I don't want to find myself at the bottom of the mountain with the same size snowball that I pushed off the top of the hill. I want to compound its size, its momentum, its magnitude, and its greatness until it overwhelms me.

If we don't learn how to multiply God's blessings, then I am confident that the way God will do it is the way He did it before, and he will send persecution to the local church. In the book of Acts, within two years the church grew from 120 members to 100,000 members. That church would have kept on growing but for the fact that God wanted to use those people to spread the Gospel to the whole world. He sent persecution as the means to accomplish that goal. As a result, the Gospel went everywhere throughout the whole world. That is predominantly the reason why we are free to meet today in churches in America.

China has tens of millions of believers, but they have to meet together in secret. Christianity cannot be stopped, but the authorities can stop big assemblies from meeting. I don't want God to have to use that technique to get our attention because we failed in multiplying the blessing.

In chapter 16, I addressed how God answered Hezekiah's prayer to live with 15 more years. However, something happened in Hezekiah's response cycle, and God was watching to decide if He wanted to multiply the blessing or diminish the blessing. *"But Hezekiah rendered not again according to the benefit done unto him...."* (II Chronicles 32:25) God blesses us in response to our prayers and to our faith.

After God answers your initial prayer, He steps back and watches what response you have following His blessing. Therein is the critical part of multiplying a blessing or cutting it short. Hezekiah was a great man, but because he did not attend to what he should have, he was cut short. *"Howbeit in the business of the ambassadors of the princes of Babylon, who sent unto him to enquire of the wonder that was done in the land, God left him, to try him, that he might know all that was in his heart."* (II Chronicles 32:31)

I want to keep that blessing mounting and mounting and mounting until it floods; I want to be a spiritual tsunami, so to speak. I want to build and then inundate the whole world around me with the blessings of God. That continual, residual blessing of God is in direct accordance to our response to God's answer. How we respond to blessing and victory and honor determines the continued response from God.

To me, II Kings 10:32 is a troubling verse. *"In those days the* LORD *began to cut Israel short...."* God saw that His people were not responding to His blessings as He had taught them to, so He started to take the blessings from them. Eventually, not only did they not have the blessings, but the curse of God fell on them because they continually failed to do right after God had blessed them.

In other words, when God blesses you, there should be an immediate response. No response? God is merciful and just. You pray again, and God blesses. Again, there should be an immediate response. No response? God is merciful and just and careful and gracious. You pray, and God blesses. It seems like you are on a roll.

Then God asks, "Where is My response?"

You ignore His question, pray, and petulantly say, "God, that isn't all that I needed."

God says, "I am watching you, and I do not like the response I am getting to My blessing. I will not give you the full measure."

It's too late to cry, "But I need more!" God doesn't like this response, so He gives even less.

"But I need more!" God doesn't like this response at all, so He now cuts the blessing way short. Usually, at this point, people turn totally away from God and become very stagnant Christians.

My Bible teaches that I should abound more and more. God is not interested in a growth spurt; God is interested in having a lifetime of growth that eventually will take you right on Home to Heaven. Dr. Hyles was not diminishing this ministry on the cor-ner of Oakley and Sibley in Hammond, Indiana. He was "so much the more-ing." Natural strength aside, his honor and glory were great as he entered Heaven! Jack Hyles was a great man, and good men should abound with blessing more and more.

The Proper Response to the Blessing

In II Chronicles 25:5-11, God gives us a negative example to consider. *"Moreover Amaziah gathered Judah together, and made them captains over thousands, and captains over hundreds, according to the houses of their fathers, throughout all Judah and Benjamin: and he numbered them from twenty years old and above, and found them three hundred thousand choice men, able to go forth to war, that could handle spear and shield. He hired also an hundred thousand mighty men of valour out of Israel for an hundred talents of silver. But there came a man of God to him, saying, O king, let not the army of Israel go with thee; for the LORD is not with Israel, to wit, with all the children of Ephraim. But if thou wilt go, do it, be strong for the battle: God shall make thee fall before the enemy: for God hath power to help, and to cast down. And Amaziah said to the man of God, But what shall we do for the hundred talents which I have given to the army of Israel? And the man of God answered, The LORD is able to give thee much more than this. Then Amaziah separated them, to wit, the army that was come to him out of Ephraim, to go home again: wherefore their anger was greatly kindled against Judah, and they returned home in great anger. And Amaziah strengthened himself, and led forth his people, and went to the valley of salt, and smote of the children of Seir ten thousand."*

In this passage King Amaziah was preparing to fight a battle, and he did not think he had enough soldiers. He hired 100,000 more and paid them about a million and a half dollars by today's standards. The man of God instructed Amaziah not to use the mercenary troops because God was not with them. He further warned the king that God would deny him the victory.

King Amaziah rebelled at the instructions because he had already paid the soldiers; however, he finally listened to the man of God, dismissed the army, sent them home, and lost his investment. Because he listened to God's man, God gave him a great victory.

Still, in the face of God's helping hand, Amaziah's response to the victory wrought by God left much to be desired. *"Now it came to pass, after that Amaziah was come from the slaughter of the Edomites, that he brought the gods of the children of Seir, and set them up to be his gods, and bowed down himself before them, and burned incense unto them. Wherefore the anger of the LORD was kindled against Amaziah, and he sent unto him a prophet, which said unto him, Why hast thou sought after the gods of the people, which could not deliver their own people out of thine hand?"* (II Chronicles 25:14, 15) Shortly after Amaziah conquered the Edomites, he adopted their gods as his own and bowed down to them. What an affront to God Almighty! God watched Amaziah's wrong response, and He cut off the people.

The sad story of Amaziah's life is the story of many Christians. God does something great for them, and in response, they do something foolish. They have not learned the truth that God's blessings are dependent upon their response to His blessings. By responding in the right way, the blessing is multiplied!

Have you ever noticed that some people seem to have the Midas touch in their Christian life? Everything they touch seemingly turns to gold. Those who enviously look at them pout and say, "Why does everything I touch turn to rust and corruption? I don't smoke. I don't drink. I don't carouse. I don't behave immorally. I don't watch bad programming on the television. I don't listen to the wrong kind of music. What am I doing wrong?" That kind of living is only a small part of receiving God's blessing.

The right response to God's blessing is found in Solomon, whose life teaches that a specific plan must be followed. *"Now when Solomon had made an end of **praying**, the fire came down from heaven, and consumed the burnt-offering and the sacrifices; and the glory of the LORD filled the house. And the priests could not enter into the house of the LORD, because the glory of the LORD had filled the LORD's house. And when all the children of Israel saw how the fire came down, and the glory of the LORD upon the house, they bowed themselves with their faces to the ground upon the pavement, and worshipped, and praised the LORD, saying, For he is good; for his mercy endureth for ever. Then the king and all the people offered sacrifices before the LORD."* (II Chronicles 7:1-4)

According to this example in the life of Solomon, how can we multiply that blessing of our prayer?

1. **When God hears your prayer, the first response He wants is worship.** *"And when all the children of Israel saw how the fire came down, and the glory of the LORD upon the house, they bowed themselves with their faces to the ground upon the pavement, and worshipped...."* (II Chronicles 7:3) As I have previously established, *worship* is a very affectionate term. Worship is the affection between a husband and a wife or the affection between a parent and a child. It is that affection a dog has for his master where he does not judge; he just offers his undying loyalty. When God answers your prayers, the response He wants from you is to bow down. He wants you to know and recognize and honor the hand that fed you.

Literally, worship is what people do before a king when they bow down, take the king's hand, and then kiss that hand. That reverence is an act of worship and humility. It is critically important to God that when He comes through for us in a big way, we bow the knee to Him and tell Him of our love because we realize He did something important for us.

So often worship is one of the great missing elements in our fundamental circles. That is one reason why Dr. Hyles would not go out to eat after a service where God had blessed him in a great way. He would return to his room, take off his shoes, take off his jacket, get his Bible, jump up and down on the bed, and shout "Glory to God! What a great meeting! I am so excited about what YOU did, God!" His was an act of worship—an act of acknowledging God in a demonstrative, affectionate display. However, I don't often see or hear of that kind of worship happening.

Prayer is not merely coming to God to ask something from Him. *It is above all fellowship with God and being brought under the power of His holiness and love,* till He takes possession of us and stamps our entire nature with the lowliness of Christ, which is the secret of all true worship.[1]

Have you ever wondered why it seems that some groups of believers, generally not independent Baptists, seem to have such great growth blessing, and they can pack a coliseum with 20,000 or more people? Why is it that the blessings of God come and people walk the aisle? You may well wonder why would God bless those people?

I have witnessed in three decades of preaching a stiff Christianity that is right in behavior, proper in deportment, and cold and lifeless in affection shown to God. I have watched preachers who have alienated all of their human relationships, but they have remained true to their standards and convictions. Before you crucify me for making these observations and castigate me for "changing," I am 1000 percent for standards and convictions. But God is not interested in a cold, dead formalism; God wants some affection! Sustained, increased blessing from God is contingent on the proper response of the believer. The blessings of God are not contingent upon any standard or strictness; they are contingent on one's right response to the goodness of God. If only man would praise the Lord for His goodness!

"More love to Thee, O Christ, More love to Thee!
Hear Thou the prayer I make on bended knee;
This is my earnest plea: More love, O Christ to Thee,
More love to Thee, More love to Thee!"

God wants us to be motivated by affection and love for Him. When God sent down the fire in answer to Solomon's prayer, Solomon responded by saying, "We are all going to worship God!"

2. When God hears your prayer, the second response He wants is praise. II Chronicles 7:3 says, "...*and worshipped, and praised the* LORD...." "Praise is primary; we cannot glorify Him by our deeds until we have glorified Him by our words."[2] Worship and praise are different. Worship is affection; the "I love you"; the tender, kind, heartfelt expressions of endearment in a relationship. When a husband comes home from work, and his wife meets him at the door with a hug and a kiss, she is showing affection— not praising him. However, when she then steps back from the embrace and says, "Tell me what you did today? I want to hear all about it. Did you win the war singlehandedly? Did the boss say you were the best employee he has bar none?" She utilizes praise.

Likewise, we need to go to God and say, "God, I am so crazy about You! God, I just love You. I love working with You. I do not want to do anything else in the world but serve You, God. I love serving You." That is showing affection—worship.

Don't you like it when the boss says, "You really know how to get a job done." Likewise, God likes it when you say to Him, "God, how You work is beyond my imagination. How do You use mortal man? How did You choose us to do Your work? You are the greatest God ever." That is showing praise.

Every prayer is a call to praise for every prayer should be accompanied by praise—praise in the beginning, the middle and the end. That is, we should praise the first day the petition is presented, keep on praising until the answer comes, and then praise more than ever because it has come.[3]

The answer came, and Solomon praised God.

3. When God hears your prayer, the third response He wants is sacrifice. *"Then the king and all the people offered sacrifices before the LORD."* (II Chronicles 7:4) If we believe God is wonderful and we want to show Him our love, the means He has provided is giving. God wants us to put our money where our mouth is! Husband, when you show your wife how much you love her, you take her out to eat; buy her flowers, chocolates, a new dress, a new purse, a new pair of shoes, some new curtains, some new flooring, a new house, or even a new car. God wants tangible expressions of our love too!

I want to show God how much I love Him. I look at every-thing He has given me, and I say, "God, with the resources You gave me, I want to show You I really appreciate what You have done for me," and I drop an offering in the offering plate when it passes by me. I give to faith promise missions because I want to show God a tangible expression of my appreciation.

4. When God hears your prayer, the fourth response He wants is work. *"And on the three and twentieth day of the seventh month he sent the people away into their tents, glad and merry in heart for the goodness that the LORD had shewed unto David, and to Solomon, and to Israel his people. Thus Solomon finished the house of the LORD...."* (II Chronicles 7:10) After the people worshiped, after they praised, and after they gave an offering, they all worked together to do a great work!

Work is what causes us to need God's blessing. If we work hard, we will say, "God, I have been working. I surely do need You!"

God says, "I can't wait, for when I answer your prayer, you are always so affectionate and excited! Here is your answer!"

"Oh, God, You are so wonderful! I love working for You!"

And the cycle of worship, praise, offering, and work continu-ally repeats. Why would anyone rob himself of the multiplied blessings of God?

When a Christian shuns fellowship with other Christians, the devil smiles. When he stops studying the Bible, the devil laughs. When he stops praying, the devil shouts for joy.

– Corrie ten Boom

The Role of the Bible in Prayer

"*I am the true vine, and my Father is the husbandman. Every branch in me that beareth not fruit he taketh away: and every branch that beareth fruit, he purgeth it, that it may bring forth more fruit. Now ye are clean through the word which I have spoken unto you. Abide in me, and I in you. As the branch cannot bear fruit of itself, except it abide in the vine; no more can ye, except ye abide in me. I am the vine, ye are the branches: He that abideth in me, and I in him, the same bringeth forth much fruit: for without me ye can do nothing. If a man abide not in me, he is cast forth as a branch, and is withered; and men gather them, and cast them into the fire, and they are burned. If ye abide in me, and my words abide in you, ye shall ask what ye will, and it shall be done unto you.*" (John 15:1-7)

We have always taught that Bible reading and prayer go hand in hand—like peanut butter and jelly. In the Christian life, we have been taught to read our Bible and pray. We know that we should read the Bible, and we know that we should pray, but unfortunately the connection between the two is a little hazy or a little tenuous. Most people don't quite understand why they go together; they just know that if you are a good Christian, you are supposed to read your Bible, pray, go to church, etc. John 15:7 explains how Bible reading and prayer fit together and accomplish a great work as a team.

But notice, the verse does not say *if* you read the Bible and pray, you shall ask what you will. In fact, this verse does not say anything about a Christian's Bible reading and prayer. The verse says, *"If ye abide in me, and* **my words abide in you,** *ye shall ask what ye will, and it shall be done unto you."* This great statement about prayer has somehow been glossed over or ignored because we have not used the correct wording. Generations of Christians have had the Bible to read and have prayed in a prayer closet— never understanding how the two of them go together. The connection needs to be made because this verse promises you that whatsoever you ask for **will** be given to you. God is really eager to answer your prayers.

To abide in Christ is to dwell on Christ, to think of Him when we go shopping and wonder what He would want us to buy. When we eat, we wonder what He would want us to eat. He fills our minds. We dwell on Him. We practice His presence. Not only do we live close to Him, but we are constantly thinking of His presence and realizing how wonderful it is.[1]

"If ye abide in me," is a conditional statement which says God will always come through for us. The verse appears to be carte blanche because it says you shall ask what you will. But *"what ye will"* is not the same as "what you want." The will is described in the other verses of chapter 15.

The will is that for which you know you should be asking. God has a will, and those who understand His will can get anything they need from Him within the context of that will. "What God wills on earth needs prayer as its indispensable condition."[2] For those who want to get those things from Him, His words must abide in them. The role of the Bible in prayer centers around the word *abide*.

• **The word *abide* means "to remain in you."** When I think of "remain in you," I think of James 1:25 which says, *"But whoso looketh into the perfect law of liberty, and continueth therein, he being not a forgetful hearer, but a doer of the work, this man shall be* *blessed....*" How do you read your Bible? What remains in you from what you have read? What remains in you is what *abides* in you, and only those Christians who have the Word of God abiding in them have the right to say, "God, that is what I will." It is not how much Bible passes through you; it is how much Bible **remains** in you. That is what God checks. What remains in you?

• **The word** *abide* **means "to submit to."** To what Scripture do you submit that you have read? God says it is not just how many words you read or how many verses you check off your Bible reading chart. God says, "As you read My words, to how many of them do you submit?"

The book of I Corinthians contains the codes and methods of how a man should wear his hair. A man shows his submission to authority by the way he wears his hair. Every woman should wear women's apparel and be feminine and modest. To how many of God's rules are you willing to submit?

God asks, "Do you want your prayers answered? When are you going to start obeying that Scripture you read?" If God's words abide in you, you will submit to what you read in His Word.

• *Abide* **also means "to put up with."** Have you ever read something and said, "That can't be so! That just can't be so!" God knows His Book is full of things people do not like or accept. So He says, "Do you want your prayers answered?" If so, you will need to put up with His words. How many times have you read the Bible and said, "Surely He does not meant that?!" If you don't like the Scriptures that say a wife should submit to her husband, do you put up with it? If you put up with God's rules, that is abiding. God wants you to put up with Him. Do you read the passages anyway, or do you skip over them? Too many people believe the Bible is the Word of God except for some of the passages with which they have issues.

I realize I and II Chronicles contain nine intense chapters of names we can't even pronounce! I read all nine chapters, and I must admit that at times I think, "Will I ever get through these chapters?" The book of Leviticus contains offerings—the peace offering, the sin offering, the trespass offering, the meal offering, the drink offering, and the wave offering. We read that during our Bible reading time and wonder how it can help with a troubled marriage or any other area of life. God wants us to read it, and He finds great pleasure in people who "put up with" His Scripture.

Do I understand everything that I read? Of course not! God doesn't expect us to understand everything we read! He wants us to put up with the parts that seem uninteresting because *"All scripture is given by inspiration of God, and is profitable...."* (II Timothy 3:16) Read it, retain it, and remember what you read. Be able to talk about what you have read. Submit to it, and put up with it!

• **Abide also means to "live up to."** Do you live up to the standard the Word of God demands or requires?

• **Abide also means to "to carry out."** Are you carrying out or distributing the Word of God?

From these definitions, if the word *abide* is in us, we know it means we must be able to talk about what we have read, be able to put up with the parts we do not like—whether or not we don't understand them or do not agree with them, submit to the parts we do understand when God says to submit—even if we do not want to live up to the expectations of the Scripture, and we have to distribute the words we read. The word *abide* has some far-reaching consequences.

Why does the Word of God have bearing upon one's prayer life?

1. **The Word of God is more than a Book to put into ourselves; the Bible contains the words that God wants to hear from us.** *"This book of the law shall not depart out of thy mouth...."* (Joshua 1:8) Do you ever wonder what God thinks about His words? He loves those words! *"Heaven and earth shall pass away: but my words shall not pass away."* (Mark 13:31) All that will

remain someday are the words of God because God loves His words. He loves them so much He called His Son "the Word." If you want God to answer your prayers, He wants to hear His words.

"Sing them over again to me, Wonderful words of life;
Let me more of their beauty see, Wonderful words of life.
Words of life and beauty, Teach me faith and duty:
Beautiful words, wonderful words, wonderful words of life."

God hates idle words or critical words or talebearing words. God loves His words, and He wants to hear us saying them. In fact, His words should never cease to be coming from out of a Christian's mouth.

When was the last time you used God's words in a normal conversation? Talking about the Bible other than in church and church-related activities is a rare commodity nowadays.

I love the Bible, and I have been deeply convicted as I have been teaching about prayer. As I learn these truths from the Bible about prayer, I think, "Lord, I am so deeply convicted."

What words of God do you use? With whom do you ever discuss the Bible? Do you and your spouse ever talk about the Bible? God says in John 15:7, "*If ye abide in me, and my words abide in you....*" Having the words of God abiding in you simply means you are talking about the Bible. When you pray, God wonders, "What have you learned recently that you like?" Do you ever tell Him about His incredible Book? God wants to hear you use His words!

Instead, we talk about sports or the opposite gender, or the movies, or a new video recently released. God says, "Did you read My Bible at all?" God wants to hear your opinion, your thoughts, your love, and your affection for His words.

2. **The Word of God provides stability of thought during unstable times.** When you are overwhelmed by national events like the war with its bombings and bloodshed, when the world is

seemingly falling apart around you, or when your world is falling apart within you and no man can offer any help, what do you do? You go to God and read His words because the Word of God brings stability in unstable times.

To pray is to open the door to Jesus and to admit Him into your distress. Your helplessness is the very thing which opens wide the door to Him and gives Him access to all your needs.[3]

"The LORD is my light and my salvation; whom shall I fear? the LORD is the strength of my life; of whom shall I be afraid? When the wicked, even mine enemies and my foes, came upon me to eat up my flesh, they stumbled and fell. Though an host should encamp against me, my heart shall not fear: though war should rise against me, in this will I be confident." (Psalm 27:1-3) Before I pray, I go to the Word of God because the Word of God gives me a perspective of stability. I can then go to God and say, "God, I spent time in Your Word, and I can now come boldly to You regarding the instability in my life. I am asking You to bring steadiness into my life."

3. The Word of God teaches us the proper emotions to display before God. When we go to God, He expects us to come with a certain decorum and propriety. Of course, He allows us to come and pour out our complaints and, in that sense, He lets us gripe to Him. Again and again, I find statements like "I lifted up my soul," "I cried unto the Lord," and "I complained," but God wants us to come to Him displaying the proper emotion. Before you cry and complain, *"Enter into his gates with thanksgiving, and into his courts with praise...."* (Psalm 100:4)

"God, my life is disastrous inwardly. My life is surrounded by problems involving my marriage, my family, my job, and my world, but I come into Your presence and say, 'Thank You.' Before I tell you all my complaints and heartaches, I want to express properly my gratitude and my praise for You. Oh Lord, let me tell You what great things You have done!" We must recognize from our reading of the Word of God that we should see what He has done before we tell Him what we think He should do. If we do not read the Bible, we will never have the proper perspective when coming to God.

Before we can give a litany of all that He supposedly hasn't done, and ask Him where He went when He was needed, we must come with the proper spirit. What has He done for us? The Bible reminds me that I must come to Him and tell Him what I have witnessed that He has done for me. We need to come to Him with thanksgiving for His unfailing mercies. The heavens declare the glory of God! The sun came up this morning! We have never yet had a morning with no air to breathe. Imagine how much praying would go on if God ever decided to reduce the oxygen ratio for just a couple of minutes! He brings seedtime and harvest. Before we give God a list of what we don't like about the way He has treated us, the Bible says to tell Him all the good things He has done. The order is very important.

4. The Word of God provides examples of what God has done for others. As you go to God in prayer, God wants you to do some research.

The Bible is the record of praying men, and from them we learn how to pray. It is the record of the prayer-life and the prayer-words of Him Who was Son of Man and Son of God. From His life and from His words, we learn prayer; what it is, what it does, what it means.[4]

When you go to God in prayer, say, "When Abraham asked for something, You did that for him, didn't You? I know You know that, but I just want to remind You."

I have heard some people say that God does not need to be reminded of what He has said in His Word. I contend He wants us to remember His Word! God wrote about Abraham so we can say, "God, remember when Abraham prayed and You delivered Lot? Would You make a deal with me about my country?"

I believe God likes it when we study examples that He has provided in the Bible. If God wrote about them, that means He chose them as examples of what He would do again. Why? He is not a respecter of persons!

A pastor friend in Michigan shared a wonderful story with me how God answered his prayer. He testified how he listened to the older men talking about the great things God had done for them. One told how God gave him a $250,000 check. Another said God built a building for him. Another needed a new bus, and when he went to his office, the keys to a new bus were waiting in his mailbox. "Brother Schaap," he said, "I never had anything like that happen to me! We were building a new building, and I could not get one dime from anywhere." This good man told how he went to God and said, "God, I don't believe You care about me." But then he read a verse that said God is not a respecter of persons. He went back to God and said, "God, did You write that? If You wrote it, then why am I not getting it? I need $300,000, and You know it isn't coming in. If You are not a respecter of persons, then You are not keeping Your word, and I might as well get out of Your business. What are You going to do about my situation?" This pastor friend concluded his story by saying, "A little old lady gave me $300,000! I know God is not a respecter of persons!"

Isn't that wonderful when you can hold God to His promises, and God says, "Why didn't you say so?!" God puts those promises and examples in the Bible because He wants us to remind Him that we have been doing our homework.

Every teacher appreciates students who do their homework. A student loves it when his teacher asks a question pertaining to his homework because he knows his material. Likewise, God likes it when we do our homework, and we know what we are talking about. He has given us the liberty to remind Him of illustrations in the Bible where He came through for others!

5. The Word of God obligates Him and gives assurance to man. Ephesians 3:20, 21 says, *"Now unto him that is able to do exceeding abundantly above all that we ask or think, according to the power that worketh in us. Unto him be glory in the church by Christ Jesus throughout all the ages, world without end. Amen."* His promises must be used, and God wants to know if you recognize them as promises. If you don't know His promises, God does not feel obligated to you. If we are not diligent enough to know what He has promised us, why should He do anything for us? God does not and will not bless laziness.

I sometimes wonder why God would listen to me and contemplate my needs, but God is a good listener, and He just listens to His children.

God answers prayer. God bends over, and listens, and does as we ask because we ask.[5]

Practical Ways to Utilize the Bible Daily

1. Write down some Scripture every day. As you read the Bible, jot down a verse, a phrase, a passage, or a promise—just write some Scripture. I have a pad of paper I keep with my Bible that I read in every morning. As I read, I write down ideas, thoughts, and phrases. A king in the Old Testament was commanded to write the Bible every day; that king wrote 3,000 proverbs. He was obeying the Bible!

2. Surround yourself with Bible promises. Carry 3x5 cards with you. Post them on your doors, on your windows, on your mirrors; and put them in places where you and your family will notice them. Decorate them with borders and frames and art work, or just print them on plain notebook paper. Just put Bible verses around you where you will see them.

Deuteronomy 6:6-8 says, *"And these words, which I command*

thee this day, shall be in thine heart: And thou shalt teach them diligently unto thy children, and shalt talk of them when thou sittest in thine house, and when thou walkest by the way, and when thou liest down, and when thou risest up. And thou shalt bind them for a sign upon thine hand, and they shall be as frontlets between thine eyes." God wants us to know His words, to memorize His words, to think about His words, to taste His words, and to talk using His words— at all times. Everywhere we look, we should see the Bible. We should want to see His words.

3. Talk about the Bible with other Christians. Nothing is wrong with saying, "I was reading a verse, and I wondered what you thought about it." Discuss a Bible verse with a friend. God doesn't ask us to have all the answers; He asks you to talk about His Word.

4. Think about the Bible stories or small portions of Scripture. While you are working, think about the Bible. Relive the stories like David and Goliath, the crossing of the Red Sea, the manna falling like dew on the ground, Joshua and the conquest of Jericho, Elijah calling down fire from Heaven, Joseph's being sold into slavery, the feeding of the 5,000, to name a few. Relive the Bible stores; think about them until your mind is filled with word pictures. Take a few phrases and just "chew" on them.

5. Let your mind dwell on Scripture passages and verses while you pray. For much of my praying, I say nothing. I listen.

The continuous nature of prayer may well be illustrated by the conversation of intimate friends. Words are not constantly exchanged, but fellowship is not interrupted.[6]

I have learned that you don't have to say a lot to accomplish a lot. Allow me to illustrate: Asking, "Will you marry me?" is enough! You don't always have to say a lot. A whole lot of communication is going on when two people in love just quietly sit together.

With God, you don't have to ramble on. Long prayers do not

impress Him; those were the prayers of the scribes and Pharisees. It is not your much speaking that impresses Him. Prayer is thinking about the Bible. It is thinking about how He delivered Hezekiah when Hezekiah appealed to Him. I think about that story when I want deliverance for people with an incurable illness, and I will just say, "God, please do the same for so-and-so as you did for King Hezekiah."

It doesn't take a long, elaborate prayer; it is thinking about a story in the Bible where God came through and slipping in a name. Prayer is not fancy words and much speaking; it is a heart filled with what God has done in His Word.

Jesus has given each of us five things to use in helping to win His world back home: The life, what we are; our lips, what we say; our service, what we do; our money, what we do not keep selfishly for ourselves; and our prayer, what we claim in Jesus the Victor's name. The greatest of these is prayer.[1]

They Continued in Prayer

"Be not ye therefore like unto them: for your Father knoweth what things ye have need of, before ye ask him. After this manner therefore pray ye: Our Father which art in heaven, Hallowed be thy name. Thy kingdom come. Thy will be done in earth, as it is in heaven. Give us this day our daily bread. And forgive us our debts, as we forgive our debtors. And lead us not into temptation, but deliver us from evil: For thine is the kingdom, and the power, and the glory, for ever. Amen. For if ye forgive men their trespasses, your heavenly father will also forgive you: But if ye forgive not men their trespasses, neither will your Father forgive your trespasses." (Matthew 6:8-15)

An oft-preached passage says, "If my **people**, which are called by my name, shall humble themselves, and pray, and seek my face, and turn from their wicked ways; then will I hear from heaven, and will forgive their sin, and will heal their land." "II Chronicles 7:14 is a dateless promise; these are timeless words; they are for God's **people** of every land and for all time."² This verse emphasizes plurality; the Bible doesn't say, "If my **person** which is called by my name shall humble himself...." Both Jeremiah and Ezekiel said that God was looking for a man.

Occasionally when I preached to young people, I preached similar messages about how God is looking for one man and focused on who would pay the price to be that one man. However, my attention has been riveted by the thought that God is not looking for just one man; He is looking for **people**—a people who will meet some conditions. With this thought in mind, consider

the following verses and the emphasis on the word *they*.
- Acts 2:42 says, *"And **they** continued stedfastly in the apostles' doctrine and fellowship, and in breaking of bread, and in prayers."*
- Acts 4:24 states, *"And when **they** heard that, **they** lifted up their voice to God with one accord...."* In other words, all of them together were praying as one person.
- Acts 4:31, *"And when **they** had prayed, the place was shaken where **they** were assembled together; and **they** were all filled with the Holy Ghost, and **they** spake the word of God with boldness."*

God most surely is looking for individuals to do a great work with Him, but God is also looking for corporate work. I have already alluded to the fact that God is not just looking for *me* to do it; He is looking for *us* to do the work of prayer.

When Jeremiah really saw the nation of Israel as she was, he tried to explain to the people that there was another side to what they were going through, and He tried to give God's perspective on their circumstances. His enemies put God's man in a pit, conspired to kill him, and tried to drown him. Jeremiah was eventually exiled to Egypt, and there he lost his life for speaking the truth.

A certain kind of a Christian lifestyle built on fun and busyness flourishes in many of our nation's churches. Even Christians in fundamental works embrace this type of Christianity. Any reader of Scriptures or any historian who studies the shifting direction of the United States, the alliances being formed, the mistakes being made, and the attitude shown toward God, will testify that America's culture is godless and anti-Christian.

At this moment, America still maintains a strong core of Christianity, but that core is weakening. The Christians who are maintaining that spiritual strength are far removed from the Christianity that I knew as a boy. It is a watered-down

Christianity, with a new Bible and almost no standards, which is following the world at a steady clip—while keeping a certain acceptable distance. This Christianity casts a very disparaging look at our kind of Christianity, and they will not be our friends.

When the "heat" comes in this country someday, it will focus on whether or not we will stand for Christ. I am afraid that much of what passes off as evangelical Christianity will not stand. If we continue in our Christian life without understanding the importance of prayer, we will eventually forfeit our right to be fun, busy Christians enjoying a good time. My great heart's desire is for **people** to see God as He is and for Christians to get ahold of Him.

In this chapter, I want to address "they"—*"they lifted up their voice to God with one accord...."* *"And when* **they** *had prayed, the place was shaken...."* Our present-day society is too busy and too proud to pray. Many Christians are too busy and too proud to pray. We live in a society where we have been given every excuse not to pray. Technology has given us more excuses not to pray. It has not freed up our time as we were promised in the '60s. With all of its modern conveniences, the twenty-first century was supposed to bring an even greater freeing of time. We should have had incredible amounts of time to do nothing but what we wanted to do.

If that is the case, then we are exceedingly proud because we definitely have not used our time for God. Instead, we fill our life with commuting; listening to CDs, tapes, audiotapes, talk radio, and sports radio; watching television and videos; and playing games. Life is filled with technology that causes us to be too busy for God. The truth of the matter is, if you did have the time you think you need, you would not spend the time in prayer.

Those of us who do think we have time to pray fill our lives chasing everything we think we need. For instance, if we have a free night, we pick up a second job with the excuse, "I have to." We don't have to do anything but die and face God someday!

Many things have led to the neglect of prayer: the swift and only half-digested progress of scientific knowledge, the sudden accumulation of material gains, the failure to maintain habits of church-going and Bible reading; the decay of family religion. Its neglect, if continued, is fatal. Our only power, now or ever, is of God, and any study which will bring professing Christians face to face with the facts will bring us to our knees.[3]

The kind of praying that I find the Bible tells us to do I can only find in countries which have lost the privilege to pray. When I want to find an example of a group of people who pray like I believe the Book commands us to pray, I do not look in America because Americans are too busy having fun.

Jim Frankel, columnist for the *Cleveland Press* says, "If and when American civilization collapses, historians of a future date can look back and sneer, 'They entertained themselves to death' "! If you prefer such a condemnation in an ecclesiastical flavor, well, here is Dr. Tozer saying, "America is laughing her way to hell."[4]

I know of a church with many tens of thousands of members which has a special retreat in a mountain cave. When people take a two-week vacation, families spend the first week there in fasting and praying. That church has thousands praying daily! When I read about the kind of praying those church members do, I say, "Lord, that is so similar to the praying of Paul and Silas. That is Jeremiah praying. It is the kind of praying that Peter and James and John did in the early church when You shook that place, and the Holy Ghost came and moved in a marvelous way. God, is there any place left in the world with that kind of praying?" Yes, there is, but you have to look for a place where oppression exists, where people have lost their freedom, and where Christianity is banished or outlawed.

There may well come a day when those of us who do not want to pray that way will be forced to pray because there will be no more of the lifestyle as we now know it. There have always been visionaries or doomsday prophets, and I am certainly not pronouncing doom on America. I am simply addressing the fact that the kind of praying God demands from His people is only done by people who come to the point where they have nothing left but God. We who have everything are madly chasing everything but God. We flee from Him on vacation. We flee from Him in the summertime. During our vacation from God, we ignore the Bible.

When we have fewer mouth-watering commodities, we will have less time for our feet under the table and more time for our knees on the floor in prayer. When we have less eye-catching TV and less thrilling music, and when we have the spirit of heaviness and know more of poverty than plenty, we might get our foot on the first rung of the ladder of intercession.[5]

I have a difficult time being with a crowd who does not have time for God. I have a very hard time countenancing the kind of Christianity which blames a lack of prayer on various situations.

- "I am busy with my kids," says the couple in their twenties.
- "I am building my business," says the ladder climber in his thirties.
- "I am climbing the ladder," says the corporate executive in his forties.
- "I am trying to build my retirement package to care for my family," says a man in his fifties.
- "I am a senior citizen," says the retired one.

May I ask you in God's holy name, when will you have time for Him?! Will you ever have time for Him?

The vast majority do not make use of this mighty instrument that God has put into our hands. We do not live in a praying age. We live in an age of hustle and bustle, of man's efforts and man's determination, of man's confidence in himself and in his own power to achieve things, an age of human organization, human machinery, human scheming, and human achievement. In the things of God, this means no real achievement at all.[6]

When do you pray? When will America have a people about whom God says, "Those are My people, and they pray to Me"? How far down into the septic tank do we have to dip our morals before we realize we have gone too far? The Parents Television Council (PTC), a group of like-minded people who believe that too much prime-time television is indecent, released the following facts:

- The estimated number of television homes = 109.6 million
- Average time kids spend watching TV each day = 4 hours
- 54% of kids have a TV in their bedroom.
- Children watching MTV are viewing an average of 9 sexual scenes per hour with approximately 18 sexual depictions and 17 instances of sexual dialogue innuendos. (2005 PTC Study, MTV *Smut Peddlers*)
- A majority of parents say they are very concerned about the amount of sex (60%) and violence (53%) their children are exposed to on TV.[7]

The Entertainment Tracking System (ETS) is the PTC's database on more than 100,000 hours of programming. The ETS tracks every incident of sexual conduct, violence, profanity, disrespect for authority and other negative content. The incidents are compiled and cross-referenced as a way of tracking trends.[8] To me, the thought of the average viewer watching over 9,000 sexually oriented scenes a year on television is incomprehensible! I dare say the average person hasn't read 9,000 verses or prayed 9,000 minutes. We Christians are so absolutely out of focus because we are too busy playing and too busy doing everything but praying.

There are great social evils that threaten not only the church, but the whole fabric of modern life. The rapid increase of wealth has brought the power of gratifying sensuous desires within the reach of greater numbers of people than ever before. All the forces which wealth and luxury have used to wreck every great civilization of the past are battering at the foundations of our present structure. The increase of wealth within the last few decades has been unprecedented in the history of man. The luxuries of yesterday have become the necessities of today. The wealth that is allied with ruthless greed, and selfish and sensuous pleasure is a thrice deadly foe to spiritual life and holy endeavor.

It is a fact, too well known to be disputed, that the great mass of [movies] are pandering to sensuality; that much of their exhibit is prurient sex stuff, prepared by specialists who are past masters in the art of making virtue dull, drab, and uninteresting, and vice thrilling, heroic and attractive.[9]

In modern times those who have made a great impact for the cause of Jesus Christ have all been people of prayer.

• Luther said, "If I fail to spend two hours in prayer each morning, the devil gets the victory through the day. I have so much business I cannot get on without spending three hours daily in prayer." He had a motto: "He that has prayed well has studied well."[10] Martin Luther built a denomination with 650 million adherents. Almost singlehandedly Luther stood against the entire Roman Catholic Church—even when they wanted to kill him. In those days they didn't have PlayStations and X-box and television and all the modern conveniences we feel we must have.

• Hudson Taylor, the well-known missionary to China, rose at 4:00 a.m. to pray.

• Adoniram Judson, missionary to Burma, prayed at seven specific times each day. "Adoniram Judson left the testimony that in all his long life he had never prayed faithfully for anything and been denied."[11]

• David Livingstone died while he was kneeling with an open Bible in front of him.

• Sir H. M. Stanley, the great explorer, wrote: "I for one must not dare to say that prayers are inefficacious. Where I have been in earnest, I have been answered. When I prayed for light to guide my followers wisely through the perils that beset them, a ray of light has come upon the perplexed mind, and a clear road to deliverance has been pointed out. You may know when prayer is answered, by the glow of content which fills one who has flung his cause before God, as he rises to his feet. I have evidence, satisfactory to myself, that prayers are granted."[12]

• When Charles Haddon Spurgeon, the great Baptist preacher of London, was asked for the secret of his ministry, he immediately responded, "I have always had a praying people."

• John Eliot, the great apostle to the North American Indians, wrote "Prayer and pains through faith in Jesus Christ will accomplish everything."[13]

• While he was cobbling shoes, William Carey used a map of the world as his prayer book, as he passed in review the long list of the nations who sat in darkness.[14]

• One of the most remarkable men in Scotland's history was John Welch, son-in-law of John Knox, the great Scotch reformer. He was not so well-known as his famous father-in-law, but in some respects he was a far more remarkable man than John Knox himself. Most people have the idea that it was John Knox who prayed, "Give me Scotland or I die." It was not; it was John

Welch, his son-in-law. John Welch put it on record before he died, that he counted a day ill-spent if he did not spend seven or eight hours in secret prayer; and when John Welch came to die, an old Scotchman who had known him from his boyhood said of him, "John Welch was a type of Christ." Of course that was an inaccurate use of language, but what the old Scotchman meant was, Jesus Christ had stamped the impression of His character upon John Welch. When had Jesus Christ done it? In those seven or eight hours of daily communication with Himself.[15]

• Bishop Hannington spent the last hours of his martyr life in prayer, and died exclaiming, "I have purchased the road to Uganda with my life."[16]

• David Brainerd prayed; "Here am I, Lord, send me; send me to the ends of the earth; send me to the rough, the savage pagan of the wilderness; send me even to death itself, if it be but in Thy service."[17]

• Praying Payson of Portland, Oregon, was a man who after death was found with calloused knees. By his bedside were two grooves which his delicate knees had rubbed into the floor as he seesawed in travail for the lost.[18]

• John Hunt died in 1845 with a prayer on his lips for the Fiji Islands; "God bless Fiji! Save Fiji! Thou knowest my soul has loved Fiji."[19]

• George Whitefield gave long hours to prayer and read his Bible on his knees.[20]

• In fifty thousand cases, Mr. [George] Mueller calculated that he could trace distinct answers to definite prayers; and in multitudes of instances in which God's care was not definitely traced, it was day by day like an encompassing by invisible presence or atmosphere of life and strength.[21]

• Mary Slessor was once asked what prayer meant to her. She replied, "My life is one long, daily, hourly record of answered prayer for physical health, for mental overstrain, for guidance given marvelously, for errors and dangers averted, for enmity to the Gospel subdued, for food provided at the exact hour needed, for everything that goes to make up life and my poor service. I can testify with a full and often wonder-stricken awe that I believe God answers prayer. I know God answers prayer!"[22]

• Savonarola said, "Enlighten, inflame me; teach me what I ought to pray."[23]

• John Fletcher stained the walls of his room by the breath of his prayers. Sometimes he would pray all night; always, frequently, and with great earnestness. His whole life was a life of prayer. "I would not rise from my seat," he said, "without lifting my heart to God." His greeting to a friend was always: "Do I meet you praying?"[24]

Has the blessed Spirit toned down His operations? Did God close down His production lines after the Spirit had come upon Wesley, upon Finney, and such men? Were those leaders spiritual freaks? Were they oddities of grace, eccentrics who were a little "off" in their spiritual operations? These days we are spiritually so *sub*normal that to be just normal seems to make us *ab*normal.[25]

When Romania was still ruled by the iron fist of Russia's Communism, the Second Baptist Church of Oradea had 8,000 praying members and was the largest Baptist church in Europe.

In those days Bibles were banned in Romania. Christians from other countries would gather Bibles to be smuggled into Romania. Words would be sent to a wife that on a certain day a car would come to the border crossing where her husband worked. That car would be loaded with Bibles. Due to his love for his wife, the border guard would wave the car through the crossing. The Bibles would then be distributed to Christians in Romania.[26]

Some of the amazing stories we have heard about border guards being seemingly blind to Bibles because an angel blinded them might well have been instances where a husband married to a believer did not want her to get in trouble with the authorities, and he let them go through.

Ceausescu, the godless dictator of Romania, invited Billy Graham to come and see the religious freedom he offered to the people of Romania. Billy Graham pronounced Romania a free country and an open nation—all because he had seen the propaganda machine at work. As soon as Billy Graham and his entourage left the country, the Bibles they brought with them were destroyed and made into toilet tissue. Portions of Scripture could actually be read on the toilet tissue used for personal hygiene.

Billy Graham had also toured the Second Baptist Church, but as soon as they left, Ceausescu gave the order to "tear down that den of rats," burn it, dig a hole, and bury the ashes. When bulldozers surrounded the building, 5,000 people, standing shoulder to shoulder, had jammed into the structure to pray. The men who were driving the bulldozers went up against the building, stopped, shut off the engines and refused to raze the building. The beginning of the overthrow of the Romanian Russian government had begun.

Dr. Tom Williams went to preach there, and when he came back, I had the privilege of speaking in a meeting with him. I will never forget his words about the Second Baptist Church. He told of a prayer meeting he attended at 5:00 in the morning. "There were 2,000 members at that church on their face. Do you know what they were praying for?"

"I have no idea," I said.

"They were praying for us!"

"What do you mean?" I asked.

"They know the only hope of deliverance from the oppression

of Communism," he explained, "is for a Western world to wake up spiritually and spread the Gospel."

Bakht Singh, a Christian leader in India, says, "The indigenous churches in India have a great burden for America and are praying that God will visit your country with revival. You feel sorry for us in India because of our poverty in *material* things. We who know the Lord in India feel sorry for you in America because of your *spiritual* poverty. In our churches we spend four or five or six hours in prayer and worship, and frequently our people wait on the Lord in prayer all night; but in America after you have been in church for one hour, you begin to look at your watches. We pray that God may open your eyes to the true meaning of worship.[27]

We have wrapped ourselves in a security blanket of professed godliness. Because we are good, busy Christians, we live acceptable lives. But Jesus warned, "You had better get your Father listening to you!"

Where are the **they** who will continue in prayer? I know we are busy. Because we do not make the time to pray, we are forcing ourselves into a predicament that will demand we make the time to pray. I do not want to have to become a POW to remind myself I can pray. I do not want to be the next Adoniram Judson who was incarcerated for the simple reason he was a Christian. Every night his captors put his legs in iron and hung him upside down. If those were your circumstances, would you learn to pray?

We *will* learn to pray, I am sure, for God will see to that. He is not concerned about our happiness but about our holiness.[28]

Judson buried three wives and all but two children, every one of his staff members, and every one of his fellow missionaries; in fact, he buried more of his friends than he had converts. But 150 years later, every one of the six million Christians in Burma testify that they have a common father, and his name is Adoniram Judson!

I am deluged by people bringing their daily irritations to me.
- "I am unhappy with my marriage."
- "I am unhappy with my monetary circumstances."
- "I am unhappy with my health."
- "I am unhappy with where I live."
- "I am unhappy with my job."
- "The people in my life do not treat me right."

I can ask in every one of these situations, "Have you prayed about this matter?" In most cases, the answer is a resounding "NO!" You would rather miss church to make a dollar, watch television, and blame God for being miserable! You have the riches of America, drive a beautiful car, wear nice clothes, have too much food, and you are unhappy. Why? Because your prayer closet has cobwebs in it! You don't have time to pray!

Pre-World War II, Gladys Aylward was a missionary in China. When Japan invaded China, the slaughter started. Miss Aylward was in charge of an orphanage, and she knew she had to evacuate the children. Her modern-day exodus of marching these children over the mountains, how they crossed flooded rivers, and how their needs were met is nothing less than phenomenal. When she reached the end of her rope, humanly speaking, she apologized to her charges for trying to save them.

One young teenage girl said, "Miss Aylward, we need to remember our favorite story of Moses crossing the Red Sea."

Miss Aylward looked at the girl and apologetically said, "I am no Moses."

"I know," said the girl, "but Jehovah is still God."

Jehovah God, using Gladys Aylward, brought all 100 orphans to safety!

Great miracles are waiting to be done, and extraordinary

opportunities are right around the next corner—if we continue in prayer and if we are not so busy with all the good things that have systematically shut the door to the greatest work we can do. For no doubt, "The greatest thing any one can do for God and for man is to pray."[29] God still lives. He still hears, and He still answers!

"Every great movement of God
can be traced to a kneeling figure.
– D. L. Moody

Endnotes

Introduction

[1] Alexander Whyte, *Lord, Teach Us to Pray* (London: Hodder & Stoughton Limited, 1922), 225- 26.

Foreword

[1] E. M. Bounds, *The Weapon of Prayer* (Grand Rapids: Baker Book House, 1931), 156-57.

[2] Unknown Christian, *The Kneeling Christian* (Grand Rapids: Zondervan Publishing House, 1971), 53.

[3] S. D. Gordon, *Quiet Talks on Prayer* (Westwood, NJ: Fleming H. Revell Company, 1967), 98-102.

[4] R. A. Torrey, *The Power of Prayer* (New Kensington, Penna.: Whitaker House, 2000), 46.

[5] Andrew Murray, *With Christ in the School of Prayer* (New Kensington, Penna.: Whitaker House, 1981), 7.

Chapter One—*The Riddle of Unanswered Prayer*

[1] Enos Kincheloe Cox, *Where Is the Lord God of Elijah?* (Chicago: The Bible Institute Colportage Association, 1929), 86.

[2] Oliver B. Greene, *Daniel: Verse by Verse Study* (Greenville, South Carolina: The Gospel Hour, Inc., 1964), 225.

[3] Dr. Charles Blanchard, *Getting Things From God* (Chicago: The Moody Bible Institute of Chicago, 1915), 32.

[4] Dr. Jack Hyles, *Exploring Prayer With Jack Hyles* (Hammond: Hyles-Anderson Publishers, 1983), 17.

[5] Merrill F. Unger, *Unger's Guide to the Bible* (Wheaton, Ill.: Tyndale House Publishers, Inc., 1974), 514.

[6] Oliver B. Greene, *The Epistle of Paul the Apostle to the Romans*

(Greenville, South Carolina: The Gospel Hour, Inc., 1962), 179.

[7] Gordon, *Quiet Talks on Prayer*, 127.

[8] Matthew Henry, *The Secret of Communion With God*, Ed. by Elisabeth Elliot (New York: Fleming H. Revell Co., 1963), 63.

[9] Whyte, 23.

[10] Gordon, *Quiet Talks on Prayer*, 96.

[11] *Ibid.*, 12.

Chapter Two—*Teach Us to Pray*

[1] E. M. Bounds, *The Reality of Prayer* (Grand Rapids: Baker Book House, 1924, 56.

[2] E. M. Bounds, *The Possibilities of Prayer* (Grand Rapids: Baker Book House, 1923), 98.

[3] Gordon, *Quiet Talks on Prayer*, 104.

[4] Dr. Dennis Corle, The Discipline of Prayer (Claysburg, Penna.: Revival Fires! Publishing, 1995), 20.

[5] Louise Harrison McGraw, *Does God Answer...Prayer?* (Grand Rapids: Zondervan Publishing House, 1941), 18.

[6] Greene, *The Epistle of Paul the Apostle to the Romans*, 21.

[7] Bounds, *The Possibilities of Prayer*, 77.

[8] Greene, *The Epistle of Paul the Apostle to the Romans*, 21.

[9] E. M. Bounds, *Power Through Prayer* (Grand Rapids: Baker Book House, n.d.), 29-30.

[10] Hyles, 161.

[11] Blanchard, 221.

[12] Bounds, *The Possibilities of Prayer*, 52.

[13] R. A. Torrey, *How to Pray* (New York: Pyramid Books, 1900), 63.

[14] Hyles, 76.

[15] Solomon Cleaver, *Life's Great Adventure~Prayer* (New York: Richard R. Smith, Inc., 1931), 35.

[16] Bounds, *The Reality of Prayer*, 74.

[17] Henry, 57.

[18] O. Hallesby, *Prayer* (London: Inter-Varsity Fellowship, 1948), 37.

[19] Charles M. Laymon, *A Primer of Prayer* (Nashville: Tidings, 1949), 17.

Chapter Three—*Hallowed Be Thy Name*
[1] Bounds, *The Reality of Prayer*, 69.

[2] *Ibid.*, 97.

[3] Charles Spurgeon, *The Power of Prayer in a Believer's Life* (Lynwood, Wash.: Emerald Books, 1993), 66.

[4] Cox, 90-91.

[5] Colonel Richard MacCormack is a member and a deacon at First Baptist Church of Hammond. He turned down a promotion to brigadier general because the social lifestyle he would have had to live was not consistent with his Christian testimony. Therefore, he chose to retire as a colonel.

[6] William Morris, ed., *The American Heritage Dictionary of the English Language*, Boston: Houghton Mifflin Company, 1969), 508.

[7] Jacob J. Finkelstein, "Assyria," *The World Book Encyclopedia* (Chicago: Field Enterprises Educational Corporation, 1972) 778-81.

[8] Clarice Swisher, *The Ancient Near East* (San Diego: Lucent Books, Inc., 1995), 87.

[9] Bounds, *The Weapon of Prayer*, 30.

Chapter Four—*Who Supplies the "Willing"?*
[1] S. D. Gordon, *Prayer and the Bible* (New York: Fleming H. Revell Company, 1935), 19.

[2] Andrew Murray, *The Prayer Life* (Chicago: Moody Press, n.d.), 50.

[3] Bounds, *The Possibilities of Prayer*, 42.

[4] Leonard Ravenhill, *Revival Praying* (Minneapolis: Bethany Fellowship, Inc., 1962), 27.

[5] Jack Williams, "Measuring the Temperature of Lightning,"

USA Today, http://www.usatoday.com/weather/resources/askjack/walighn.htm, May 9, 2002.

[6] E. M. Bounds, *Prayer and Praying Men* (Grand Rapids: Baker Book House, 1921), 52.

[7] *Ibid.*, 45.

[8] McGraw, 34.

[9] John R. Rice, *A Christian's Wells of Joy* (Murfreesboro: Sword of the Lord Publishers, 1971), 38.

Chapter Five—*God's Recipe for Answered Prayer*

[1] G. Granger Fleming, *The Dynamic of All-Prayer* (Chicago: Moody Press, n.d.), 68.

[2] Hyles, 29.

[3] Unknown Christian, *The Kneeling Christian*, 53-54.

[4] James G. McClure, *Intercessory Prayer: A Mighty Means of Usefulness* (Chicago: Moody Press Publications, n.d.), 13, 14.

[5] *Ibid.*, 15.

[6] *Ibid.*, 119-20.

[7] Blanchard, 79.

[8] *Ibid.*, 84.

Chapter Six—*Miracle Praying*

[1] Bounds, *The Possibilities of Prayer*, 11.

[2] Spurgeon, *The Power of Prayer in a Believer's Life*, 54.

[3] Cox, 59.

[4] Bounds, *Prayer and Praying Men*, 15-16.

[5] R.A. Torrey, *How to Pray*, 56-57.

Chapter Seven—*The Work of Prayer*

[1] Whyte, 152.

[2] Unknown Christian, *The Kneeling Christian*, 55.

[3] Laymon, 68.

[4] *Ibid.*, 69.

[5] Unknown Christian, *The Kneeling Christian*, 40.

[6] Gordon, *Quiet Talks on Prayer*, 86.

[7] Unknown Christian, *The Kneeling Christian*, 17.

[8] *Ibid.*, 114.

[9] *Ibid.*, 56.

[10] *Ibid.*, 115.

[11] *Ibid.*, 66-67.

[12] Bounds, *The Weapon of Prayer*, 35.

[13] Cox, 61.

[14] J. C. Macaulay, *After This Manner: Thoughts on the Lord's Prayer* (Grand Rapids, William B. Eerdmans Publishing Company, 1952), 45.

[15] Whyte, 119.

Chapter Eight—*As in Heaven*

[1] Spurgeon, *The Power of Prayer in a Believer's Life*, 138.

[2] Unknown Christian, *The Kneeling Christian*, 8.

[3] Blanchard, 74.

[4] John R. Rice, *Whosoever and Whatsoever When You Pray* (Murfreesboro: Sword of the Lord Publishers, 1970), 119.

[5] Torrey, *How to Pray*, 15.

[6] Macaulay, 22.

[7] Whyte, 155.

[8] Macaulay, 42.

[9] Henry, 60.

[10] Blanchard, 87-88.

[11] G. Campbell Morgan, *The Practice of Prayer* (New York: Fleming H. Revell, Company, 1906), 98-99.

[12] Rosalind Rinker, *Prayer: Conversing With God* (Grand Rapids: Zondervan Publishing House, 1959), 64.

[13] Cox, 85.

[14] Macaulay, 66-67.

[15] Unknown Christian, *The Kneeling Christian*, 54.

[16] Gordon, *Quiet Talks on Prayer*, 86.

Chapter Nine—*Four Prayer Partners*
[1] Rice, *A Christian's Well of Joy*, 57.
[2] D. L. Moody, *Prevailing Prayer* (Chicago: Moody Press, n.d.), 93.
[3] Hallesby, 90-91.
[4] Hyles, 53.
[5] Henry, 75.
[6] Rice, *A Christian's Wells of Joy*, 32.
[7] Gordon, *Quiet Talks on Prayer*, 58.
[8] Bounds, *Prayer and Praying Men*, 75-76.
[9] "Inaugural Addresses of the Presidents of the United States," Bartleby. com/124/pres/32.html.
[10] "The Civil War," *The World Book Encyclopedia*, Vol. 4 (Chicago: Field Enterprises Educational Corporation, 1972), 492.

Chapter Ten—*The Good Neighborhood of Prayer*
[1] Bounds, *The Possibilities of Prayer*, 45.
[2] Hallesby, 109-10.
[3] Fleming, 52-53.
[4] Unknown Christian, *The Kneeling Christian*, 41.
[5] Gordon, *Quiet Talks on Prayer*, 146.
[6] Torrey, *How to Pray*, 53.
[7] Bounds, *The Possibilities of Prayer*, 41.
[8] Unknown Christian, *The Kneeling Christian*, 135.

Chapter Eleven—*The Enemies of Prayer*
[1] Ravenhill, 31.
[2] Bounds, *Prayer and Praying Men*, 63.
[3] Bounds, *The Reality of Prayer*, 21.
[4] Moody, 98.
[5] Bounds, *The Weapon of Prayer*, 109.

[6] Gordon, *Quiet Talks on Prayer*, 83-84.
[7] Unknown Christian, *The Kneeling Christian*, 82.
[8] *Ibid.*, 115.
[9] Murray, *The Prayer Life*, 23.
[10] John R. Rice, *Whosoever and Whatsoever When You Pray* (Murfreesboro: Sword of the Lord Publishers, 1970), 143.
[11] Morgan, 88.
[12] Bounds, *Prayer and Praying Men*, 51.

Chapter Twelve—Team Pray-ers
[1] Ravenhill, 13.
[2] Whyte, 230.
[3] *Ibid.*, 124.
[4] Unknown Christian, *The Kneeling Christian*, 124.
[5] Laymon, 42.
[6] Bounds, 37.
[7] Unknown Christian, *The Kneeling Christian*, 17.

Chapter Thirteen—Five Phases of Prayer
[1] Bounds, *The Possibilities of Prayer*, 101.
[2] Bounds, *The Weapon of Prayer*, 60.
[3] Charles Spurgeon, *Praying Successfully* (New Kensington, Penna.: Whitaker House, 1997), 53.
[4] Laymon, 48.
[5] Gordon, *Quiet Talks on Prayer*, 59.
[6] Bounds, *The Weapon of Prayer*, 9.
[7] *Ibid.*, 11.

Chapter Fourteen—How to Talk to God
[1] Unknown Christian, *The Kneeling Christian*, 63-64.
[2] "All About Alexander the Great," http://www.pothos.org/alexander.asp?paraID=96, 1.
[3] Bounds, *The Weapon of Prayer*, 13.

[4] Laymon, 70.
[5] Murray, *The Prayer Life*, 46.
[6] Rinker, 23.
[7] Bounds, *Prayer and Praying Men*, 36-37.

Chapter Fifteen—Show Yourself Strong Through Me
[1] Torrey, *How to Pray*, 48.
[2] Laymon, 32-33.
[3] Ravenhill, 88.
[4] Unknown Christian, *The Kneeling Christian*, 54.
[5] Spurgeon, *The Power of Prayer in a Believer's Life*, 53.
[6] *How to Get Your Prayers Answered* (Los Angeles: Christian Pocket Books, n.d.), 13.
[7] Bounds, *The Weapon of Prayer*, 10.
[8] Hyles, 36.
[9] Frank C. Laubach, *Prayer: The Mightiest Force in the World* (New York: Fleming H. Revell Company, 1946), 76.

Chapter Sixteen—Why God Wants Me to Pray
[1] Cleaver, 91.
[2] Spurgeon, *The Power of Prayer in a Believer's Life*, 15.
[3] Blanchard, 148.
[4] Bounds, *The Weapon of Prayer*, 29.
[5] Rinker, 7.
[6] Blanchard, 224.
[7] Unknown Christian, *The Kneeling Christian*, 77.
[8] Morgan, 13.
[9] McClure, 9.
[10] Morgan, 13.
[11] Bounds, *Power Through Prayer*, 30-31.
[12] Ravenhill, 60.
[13] James Oliver Buswell, *Problems in the Prayer Life* (Chicago: The Bible Institute Colportage Association, 1928), 69.

[14] Unknown Christian, *The Kneeling Christian*, 24.
[15] Cox, 55-56.
[16] Dr. Dennis Corle, *The Discipline of Prayer* (Claysburg, Penna.: Revival Fires! Publishing, 1995), 154.
[17] Bounds, *The Weapon of Prayer*, 114-15.
[18] Spurgeon, *The Power of Prayer in a Believer's Life*, 116.
[19] Cox, 71.
[20] Hallesby, 13.
[21] Hyles, 19.

Chapter Seventeen—Ask for It
[1] Hyles, 20.
[2] Bounds, *The Possibilities of Prayer*, 126.
[3] Moody, 94-95.
[4] Torrey, *How to Pray*, 8.

Chapter Eighteen—How to Multiply the Blessing
[1] Murray, *The Prayer Life*, 40-41.
[2] McGraw, 209.
[3] *Ibid.*, 210.

Chapter Nineteen—The Role of the Bible in Prayer
[1] Hyles, 191.
[2] Murray, *The Prayer Life*, 48.
[3] Hallesby, 16.
[4] Helen Barrett Montgomery, *Prayer and Missions* (West Medford, Mass.: The Central Committee on the United Study of Foreign Missions, 1924), 13.
[5] S. D. Gordon, *Prayer and the Bible* (New York: Fleming H. Revell Company, 1935), 11.
[6] Buswell, 10.

Chapter Twenty—They Continued in Prayer
[1] Gordon, *Prayer and the Bible*, 28-29.
[2] Cox, 21.

[3] Montgomery, 11.

[4] Ravenhill, 16.

[5] *Ibid.*, 41.

[6] Torrey, *The Power of Prayer*, 15.

[7] "Sex, Violence, and Profanity in the Media Fact Sheet, TV Statistics—Parents Television Council," http://www.parentstv.org /PTC/ facts/media facts.asp.

[8] James Poniewozik, "The Decency Police," *Time*, 28 March 2005, 25, 26.

[9] Cox, 11-12.

[10] Bounds, *Power Through Prayer*, 46.

[11] Montgomery, 107.

[12] Unknown Christian, *The Kneeling Christian*, 101.

[13] Montgomery, 106.

[14] *Ibid.*

[15] Torrey, *The Power of Prayer*, 20.

[16] Montgomery, 106-07.

[17] *Ibid.*, 107.

[18] Ravenhill, 102.

[19] Montgomery, 107.

[20] *Ibid.*

[21] Montgomery, 120-21.

[22] Unknown Christian, *The Kneeling Christian*, 101.

[23] Laymon.

[24] Bounds, *Power Through Prayer*, 46.

[25] Ravenhill, 57.

[26] Dr. Mike Sisson, comp., *His Amazing Grace* (Hammond, Ind.: Hyles Publications, 2006), 50.

[27] Ravenhill, 41.

[28] *Ibid.*, 40.

[29] Gordon, *Quiet Talks on Prayer*, 11.

"Prayer does not fit us for the greater work;
prayer is the greater work."
–Oswald Chambers

Sources Consulted

"All About Alexander the Great." http://www.pothos.org/alexander.asp? paraID=96.html.

Blanchard, Dr. Charles. *Getting Things From God.* Chicago: The Moody Bible Institute of Chicago, 1915.

Bounds, E. M. *Power Through Prayer.* Grand Rapids: Baker Book House, n.d.

_____. *The Possibilities of Prayer.* Grand Rapids: Baker Book House, 1923.

_____. *Prayer and Praying Men.* Grand Rapids: Baker Book House, 1921.

_____. *The Reality of Prayer.* Grand Rapids: Baker Book House, 1924.

_____. *The Weapon of Prayer.* Grand Rapids: Baker Book House, 1931.

Buswell, James Oliver. *Problems in the Prayer Life.* Chicago: The Bible Institute Colportage Association, 1928.

Clark, Glenn. *I Will Lift Up Mine Eyes.* Carmel, New York: Guideposts Associates, Inc., 1937.

Cleaver, Solomon. *Life's Great Adventure~Prayer.* New York: Richard R. Smith, Inc., 1931.

Conlan, Roberta, ed. *Persians: Masters of Empire.* Alexandria, Vir.: Time-Life Books, 1995.

Corle, Dr. Dennis. *The Discipline of Prayer.* Claysburg, Penna.: Revival Fires! Publishing, 1995.

Cox, Enos Kincheloe. *Where Is the Lord God of Elijah?* Chicago: The Bible Institute Colportage Association, 1929.

Finkelstein, Jacob J. "Assyria," *The World Book Encyclopedia.* Chicago: Field Enterprises Educational Corporation, 1972.

Fleming, G. Granger. *The Dynamic of All-Prayer*. Chicago: Moody Press, n.d.

Gordon, S. D. *In the Quiet Corner*. New York: Fleming H. Revell Company, 1932.

_____. *Prayer and the Bible*. New York: Fleming H. Revell Company, 1935.

_____. *Quiet Talks on Prayer*. Westwood, NJ: Fleming H. Revell Company, 1967.

Greene, Oliver B. *Daniel: Verse by Verse Study*. Greenville: The Gospel Hour, Inc., 1964.

_____. *The Epistle of Paul the Apostle to the Romans*. Greenville: The Gospel Hour, Inc., 1962.

Hallesby, O. *Prayer*. London: Inter-Varsity Fellowship, 1948.

Haskin, Dorothy C. *A Practical Primer on Prayer*. Chicago: Moody Press, 1951.

Henry, Matthew. *The Secret of Communion With God*. Edited by Elisabeth Elliot. New York: Fleming H. Revell Co., 1963.

Hicks, Jim. *The Persians*. New York: Time-Life Books, 1975.

How to Get Your Prayers Answered. Los Angeles: Christian Pocket Books, n.d.

Hyles, Dr. Jack. *Exploring Prayer With Jack Hyles*. Hammond, Ind.: Hyles-Anderson Publishers, 1983.

"Inaugural Addresses of the Presidents of the United States." Bartleby. com/124/pres/32.html.

Laessoe, Jorgen. *People of Ancient Assyria*. n.c.: Assyrian International News Agency, 1963.

Laubach, Frank C. *Prayer: The Mightiest Force in the World*. New York: Fleming H. Revell Company, 1946.

Laymon, Charles M. *A Primer of Prayer*. Nashville: Tidings, 1949.

Macaulay, J. C. *After This Manner: Thoughts on the Lord's Prayer*. Grand Rapids, William B. Eerdmans Publishing Company, 1952.

"Map of the Assyrian Empire." http://www.bible-history.com/maps/map_ assyrian_empire_650_ bc.html.

McClure, James G. McClure. *Intercessory Prayer: A Mighty Means of Usefulness.* Chicago: Moody Press Publications, n.d.

McGraw, Louise Harrison. *Does God Answer...Prayer?* Grand Rapids: Zondervan Publishing House, 1941.

Montgomery, Helen Barrett. *Prayer and Missions.* West Medford, Mass.: The Central Committee on the United Study of Foreign Missions, 1924.

Moody, D. L. *Prevailing Prayer.* Chicago: Moody Press, n.d.

Morgan, G. Campbell. *The Practice of Prayer.* New York: Fleming H. Revell, Company, 1906.

Morris, William, ed., *The American Heritage Dictionary of the English Language,* Boston: Houghton Mifflin Company, 1969.

Mueller, George. *Answers to Prayer.* Chicago: Moody Press, n. d.

Murray, Andrew. *The Prayer Life.* Chicago: Moody Press, n.d.

_____. *With Christ in the School of Prayer.* New Kensington, Penna.: Whitaker House, 1981.

Poniewozik, James. "The Decency Police." *Time.* 28 March 2005.

Ravenhill, Leonard. *Revival Praying.* Minneapolis: Bethany Fellowship, Inc., 1962.

Rice, John R. *A Christian's Wells of Joy.* Murfreesboro: Sword of the Lord Publishers, 1971.

_____. *Prayer: Asking and Receiving.* Murfreesboro: Sword of the Lord Publishers, 1942.

_____. *Whosoever and Whatsoever When You Pray.* Murfreesboro: Sword of the Lord Publishers, 1970.

Rinker, Rosalind. *Prayer: Conversing With God.* Grand Rapids: Zondervan Publishing House, 1959.

"Sex, Violence, and Profanity in the Media Fact Sheet, TV Statistics—Parents Television Council," http://www.parentstv.org/PTC/facts/media facts.asp.

Sisson, Dr. Michael, ed. *His Amazing Grace*. Hammond, Ind.: Hyles Publications, 2006.

Spurgeon, Charles. *The Power of Prayer in a Believer's Life*. Lynwood, Wash.: Emerald Books, 1993.

_____. *Praying Successfully*. New Kensington, Penna.: Whitaker House, 1997.

Swisher, Clarice. *The Ancient Near East*. San Diego: Lucent Books, Inc., 1995.

"The Civil War." *The World Book Encyclopedia*. Vol. 4. Chicago: Field Enterprises Educational Corporation, 1972.

Torrey, R. A. *How to Pray*. New York: Pyramid Books, 1900.

_____. *The Power of Prayer*. New Kensington, Penna.: Whitaker House, 2000.

Tozer, A. W. *The Pursuit of God*. Harrisburg: Christian Publications, Inc., 1948.

Trieber, Jack. *Men Ought Always to Pray*. Santa Clara: North Valley Publications, 1998.

Unknown Christian. *The Kneeling Christian*. Grand Rapids: Zondervan Publishing House, 1971.

Unger, Merrill F. *Unger's Guide to the Bible*. Wheaton, Ill.: Tyndale House Publishers, Inc., 1974.

Whyte, Alexander. *Lord, Teach Us to Pray*. London: Hodder & Stoughton Limited, 1922.

Williams, Jack. "Measuring the Temperature of Lightning." *USA Today*. http://www.usatoday. com/weather/ resources/ askjack/ walighn.html. May 9, 2002.